Everyday Cognition

Everyday Cognition:
Its Development in Social Context

Edited by
Barbara Rogoff and Jean Lave

Harvard University Press
Cambridge, Massachusetts, and London, England
1984

To our children: *Rebecca Lave*

Luisa, Valerie, and David Magarian

Library of Congress Cataloging in Publication Data
Main entry under title:

Everyday cognition.

Bibliography: p.
Includes index.
1. Cognition — Social aspects — Congresses.
2. Cognition in children — Social aspects — Congresses.
I. Rogoff, Barbara. II. Lave, Jean.
BF311.E87 1984   153   83-18521
ISBN 0-674-27030-4 (alk. paper)

Contents

Introduction: Thinking and Learning in Social Context

Barbara Rogoff

Cognitive developmental work has been overly concerned with describing mental changes which are assumed to occur within the individual independent of contextual influences. The predominant focus has been on establishing stages of development or transformations in capabilities associated with development. Most depictions of stages (e.g. the concrete operational stage of Piaget) or capacities (e.g. spatial skill, metamemorial ability) assume that the stage or capacity characterizes the person's thinking across a large number of task situations (Piaget, 1970; Feldman, 1980; Fischer, 1980). Usually the existence of the stage or capacity is evaluated through the use of one or a small sample of task situations that are assumed to represent the domain of problems which people meet. However, when multiple tasks are given, the assumption of widespread generality of stage or capacity is usually not upheld (Reese, 1977; Brainerd, 1978; Feldman, 1980; Fischer, 1980; Siegler, 1981). Cognitive skills which are logically similar or isomorphic (e.g. conservation, problem solving, role taking) often appear at different ages or do not cluster together on similar tasks performed by the same individuals. Instead, cognitive skills seem to fluctuate as a function of the situation, which suggests that skills are limited in their generality.

Increasingly, psychologists emphasize the role of context in cognitive activities (Siegel, 1977; Cole, Hood & McDermott, 1978a; Gelman, 1978; Rogoff, 1982). Concern with contextual variation in skills has been influenced by cross-cultural observations that people who have difficulty with a task embodying a particular skill in the laboratory spontaneously evidence the skill in their everyday activities (Laboratory of Comparative Human Cognition, 1979;

Rogoff, 1981). Micronesian navigators who show phenomenal skills in memory, inference, and calculation when traveling from island to island perform abominably on standard tests of intellectual functioning (Gladwin, 1970). Subjects who perform poorly on logic or communication problems in a test situation often reason precisely and communicate persuasively in more familiar contexts (Labov, 1970; Cole, 1975; Scribner, 1976).

Observations that children's capabilities appear quite different in their familiar environments than in the laboratory have increased developmentalists' concern with the role of context (Gelman, 1978; DeLoache, 1980; Todd & Perlmutter, 1980). For example, young children routinely have difficulty in referential communication tasks, yet in everyday situations they adjust their communication to meet the needs of their listeners (Gleason, 1973; Shatz & Gelman, 1977). Similarly, toddlers have difficulty in laboratory memory tests but remember locations of objects hidden at home by their parents and demonstrate impressive recall and strategic capacities in other quasi-naturalistic tasks (DeLoache & Brown, 1979; Wellman & Somerville, 1980). Infants use an egocentric frame of reference when looking for an object in the laboratory but a nonegocentric frame of reference when tested at home (Acredolo, 1979). Skills that children seem not to possess in laboratory tasks thus appear well developed when these same children meet similar problems in familiar contexts.

These findings that laboratory skills seem rather separate from thinking outside of the laboratory may lead to an assumption that only in natural environments can valid measures of people's real cognitive processes be found (Charlesworth, 1976). However, the dichotomy of laboratory vs. "natural" cognition is an oversimplification. Focusing the issue on a field vs. laboratory distinction assumes that in certain situations people's *real* cognitive capabilities and processes can be uncovered (McCall, 1977; Weisz, 1978; Parke, 1979; Wohlwill, 1981). But to assume that under ideal circumstances people's underlying capacities or processes can be attributed to their internal functioning without concern for the context of their activity is unrealistic. Thinking is intricately interwoven with the context of the problem to be solved. The context includes the problem's physical and conceptual structure as well as the purpose of the activity and the social milieu in which it is embedded. One must attend to the content and the context of intellectual activity in order to understand thought processes. This is the case for any situation in which thinking is studied, including the laboratory context, which is not context-free as researchers frequently assume. Understanding the circumstances of cognitive activity is essential to developing a more sufficient theory of cognitive development. This is quite different from searching for the "most natural" context or attempting to control for context. Context is an integral aspect of cognitive events, not a nuisance variable.

Psychologists often think that it is possible, in principle and in practice, to examine cognitive processes without concern for the context, i.e. to neutralize the task so that performance reflects "pure process" (Cole & Scribner, 1975; Price-Williams, 1980; Rogoff, 1981). Evidence suggests that our ability to control and orchestrate cognitive skills is not an abstract context-free competence which may be easily transferred across widely diverse problem domains but consists rather of cognitive activity tied specifically to context. Both the arithmetic skills learned in school and those learned in tailoring show a limited generality to different types of arithmetic problems (Lave, 1977). Experience with literacy of various types has specific but not general cognitive effects (Scribner & Cole, 1981). Experience as a weaver relates to performance on only those pattern continuation tests that resemble weaving (Rogoff & Gauvain, ms.).

This is not to say that cognitive activities are completely specific to the episode in which they were originally learned or applied. In order to function, people must be able to generalize some aspects of knowledge and skills to new situations. Attention to the role of context removes the assumption of broad generality in cognitive activity across contexts and focuses instead on determining how generalization of knowledge and skills occurs. The person's interpretation of the context in any particular activity may be important in facilitating or blocking the application of skills developed in one context to a new one.

Several theories have recently been proposed which involve the context in explanations of cognitive development. Feldman (1980) argued that stages do not reside in the head of the child but must also involve the domain in which stages are achieved. Fischer (1980) proposed that features of both the organism and the environment are involved in cognitive developmental sequences. Both of these approaches, while making appreciable advances in understanding cognitive development, limit their consideration of context to the structure or features of the task or domain of knowledge. A broader view of context requires that task characteristics and cognitive performance be considered in light of the goal of the activity and the interpersonal and cultural context in which the activity is embedded.

Central to the everyday contexts in which cognitive activity occurs is interaction with other people and use of socially provided tools and schemas for solving problems. Cognitive activity is socially defined, interpreted, and supported. People, usually in conjunction with each other and always guided by social norms, set goals, negotiate appropriate means to reach the goals, and assist each other in implementing the means and resetting the goals as activities evolve (Rogoff, 1982; Cole, Hood & McDermott, 1978b). For example, people seldom commit a list of shopping items to memory in preparation for a trip to the grocery store. Rather, they make use of aids such as written lists of items, they ask other people to remind them of what to purchase, or they use the grocer's arrangement of items to jog their memory as they peruse the aisles for the needed items.

The social context affects cognitive activity at two levels, according to Vygotsky (1978). First, sociocultural history provides tools for cognitive activity (e.g. writing and calculators) and practices that facilitate reaching appropriate solutions to problems (e.g. norms for the arrangement of grocery shelves to aid shoppers in locating what they need, common mnemonic devices, scripts and frames for interpreting events). Second, the immediate social interactional context structures individual cognitive activity. Information regarding tools and practices is transmitted to children and other novices through interaction with more experienced members of society. In practical situations the context provides information and resources that facilitate the appropriate solution of the problem at hand.

The social system in which the child is embedded thus channels cognitive development. The culture and the influence of socialization agents are not overlays on basic individual development. Rather, the development of the child is guided by social interaction to adapt to the intellectual tools and skills of the culture. The Soviet view of cognition suggests that psychology, rather than deriving explanations of activity from the individual plus secondary social influences, focus on the social unit of activity, from which individual functioning springs. The formal institutions of society and the informal interactions of its members are thus central to the process of development. In order to understand cognitive development, we must attend to the role played by such influences as schooling, television, toys, and especially the formal and informal instruction provided by adults and peers expert in the activity.

This volume represents the outcome of a conference which focused on the issue of how everyday cognition develops in social contexts. The authors, who come from the fields of developmental psychology, anthropology, sociology, and computer science, are involved in exploring the development of thinking in practical situations, including school and laboratory. They are working in the nexus of these disciplines in which there is consensus regarding the problems to be studied, the directions for research, and the conceptual frameworks.

The approaches taken here focus on studying the influences of differently organized learning experiences on the development of cognitive skills. The research examines the effects and processes not only of schooling but also of on-the-job learning, of adult and peer interaction with children, and of acquiring skills and information in socially structured situations that do not involve a teacher. The context of cognitive functioning includes, besides the physical objects, the task characteristics, and the people present, the less immediate social context in which the task and the problem solver are embedded. In fact, in some instances the word *culture* is used interchangeably with the term *context.* It is no accident that the issues dealt with in the study of everyday cognition resemble those faced by researchers who wish to understand the relation between culture and cognition, for the interest in studying thinking in context has derived in part from efforts to examine thinking in diverse cultures. Many of the authors have conducted research in different cultures, and others have dealt with the issue of culture in their writing and research.

Three themes receive primary focus in the book: the problem of determining the situational specificity and generality of cognitive skills; the role of the social orchestration of thinking through cultural institutions and normative techniques for problem solving and through the transfer of cognitive skills from one person to another; and the practical, opportunistic nature of everyday cognitive activity. The problem of determining the situational specificity and generality of cognitive skills stems directly from the demonstrated variation in skills across settings. It involves the question of how to assess a person's skills, given that skills are not employed independently of the context in which a problem is embedded. There are similarities and differences in performance and organization of formally similar tasks in test or school settings as opposed to other situations (Scribner; Lave, Murtaugh & de la Rocha; Wertsch, Minick & Arns; Ginsburg & Allardice). In laboratory situations researchers generally do not examine the influence of the experimenter or tester on the subject's performance (Newman, Griffin & Cole). The instructions to the subject are cleanly separated from the assessment of performance. In contrast, in many other circumstances, such as joint problem-solving in a classroom, the performance of any individual is aided and constrained by the actions of other people. What appears to be a formally similar problem in two settings is managed quite differently when the two settings involve different social arrangements. What makes two tasks "the same" is that the investigators in a field "diagram" the tasks identically (White, personal communication). To produce a diagram of any two tasks, investigators must focus on one feature that the tasks have in common (e.g. systematically organizing combinations of objects) and ignore other features that vary (e.g. the purpose of combining the objects, who is involved in the task). The diagram is thus a somewhat arbitrary classification for the researchers' convenience rather than an aspect of the task itself. That people's performance varies in tasks which are considered similar is therefore not surprising.

The existence of contrasting performances in different settings also relates to the role of the social orchestration of thinking through society's institutions and tools. For example, arithmetic procedures used in a dairy are constrained and aided by the arrangements of order sheets and of the cases of dairy items to be counted (Scribner). Arithmetic use in shopping is structured by the practical problems to be solved (Lave, Murtaugh & de la Rocha). Decision-making by groups of people in institutions, such as school systems, rely on budgetary constraints and pragmatic concerns, such as class size, rather than on a systematic, logical examination of all alternatives (Mehan). Cognitive development may be tied closely to chil-

dren's widening experience with the institutions and socially structured learning situations of their society (White & Siegel).

The institutional and technological basis for solving problems is
introduced and guided in cognitive development by interaction
with more experienced members of society. Novices learn under
the guidance of others who support their progress through adjustment of task difficulty and who provide experience in the joint
solution of the problem (Wertsch, Minick & Arns). Sensitive instruction at the novice's cutting edge of understanding, in Vygotsky's zone of "proximal development," encourages participation at a comfortable yet challenging level and provides a bridge for
generalizing skills and approaches from familiar to novel situations
(Rogoff & Gardner). Ski coaches guide the novice skier's advancement in skills by adjusting the problem posed and focusing on the
learner's needs (Burton, Brown & Fischer). Teaching in the zone of
proximal development provides a "scaffold" to support the child in
learning to talk and learning to weave (Greenfield). Children's
social skills and success in social problem-solving may be a function
of having appropriate levels of social understanding and skill relative to the expectations and culture of the peer group (Lubin &
Forbes).

The final theme of the book is that thinking is a practical activity
which is adjusted to meet the demands of the situation (Scribner;
Mehan; Lave, Murtaugh & de la Rocha; Rogoff & Gardner; Burton,
Brown & Fischer; Wertsch, Minick & Arns; Newman, Griffin &
Cole). As such, what is regarded as logical problem-solving in
academic settings may not fit with problem solving in everyday
situations, not because people are "illogical" but because practical
problem-solving requires efficiency rather than a full and systematic consideration of all alternatives. In everyday situations,
thought is in the service of action. Rather than employing formal
approaches to solving problems, people devise satisfactory opportunistic solutions. Everyday thinking, in other words, is not illogical and sloppy but instead is sensible and effective in handling the
practical problem. In many cases, the more systematic and precise
approach would result in less effective practical action since it
would take more effort to develop and would be less flexible in the
face of unanticipated opportunities or constraints. Effective practical problem-solving may proceed by using tacit knowledge available in the relevant setting rather than by relying on explicit propo-

sitions. Skilled activities, such as arithmetic, communication, or skiing, may proceed through the use of contextual cues that inter-face with tacit knowledge rather than through the systematic appli-cation of explicit steps in problem solving.

This volume examines the influence of the social context as it contributes to the course of cognitive development. The focus on everyday contexts of thinking — at home, in school, in the labora-tory, or wherever — involves an emphasis on the purposes for which people engage in activities and the pragmatic considerations involved in people's solutions to problems.

1. Studying Working Intelligence

Sylvia Scribner

In the Western philosophical tradition, theoretical and practical thinking have often been opposed to each other as two distinct forms of thought. Aristotle (1963) considered theoretical thinking characteristic of philosophers and those who pursue the why of things; practical thinking is characteristic of artisans and others whose social task is to get things done. He believed theoretical thought to be the superior of the two, the fount of wisdom and the true object of metaphysics. Practical thinking simply fell outside his sphere of interest.

Modern psychologists, though far from Aristotle's world view, still share his philosophical preoccupation with modes of thought central to theoretical inquiry — with logical operations (Piaget, 1950), scientific concepts (Vygotsky, 1962), and problem solving in symbolic domains (Newell & Simon, 1972). Most appear, too, to maintain Aristotle's high esteem for theoretical thought and disregard for the practical.

The studies described here shift this focus. They are concerned with practical knowledge and thought for action. They were carried out among workers in an industrial milk-processing plant, referred to as a dairy, and were undertaken for two related purposes: to contribute to a functional theory of practical thinking and to test a research strategy appropriate to its investigation. The concept of practical thinking guiding this research, unlike Aristotle's, entails no presuppositions about its relationship to theoretical thinking, nor does it imply a dichotomy between the intellectual and manual spheres of human action. As used here, "practical thinking" refers to all thinking that is embedded in larger activities and that functions to carry out the goals of those activities. Goals may involve mental accomplishments (e.g. computing the cost of a milk delivery) as well as manual accomplishments (e.g. loading a truck). The phrase "working intelligence" thus has two senses: it refers both to the intellect at work in whatever contexts and activities those may be and, more narrowly, to the particular context of the dairy studies — the workplace.

A Practice Framework of Cognition

The theoretical approach to these studies of practical thinking has its roots in earlier efforts to understand the formative role of culture in cognitive development. Research and concepts developed in this field seem to have implications for a general functional account of thinking (Cole & Scribner, 1974). In particular, cross-cultural research highlights the dependencies of particular thinking skills on the socially organized experiences that mark the lives of people in different cultures.

Considered in an atheoretical sense, the role of experience has long been accorded its due in psychology; it did not await discovery in other cultures. But as William James (1890, 619) warned in the founding of the science, "the first thing to make sure of is that when we talk of 'experience,' we attach a definite meaning to that word." Attaching "a definite meaning" and specifying the links between concrete forms of experience and selective functional aspects of cognition have proved even more difficult than James's warning portended. Within any given society, significant experiences tend to co-occur in patterned ways. For example, in the United States, the increasing independence of children from parents parallels their progress through school.

It is difficult to go beyond observations of cognitive change that are associated with such patterned configurations to uncover specific mechanisms at work. Here cross-cultural research has proved helpful. In spite of the many ambiguities in this field (Cole & Scribner, 1974; Dasen, 1977), investigators have taken advantage of changing co-occurrences of events in different cultures to make some headway in identifying formative "prior experiences." Most prominent in this line of work is the well-demonstrated association between Western-style schooling and features of performance on cognitive tasks and tests (Rogoff, 1981; Scribner & Cole, 1973). School-related cognitive skills have been demonstrated among many cultural groups and through a variety of research techniques, including survey interviews (Inkeles & Smith, 1974); clinical interviews (Ginsburg, Posner & Russell, 1981); ethnographic observations combined with paper-and-pencil tests (Lave, 1977); and, commonly, psychological experiments (Greenfield, 1966; Scribner, 1974; Laurendeau-Bendavid, 1977; Stevenson, Parker, Wilkinson, Bonnevaux & Gonzalez, 1978; Wagner, 1978; Sharp, Cole & Lave, 1979).

While many interpretations are offered as to the nature of these skills and their theoretical significance (Brown & French, 1979; Cole, 1979), the evidence to date makes a persuasive case that school effects are just that — outcomes of certain experiences that individuals encounter in this distinctive institution called school. Accounts of how school "makes a difference," however, remain speculative. Little is known about the nature of critical learning experiences in school that might underlie aspects of performance on cognitive tasks. Active research is now underway on possible causal mechanisms, such as learning to read text (Olson & Nickerson, 1978), participating in certain forms of classroom discourse (Mehan, 1979), and acquiring meta-cognitive skills (Brown, 1977).

In one such attempt to untangle experiences occurring in school, Michael Cole and I conducted a series of comparative studies examining whether literacy — knowledge and use of a written language — constitutes the crucial set of skills (Scribner & Cole, 1981).

We carried out this research among the Vai people of West Africa, who practice literacy in three scripts: English, acquired in government-sponsored schools; the indigenous Vai script, learned from tutors; and Arabic or Qur'anic literacy, typically acquired through group study with a teacher but without actual schooling.

We began with experimental tests of speculative propositions about the intellectual operations that literacy presumably either generates or fosters. Many of these propositions involve assumptions about the dependency of general abilities, such as abstract thinking (Havelock, 1963; Greenfield, 1972) or logical reasoning (Olson, 1977), on mastery of a written language. In the Vai setting, we failed to confirm such speculations. Moreover, we found that literacy without schooling (Vai script, Qur'anic) was not associated with the same cognitive skills as literacy with schooling.

The second phase of the research succeeded in identifying linguistic and cognitive skills related to the two nonschooled literacies. With the exception of some common encoding and decoding skills, these skills were specific to one or the other literacy. Interpretation of literacy effects in these studies was not as troublesome as the interpretation of school effects because the skills displayed on our contrived tasks were clearly implicated in reading and writing activities normally carried on in Vai villages. We did not have to "hypothesize" formative experiences; we could, at least on some occasions, point to them. We were able to make these links because we derived our experimental tasks in the first place from informal observations of literacy in operation. For example, while watching young boys memorize the Qur'an, we noticed that beginners were often taught to learn a verse by an incremental chaining technique: learning the first three words, then the next three, then putting all six together, and so on. When this technique was modeled in an experimental memory task, men with experience in Qur'anic study recalled more material in accurate order than inexperienced comparison groups, both nonliterate and those literate in other scripts. This positive result was buttressed by negative outcomes on other memory tasks (e.g. repeat a story, freely recall a list of words) in which Qur'anic students displayed no superiority over others. Through similar procedures, certain communication skills on experimental tasks were found to be related to prior experience with letter writing in the Vai script, and language comprehension skills were related to reading proficiency in the script.

In Vai society, links between well-practiced activities, such as memorizing the Qur'an or writing letters, and specific cognitive skills were especially visible because the three literacies are put to specialized uses and are based on different orthographies. The pattern of skills found across literacies closely paralleled these uses and the distinctive features of each script. This outcome suggested the need to rethink the nature of literacy within a functional framework. Instead of conceiving of literacy as involvement with written language that is the same everywhere at all times and therefore likely to implicate some fixed inventory of skills ("reading is reading, writing is writing"), we began to think of literacy as a term applying to a varied and open set of activities with written language. These activities might range from simple record-keeping to the composition of historical chronicles (Goody, 1968; 1977). The functional skills that literacy fosters beyond some possible common set might then be expected to vary with the nature of the activities with written language that particular cultures develop and individuals within cultures undertake.

This view attaches one definite, if not exhaustive, meaning to the ambiguous concept of experience. It particularizes experience as the active engagement of an individual in some pursuit involving socially organized domains of knowledge and technologies, including symbol systems. It conceives of functionality in the instrumental sense of supporting accomplishment of some goal-directed action. Writing a letter to secure repayment of a debt is a goal-directed action that is common among Vai script literates. Letter writing involves knowledge of the script and conventions of composition as well as topics discussed; it requires ability to use the implements that the culture makes available for producing written messages. Letter writing is related to other goal-directed actions that share certain of these knowledge and skill components and manipulate the same object, the Vai script; together these actions constitute "literacy."

We offered this account of our work at the conclusion of the Vai research, calling it a practice account of literacy. We used the term "practice" to highlight the culturally organized nature of significant literacy activities and their conceptual kinship to other culturally organized activities involving different technologies and symbol systems. Just as in the Vai research on literacy, other investigators have found particular mental representations and cognitive skills involved in culture-specific practices: navigation in Puluwat (Hutchins, 1979), weaving in Zinacanteco (Childs & Greenfield, 1980), and tailoring in Liberia (Lave, 1977; Reed & Lave, 1979). Lave's studies of tailoring, in particular, were carried to a level of specification which linked features of tailors' performance on a pure arithmetic paper-and-pencil task to the quantitative operations they used every day in sewing trousers for a living.

In these cross-cultural investigations, we have the skeletal outlines of one functional approach to cognition. The general construct of practice offers a possibility for integrating social-cultural and psychological levels of analysis and achieving explanatory accounts of how basic mental processes and structures become specialized and diversified through experience.

Methodological Implications

A functional approach to cognition implies a methodological principle. If cognitive skill systems are closely tied to the intellectual requirements of the practices in which they are embedded, one way to determine their characteristics is to study them as they function in these practices. Put somewhat differently, the practices themselves need to become objects of cognitive analysis. What intellectual tasks do these practices pose? What knowledge do the various tasks require, and what intellectual operations are involved in their accomplishment?

With this set of questions, a practice approach to cognition makes common cause with other efforts to develop techniques for studying thinking in context. Difficulties in this enterprise (Cole, Hood & McDermott, 1978; Bronfenbrenner, 1979) involve both conceptual and technical issues. A well-known conceptual difficulty is determining useful units of analysis. How does one locate cognitive phenomena that can be classified as similar in kind and that are sufficiently bounded to be amenable to analysis? The constructs of practice and task, (here an alternative term for goal-directed action), offer one potential approach to these dilemmas. If a particular practice is selected for study, it should in principle be possible to increase the power of decision rules for determining which of the multiple tasks that people carry on in certain settings are relevant to a cognitive analysis. Lave, for example, was concerned with how tailors measure cloth, a task essential to the practice of tailoring, not how tailors play cards, although both activities might be carried out in the tailor shop or its vicinity. There is also a basis for assuming that tasks within a practice will share some common intellectual requirements, such as, in tailoring, the need to use measuring operations in taking the customer's size and in laying out a pattern. The dairy studies attempted to test the problems involved in operationalizing these notions and using tasks-within-practices as basic units of analysis.

A claim has been made (Bronfenbrenner, 1979) that in the present state of the art, studies of everyday cognition involve a trade-off between the relevance that naturalistic settings provide and the rigor that laboratory settings make possible. The rigor-relevance controversy is often posed as an opposition between explanatory (usually equated with experimental) and descriptive (observational) methods of study. A cognitive analysis of actual practices, however, requires the two approaches. Observational methods are needed to determine what tasks are involved in certain practices, to describe their characteristics, and to discover the constraints the setting imposes. Experimental methods are needed to refine these descriptions and to analyze the component knowledge and cognitive processes involved in task accomplishment. In a rudimentary way, we attempted to carry out this progression from observation to experiment in the Vai literacy research, but were hampered by conditions of work in an unfamiliar culture. The dairy studies had as one of their aims a deliberate test of method: can we derive models of cognitive tasks empirically from a study of ongoing activities that will help us understand the characteristics of practical thinking?

Industry as a Research Setting

Our first research decision was to define the target cognitive activities as those occurring in the course of work-related tasks. Three considerations motivated this decision: significance, strategy, and social concern.

The significance of these activities is apparent. Just as schooling represents a dominant activity for children, work is a principal activity for adults. Work offers many occasions for the development of expertise in tasks involving complex intellectual skills. The labor market provides incentives, both positive and negative, for acquiring such expertise.

Considerations of research strategy pointed in the same direction, leading us to concentrate on a single industrial plant. In developing methods for studying intellectual activities in context, researchers can benefit from an environment that imposes tight constraints on these activities. An industrial plant commends itself as such a constrained environment. The functional requirements of the production system shape work activities in both their technical and their social aspects. A plant can be viewed for some purposes as analogous to a "culture." Occupational activities are socially organized for socially defined objectives and make use of "culture-specific" knowledge domains and technologies. An industrial plant has the added feature, useful for research purposes, of making required tasks and norms of performance explicit, often in the form of official job descriptions. Work tasks are repetitive and tend to recur under conditions of practice whose range of variation is known and can also be made explicit. Under these conditions, the research does not have to begin with the problematic exercise of defining discrete units of behavior or determining which qualify as the "same" or "different." Initially, the investigator can accept the social system's definition of a work task as a unit of behavior and allow the evolving research to test its adequacy.

Most important, in factory work, cognitive activity is often embedded in larger manual activities which have observable behavioral outcomes. Thought is related to action in ways that facilitate psychological reconstruction of the knowledge and operations brought to bear in the accomplishment of a task. If we can achieve some rigorous analysis of tasks involving external operations, it might then be possible to consider how such analyses might function as models for understanding cognitive tasks whose operations are primarily internal.

Social concerns also motivated selection of factory work for study. Class-related differences in educational achievement are well known. Children from families on the lower rungs of the economic ladder tend not to do as well in school as the offspring of professional and middle-class families. Yet many working-class children go on to learn jobs requiring technical knowledge and skills and to perform them competently. Some psychologists (e.g. Neisser, 1976) have attempted to take account of these differences in performance by making a distinction between academic and general intelligence. The usefulness of this distinction for instructional purposes is limited, however, by lack of knowledge of the nature of general intelligence or practical thinking. If researchers can achieve a fine-grained specification of how certain job-related tasks—say tasks involving reading or arithmetic—are accomplished in the workplace, there will be a better basis for comparing cognitive requirements that young people encounter in the two settings. Educational implications might follow.

With these considerations in mind, we selected a medium-sized milk-processing plant in a large urban city as the research site. This plant, employing some three hundred people, has a representative array of blue-collar and white-collar jobs, including machine production, warehouse, distribution, clerical, and computer operations.

The research began with a descriptive case study (ethnography) of the dairy as a whole, detailing the way it carries on its business and the role of various occupations in the enterprise. The ethnography included a general picture of literacy, math, and other cognitive skill requirements in various occupations. On the basis of this

Table 1.1. Comparative Experimental Design (all groups received all tasks).

Groups[a]	Tasks
Preloaders ($n = 5$)[b]	Product assembly
Inventory ($n = 4$)[b]	Counting the product
Wholesale drivers ($n = 10$)	Pricing delivery tickets
	Representing product quantities on computer form
Clerks ($n = 11$)	[Comparison group only]
Students ($n = 30$)	Paper-and-pencil math test

a. Either exhaustive or random selection methods were used, depending on the number of individuals employed in each occupational group. Students were a random stratified sample of all math ability groups in the ninth grade of a junior high school in the same neighborhood as the dairy.

b. Preloaders and inventory people, both of whom work in the icebox, are occasionally referred to here collectively as icebox workers.

background knowledge, four common blue-collar tasks were selected as candidates for cognitive analysis. All tasks were essential to job performance, and all involved operations with written symbols and numbers: product assembly (performed by preloaders), counting product arrays (inventory people), pricing delivery tickets, and using a computer form to represent numbers (wholesale drivers; Table 1.1).

The research objective was to describe skilled performance on each task and identify its systematic characteristics. As a first step, we conducted naturalistic observations of task performance under normal working conditions. These observations resulted in a first-level description of the major strategies workers employed on the task and their variability across individuals and occasions. On the basis of this description, we generated hypotheses or, more accurately, "hunches" about factors that might regulate variability. To explore these hunches, we introduced modifications in the task and observed performance under more constrained conditions than those occurring in the ordinary work environment. These modifications took the form of job simulations, which were administered, along with other experimental tasks, to employees in the occupations of interest. As we proceeded with job simulations and experimental tasks, we occasionally returned for more narrowly focused on-the-job observations to resolve particular questions.

For greater analytic power, a novice/expert contrast was built into the experimental design. All job simulations were given to all occupations; each occupation served as expert on its own task and novice on the others. For example, preloaders were experts on product assembly and were novices on delivery tickets, whereas the situation was reversed for wholesale drivers. Inclusion of office clerks provided the most marked novice-expert contrast. Their work does not involve them in manipulating physical products, a common task component for preloaders, inventory people, and drivers, while at the same time they share a common "cultural knowledge" of dairy products and operations and are familiar with the products in their symbolic representations (written names and abbreviations). A school math–work math comparison was also incorporated into the study by inclusion of a stratified sample of ninth graders in a nearby junior high school. Students received a small set of simulated dairy tasks and a paper-and-pencil math test which represented their own well-practiced activity; the test was also given to dairy workers. Average schooling for preloaders and inventory people was tenth grade; for drivers, eleventh grade; and for billing clerks, twelfth grade. Two tasks, product assembly and pricing delivery tickets, represent the more successful efforts at cognitive analysis and offer interesting contrasts in the problems they posed for research.

Product Assembly

Product assembly is a warehouse job. It is classified as unskilled manual labor and is one of the lowest paying jobs in the dairy. The perishable nature of dairy products requires that warehouse temperature be maintained at 38 degrees Fahrenheit; accordingly, the warehouse is, and is referred to as, an icebox. During the day, thousands of cases of milk products (e.g. skim milk, chocolate milk) and fruit drinks are moved on conveyor belts from the plant filling machines into the icebox, where they are stacked in designated areas along with many other dairy products (e.g. yogurt, cottage cheese). Preloaders arrive at the icebox at 6 P.M. Awaiting them is a sheaf of route delivery orders, called load-out order forms. Each form lists the products and their amounts that a wholesale driver has ordered for his next day's delivery. The preloader's task is to locate each product. Using a long metal "hook," he pulls the required number of cases and partial cases of that product and transports them to a common assembly area near a moving track that circles the icebox. When all the items of a given truck order are assembled, they are pulled onto the track and carried past a checkpoint out to the loading platform.

Our attention was first drawn to an interesting feature of this job when we studied the load-out form used by preloaders. This form is generated by a computer program which follows a certain rule in expressing quantities. Drivers place their orders for products in terms of the number of units needed (e.g. how many half-pints of chocolate milk are needed, how many quarts of skim milk). Fluid products, however, are not handled by unit within the plant. Gallons, quarts, pints, and other containers are packed in plastic cases as they move off the filling-machine production line. These are stacked in cases in the icebox and loaded in cases on the drivers' trucks. Cases are a standard size, and therefore the number of units they hold varies with the type of container (one case equals 4 gallons, 9 half-gallons, 16 quarts, 32 pints, or 48 half-pints).

When load-out order forms are produced, the computer "cases out" the driver's orders by converting units into case equivalencies. If the required number of units does not amount to an even number of cases, the leftover amount is expressed in units. Consequently, the load-out order form represents some orders as mixed case-and-unit quantities. If the leftover amount equals half a case or less, it is expressed as the number of cases plus the number of units; if the leftover amount is more than half a case, it is expressed as the number of cases minus the number of units. Consider quarts, which come 16 to a case. Orders for 17 to 24 quarts are expressed as 1 case + 1 unit up to 1 case + 8 units. For example, 1 case + 3 units equals 19 quarts. Orders for 25 to 31 quarts are expressed as 2 cases − 7 units up to 2 cases − 1 unit. For example, 2 cases − 5 units equals 27 quarts. The terms *case* and *unit* are not expressed on the load-out order form: "1 case + 3 units" is written simply "1 + 3."

How do preloaders handle these mixed numbers? Do negative numbers pose a special problem? Do preloaders always fill the orders as written; that is, do they always add units to an empty case when the order calls for a case plus units (e.g. 1 + 6) or remove units from a full case when the order calls for that (e.g. 1 − 6)? Informal observations suggested at the start that preloaders had worked out interpretive procedures for the number representations and often departed from literal instructions.

We prepared for a night of organized observation to obtain more systematic information. Logistics were not simple. The icebox is tightly packed. Preloaders run over slippery floors through aisles between stacks of cases. We could not follow them without interfering with their work or risking accident. We needed a stationary point of observation, but which location would be advantageous? Since we were especially interested in mixed orders and partial cases, we wanted to be in a position to watch as many of these orders as possible. Our access to the plant afforded a solution: we were able to obtain the complete set of load-out order forms for that night prior to the beginning of the shift. We counted the frequency with which mixed and partial orders occurred for different types of products. Having previously made a map of the locations of various products in the icebox, we knew which products were stored in adjacent areas. In this way, we were able to select a suitable lookout point across the track from products (quarts of buttermilk, chocolate milk, skim milk) which had the greatest number of partial-case orders.

Two researchers worked as a team for this aspect of the observation. One drew a diagram of the physical array that the preloader would find on arrival, noting the empty or partially filled cases that were available for use; the other described into a tape recorder how many quarts the preloader moved from one case to another to fill the order and what cases were taken away. On several orders, we intervened in the situation by creating mini-experiments. Before the preloader arrived, we added to or subtracted from the number of units in a partly filled case to test hunches about factors regulating choice of case and method of assembly. These changes were made without the knowledge of the preloaders who were working this location. They had no disruptive consequences. Preloaders customarily read off orders for several products at one time and need to keep these quantities in working memory until all are assembled. They said that they could not process other information at the same time and made no effort to remember how many units they were leaving in partial cases.

Using the diagrams and transcriptions from the observations, we were able to reconstruct for each order the initial state of the array, the preloader's moves, and the final state of the array. With these classes of evidence on hand, we could analyze the product assembly task as an example of problem solving within the tradition of laboratory-based research (Newell & Simon, 1972; Simon, 1975; Simon & Reed, 1976; Klahr & Robinson, 1981).

The first thing learned from these systematic observations is that preloaders have a large repertoire of solution strategies. Consider the set of strategies recorded on a particular order which recurred six times during the observation in the icebox: 1 – 6 quarts. On two occasions this order received a literal solution, with the preloader removing six quarts from a full case. But on four occasions the order was rewritten behaviorally. Two of these solutions took advantage of partially full cases to reduce the number of units that had to be moved to satisfy the order: 4 quarts were removed from a case of 14, 1 from a case of 11. In the two more interesting solutions, the take-away problem was transformed to an add-to problem: 2 units added to 8 and 4 units added to 6.

These forms of solution were not product-specific. They occurred for quarts of buttermilk as well as for chocolate. Nor were they restricted to particular quantities. Orders such as $1 + 6$ or $1 - 4$, for example, were also assembled in variable ways.

Nonliteral solutions such as these require that the assembler transform the original information into some representation that can be mapped onto quantitative properties of different arrays. We may infer that such solutions involve mental processing or, broadly speaking, mental work over and above retention in short-term memory of the quantity given on the load-out order sheet, which literal solutions also require. When does a preloader elect to engage in such additional mental work? Are nonliteral solutions haphazard or rule governed? We postulated a "law of mental effort": "In product assembly, mental work will be expended to save physical work."

We tested this possibility against the observational records. These records provided a precise metric for scaling physical effort: the number of units an assembler moved in completing an order. By comparing various modes of solution in terms of the number of moves they required, we could determine which strategy represented a "least-physical-effort solution" under a given set of circumstances. For example, if an order is $1 - 6$ (10) quarts and a preloader has the option of using a full case and removing 6 quarts (the literal strategy) or using a case with 2 quarts already in it and adding 8, the literal strategy is optimal from the point of view of physical effort: it saves 2 moves. If the partial case, however, has 8 quarts and only 2 quarts must be added, filling the order as $8 + 2$ is the least-physical-effort solution (the saving is 4 quarts).

According to this test, preloaders during the observations used literal strategies 30 times, and 25 of these times were also least-physical-effort solutions. Nonliteral strategies were adopted 23 times; on every occasion, such strategies represented a least-physical-effort solution. In view of the fact that in the course of a night's work preloaders must engage in some housekeeping operations (e.g. consolidating partial cases) that might run counter to least-physical-effort solutions on particular problems, the evidence overwhelmingly favors the postulated relationship between mental and manual operations on this task.

At this point, we moved to task simulation to further our analysis. On the simplest level, we wanted to determine whether preloaders would continue to apply optimizing strategies to the task when it had to be performed out of context and for study reasons only. In other words, would solution strategies transfer? We wanted to examine the effects of job experience through a comparison of preloaders with such novice groups as office workers and students. Audio and video records of performance were needed to support a microanalysis of solution processes. Finally, the simulation was designed to increase understanding of the hypothesized mental effort — physical effort trade-off by the systematic manipulation of levels of mental and physical difficulty in the problems.

These objectives reflect factors that have traditionally motivated psychologists to set up contrived situations (experiments) to help answer questions about complex phenomena which either cannot or can only with great inefficiency be answered on the basis of naturalistic observations. One example of the class of unanswerable questions is, "How do student strategies compare with those of expert preloaders?" Psychologists are unlikely to find students either working in a dairy icebox or doing product assembly in school. It would be inefficient to study interactions between problem type and solution mode by waiting until a sufficient number of each kind of problem had turned up on load-out order sheets to support systematic analysis.

The simulation was devised in such a way as to make sense to participants, retain veridicality, and at the same time satisfy experimental requirements for standardized conditions. We prepared facsimiles of load-out order sheets with orders prelisted on them.

To simplify matters, only orders of less than a case were used, and these were restricted to two container sizes, quarts and pints — all empties. After reading the order, the individual proceeded to an assembly area containing an array of milk cases. The array always consisted of a full case, an empty case, and a partial case, but the number of units in the partial case varied from trial to trial to fulfill the parameters of the problem list. Interviewees represented the four dairy occupations and the junior high school students.

First, consider the use of least-physical-effort strategies, or optimal solutions, by the various groups (Table 1.2). To what extent did members of these groups employ an optimal (least-physical-effort) solution when it involved carrying out a literal instruction (least mental work), and to what extent did they adopt this strategy when it involved the greater mental effort of producing equivalents to the presented problem? When optimal and literal strategies coincided, all occupational and student groups were optimizers virtually all of the time. But when the optimal strategy required some transforma-

Table 1.2. Product Assembly Simulation (quarts).

	Solution strategy, percent problems ($N = 16$ per person)[a]	
Population group	Literal strategy selected when it is optimal (LPE = LME)[b]	Nonliteral strategy selected when it is optimal (LPE ≠ LME)[b]
Preloaders	100	72
Inventory people and drivers	92	65
Clerks	92	47
Students[c]	94	25

a. All solutions could be classified according to this twofold classification except for 15 idiosyncratic solutions, 3 among clerks and 12 among students. These were excluded from the analysis.

b. LPE = least physical effort; LME = least mental effort.

c. The method of sampling students resulted in an interview population evenly distributed across the full range of math abilities as determined by performance on a national math achievement test. Twelve students were at or above grade level (highest grade equivalency score was 12.9), and eighteen students were below grade level (lowest grade equivalency was 3.5). Supplementary analyses show the below-grade group hardly ever gave nonliteral solutions (15%), while even the upper group used them on only 42% of applicable problems.

tion of the problem, major group differences appeared. Preloaders, as expected, made the greatest use of nonliteral optimizing strategies, using them 70% of the time. This outcome is evidence for transfer of solution strategies from a natural to an arbitrary performance context. It is also important validation of the job simulation technique as a device for cognitive analysis of "real-life" activities.

As might be suspected from other problem-solving research, group rankings confirm that expertise is a function of experience. Inventory people and drivers were not far behind the preloaders. As it turned out, all but one of the inventory people either worked at preloading occasionally or were formerly preloaders; and wholesale drivers, on occasion, made up orders for themselves. But consider the distant groups. Clerks showed little tendency to adapt strategies to the properties of the problem at hand, using nonliteral solutions in less than half of the instances in which they were strategies of choice. Students by and large were single algorithm problem-solvers; they were overwhelmingly literal.

Group disparities are highlighted in a supplementary analysis spanning two rounds of this task, which measured the extra physical effort each population group expended through failure to adopt the optimal solution on all occasions. Scores for students, who received only one round of this task, were extrapolated from their first session. Overexpenditures of physical effort by population group were: 26 units for preloaders, 37 units for inventory people and drivers, 95 for clerks, and 139 for students.

Novices are thus clearly distinguishable from experts in thinking out optimal solutions to these mundane problems. Does this mean that they have difficulty with the necessary mental arithmetic? A second set of simulated problems administered some weeks after the first included a set of problems which forced the use of non-literal solutions. For example, if the order called for 1 – 6 quarts, the problem solver was not presented with a full case but was given a choice of two partial cases, one holding 11 quarts and one 14. Clerks and most students (the novice groups) filled these orders accurately, indicating that the mental work involved was not beyond them. But their use of optimal strategies continued to be dependent on the nature of the problem and the type of conversion required.

Comparison of skilled and unskilled performance in terms of

best solution is only part of the story. Strategies may be optimal, or adequate (as when an assembler follows literal instructions even if these involve extra effort), or patently poor. A student's protocol furnishes one example of a poor solution; a billing clerk's another (Fig. 1.1). All idiosyncratic performances of this kind were restricted to these two groups; preloaders and drivers may have failed to use optimal strategies on some occasions, but they never resorted to such inefficient assemblies.

Following Wertheimer's (1959) lead, we are tempted to refer to these solutions as "blind" solutions. Such an evaluation, however, unlike Wertheimer's judgment, does not require imposition of a standard that psychologists developed in laboratory research. We have available a standard that expresses empirical regularities ob-

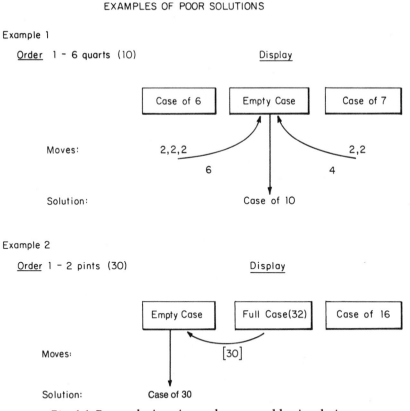

Fig. 1.1. Poor solutions in product assembly simulation.

served in the work performance of individuals whom all would acknowledge to be skilled. This is one of the advantages of taking actual occurrences of practical thinking as a starting point for cognitive analysis. They make it possible to say what "intelligent" practical thinking actually is in a particular setting, not merely what, according to existing theories, it ought to be. In product assembly, we have a suggestion as to one possible defining characteristic of practical thinking which might warrant the use of the qualifier "intelligent," that is, the extent to which thinking serves to organize and make more economical the operational components of tasks.

Even when novices selected an optimal strategy, they tended to carry it out quite differently from preloaders and drivers. Audio and video records indicate that office workers relied heavily on numerical solutions and counting operations, especially on early trials. In the following example, where the order is $1 - 6$ (1 case less 6 quarts), the clerk begins to fill the order while saying: "I'm going to remove six quarts and put them in an empty case. Oh, that won't . . . oh, no, that's wrong. (*Starts over again and returns units that she removed from the full case.*) It was one case minus six, so there's two, four, six, eight, ten, sixteen. (*Verifies that the case is full again by counting, pointing a finger as she counts.*) So there should be ten in here. Two, four, six, eight, ten. (*Counts her moves as she makes them, keeping track.*) One case minus six would be ten."

In contrast, preloaders often appeared to shortcut the arithmetic and work "directly" from the visual display. A preloader discusses how he filled an order for $1 - 8$ (half a case):

Preloader: I walked over and I visualized. I knew the case I was looking at had ten out of it, and I only wanted eight, so I just added two to it. (*Later, in an exchange with the interviewer on another order.*) I was throwing myself off, counting the units. I don't never count when I'm making the order. I do it visual, a visual thing, you know.

Interviewer: OK, well, do it the way that you would do it, I mean, as far as that's concerned.

Preloader: If I did it that way, you wouldn't understand it. See, that's why . . . this is what's throwing me off, doing it so slow.

Videotapes of five preloaders and four white-collar workers (all billing clerks) provided more systematic evidence that different processes of comparison and solution characterize expert and novice assemblies. A particularly crucial phase of the assembly is the premovement period, the interval between a person's arrival at the array and execution of the first movement. During this time, the assembler has to evaluate the partial case and adopt a solution strategy. A tally of the frequency of overt counting operations (verbal and/or gestural) in this premovement phase showed that all clerks, on some occasions, counted out loud with or without pointing gestures. There was a total absence of overt counting among preloaders. Using a second-sweep watch, we measured the duration of this period for all 89 problems in the two administrations of this task for which there was an optimal solution. Preloaders averaged 1.4 seconds processing time; clerks averaged 3.2 seconds. This differential in planning time supports indications in the protocols that preloaders used perceptual information from the array to determine quantity in the cases, while clerks used slower, enumerative techniques.

These analyses suggest that becoming a skilled product assembler involves learning the value of various configurations of containers (e.g. one layer of half-pints is 16; two rows of quarts is 8). Visual inspection then provides the quantitative information necessary to fill the order with little or no recoding into the number system. Some psychologists (deGroot, 1966; Chase & Simon, 1973) believe that master chess players are distinguished from lesser competitors by their vocabulary of perceptual units (configurations of pieces), which enable them to "see" move possibilities rapidly and without recourse to verbal analysis (Olson & Bialystok, 1980). Skill in as simple a task as product assembly may follow a similar course of acquisition from the primarily linguistic to the primarily perceptual. Follow-up training studies could be designed with this question in mind.

The last question pursued in these simulations concerned the postulated mental effort — physical effort trade-off. While we had a precise scale for measuring physical effort, no general methodology for assessing mental effort is available. We used an intuitive scheme for classifying types of problems by "mental difficulty" for which we secured partial confirmation. The analysis of preloader skill leaned heavily on the notion that nonliteral solutions (transformations of problems) require more mental work than the simple execution of literal solutions. If the time required to adopt a solution strategy (the premovement period) is provisionally considered to be an index of the difficulty of a problem, the distribution of average processing time falls into place. Preloaders required a second (1.0) to get started on problems in which literal solutions represented the optimal, least-physical-effort strategies, as compared to 1.4 seconds for problems in which the optimal solutions involved departures from the literal. The corresponding averages for billing clerks were 1.4 and 3.6 seconds.

Pricing Delivery Tickets

The second example of cognitive analysis of a work task involves wholesale drivers, a group whose earnings, including commissions, are among the highest in the dairy. In contrast to product assembly, wholesale delivery is regarded as an occupation with demanding intellectual and personality skills. Many a company executive today, we were told, began worklife as a milk driver.

Among their other daily chores, wholesale milk drivers must compute the total dollar value of their deliveries. For this purpose, they use computer-generated delivery tickets, which come to them preprinted with the customer's name and the products to be delivered that day. Quantities are left blank, but after a delivery is completed, drivers enter the amount of each item at that stop. This amount is always expressed in units. At that time, or after they have returned to the dairy to settle accounts, drivers are required to "extend the ticket" — find the total price for each line item and then the dollar value of the entire delivery. Accuracy counts. Drivers are responsible for the exact value of the products they take out of the dairy, and delivery tickets are also the basis of the company's billing system. To help drivers price out, the company provides a mimeographed wholesale price list, which gives prices for the various kinds of milk products. All prices are expressed in units on this list, as on all lists, because the price structure consists wholly of unit prices. Since the size of each product order is recorded on the delivery ticket in units and since prices are in units, the computation task seems straightforward: take the unit price from the price list or from memory, multiply it by the number of units recorded on the delivery ticket, and enter the result in the appropriate column; proceed in this fashion down the list; total the entries.

Informal observations revealed that drivers, no less than pre-loaders, frequently depart from this literal format. The most interesting departure involved importing into the problem information about the number of containers of different sizes that fit into a case. A driver who was accompanied on his route provided one of the first instances of this computational strategy. He read the item, "32 quarts homo milk" (dairy abbreviation for homogenized milk), found a price on a crib sheet in his pocket, doubled it, and entered the resultant product on his delivery ticket. His crib sheet, personally prepared, was an organized arrangement of tables listing prices by the case for products he frequently handled and prices by case multiples (8-case prices, 12-case prices) for high-volume items.

The milk case played an instrumental role in the product assembly task both in its physical aspects as a container and in its symbolic aspects as a variable that could take certain number values. Pricing out is an activity occurring wholly in the symbolic mode; as a material object, the case is without significance for this activity, yet it appears here, too, as a variable in arithmetic operations. Unremarkable as this may first appear, one can think of the case price as a prototype of human sign-creating activities that play such an important role in theories of higher mental functions. An object which first possesses instrumental value in physical activity begins to serve a sign function and becomes incorporated in mental operations (Vygotsky, 1978).

How widespread among the drivers was the case-price technique? And what specific functions did it serve? Again, we turned to task simulation to pursue the analysis.

As with product assembly, we planned to model simulations on the task as performed under normal working conditions. But unlike product assembly, where the operator's overt behavior is informative as to strategies of solution, a driver's use of a calculator or entry on a delivery ticket is mute with respect to the path of problem solution. We therefore transferred our observations from the dairy settlement room to an office in the basement where we recorded drivers talking out loud as they went through some of the day's delivery tickets. An observer noted which numbers the driver marked on scratch paper or entered into his calculator, and whether he consulted a price list. These converging lines of evidence permitted reconstruction of the driver's representation of the problem and method of solution (Table 1.3).

Drivers differed in the range and type of their solution strategies, but with the one exception of a relief driver who was not handling his own route, all used a case-price strategy on at least one occasion. Most commonly, the case price appeared on quantities convertible to an even number of cases. Older drivers, however, especially those without calculators, used the strategy flexibly and in many forms. Some devised combinations of case and unit prices, reminiscent of the mixed orders on the load-out order form, which permitted them to solve these multiplication problems through addition and subtraction:

Order	Solution strategy
17 quarts	Driver took the case price and added a unit price.
31 pints	Driver took the case price and subtracted a unit price.
48 gallons	Driver took ten times the case price and added two case prices.
98 half-pints	Driver took two times the case price and added two times the unit price.

A problem-by-problem analysis of strategies suggested that the case-price technique functioned as an effort saver in a manner analogous to the nonliteral optimal solutions in the product assembly task. Effort saved in pricing delivery tickets, however, is mental rather than physical. Use of a case price either eliminates computation altogether or simplifies it. Such effort saving would appear to be dependent on whether an individual driver has access to the case price, either in memory or on paper through a crib sheet or his own modification of the dairy's unit price list.

The task simulation examined how knowledge of case prices affected pricing strategies. In separate interviews we had elicited each driver's knowledge of case and unit prices for all products carried on wholesale routes. We were, therefore, in a position to test the knowledge-strategy interaction against an individual driver's recall record and pricing protocol. Standardized delivery tickets were prepared, composed of items for which most drivers knew the case prices and including many orders whose quantities were convertible to an even number of cases. As before, drivers who used calculators normally were allowed to use them on this task if they desired.

Table 1.3. Pricing Delivery Tickets (example of data for analysis from one driver).

Ticket item (reproduced from driver's ticket)	Unit price (reproduced from dairy wholesale price list)	Driver's computation (reproduced from scratch sheet or driver's ticket)[a]	Ticket entry (reproduced from driver's ticket)	Protocol (driver talking out loud; transcribed from audio tape)
120 gal. homo D	$2.33	932 30 27960 (30 underlined)	279.60	All right, so it's nine thirty-two a case and we have four into a hundred and twenty is thirty cases. So, I'll take thirty times nine thirty-two. I'll figure that's the easiest way to do it. Two seventy-nine sixty. See, in other words, it's two thirty-three a gallon, there's four gallons to a case, that's how you get nine thirty-two.
16 qt. homo VD	.74	11.84 74 16 11.84 (16 underlined)	11.84	Sixteen quarts of white is seventy-four. Now that's eleven eighty-four. We know it from memory, 'cause we use it over and over. So you take seventy-four times sixteen, you get eleven eighty-four. Yeah, it's eleven eighty-four a case. Seventy-four cents a quart.
12 gal. punch	.84	840 168 1008 (168 underlined)	10.08	All right, you got twelve, now it's eighty-four a gallon, so ten gallons would be eight forty. So I take the eight forty and two gallons would be one sixty-eight. That's two times eighty-four. So it's ten and two is twelve. Ten-o-eight.

a. Observer's record also available. For drivers who used calculators, the observer's record of numbers entered on calculator was used. Note the variable use of decimal point on the scratch sheet (items 1 and 3 have no decimals).

Results support an effort-saving hypothesis as well as highlighting the important role of knowledge in the choice of solution strategy. When drivers knew the applicable case prices on orders equivalent to single cases, they handled 77% of these orders by plugging the case prices into the cost column, bypassing computation altogether. All orders solved by the use of unit prices involved some recourse to paper and pencil or calculator to determine cost. Reduction in effort is apparent here.

Some orders presented quantities equivalent to two, three, and four cases; others to five and ten cases. Use of case prices on these problem classes dropped off to 59% and 38%, respectively. In all instances, case prices were used on orders for which the driver knew the price for a single case; the case price was never computed as a step to the solution of a problem involving multiple cases. Although multiple-case-price knowledge had not been assessed in the elicitation interview, some drivers spontaneously remarked that they knew or did not know how much N cases of X was because they did or did not handle this particular product in that volume. If a driver did not know the multiple-case price, the use of case-price strategy on these problems met an effort-saving criterion only in the sense of simplifying, rather than eliminating, computation. Analysis of case price solutions provided ample evidence of simplified arithmetic: two-thirds of the time drivers either entered the total price, giving no overt indication of computation, or did mental arithmetic (e.g. "That's $15.40 a case and there's two of them, so that would be $30.80"). Mental arithmetic did not suffice for unit-price solutions; these always involved some paper-and-pencil or calculator operations.

In addition to knowledge, the technological means drivers used in delivery ticket settlement affected their solution strategies. Except for three senior drivers who did paper-and-pencil arithmetic, other drivers owned and used calculators. The calculator encouraged greater reliance on the repetitive and literal solution strategy (number of units times unit price). Nonetheless, drivers with calculators also shifted to a case-price strategy on even-case orders in the simulation, providing additional evidence of an effort-saving hypothesis. In a subsequent study, drivers with calculators were required to price out the same set of facsimile tickets in different ways on two occasions; in the first session, in their customary manner; in the second session, without their calculators. The presence or absence of a calculator did not affect the incidence of case-price use on single-case orders, which was high under both conditions. But on more complex problems, either involving multiple-case orders or allowing solution by mixed case-and-unit price strategies, the removal of calculators resulted in a marked jump in case-price shortcutting strategies.

To explore the versatility of pricing-out techniques and compare novices with experts, we equalized all groups for ignorance. We prepared tickets exhibiting orders for products that were not handled by the dairy but represented sensible additions (e.g. iced coffee, 1% low-fat milk). Pseudo-price lists displaying both unit and case prices for these products were made available to informants, along with charts showing how many containers of various sizes fit into cases. In this group comparison, only students were unfamiliar with the case system and true novices. Preloaders and inventory men knew the case system but not the price system and had never before worked delivery tickets. White-collar workers were familiar with the price system, and one subgroup (billing clerks) worked on wholesale delivery tickets daily, checking and posting totals.

We devised orders to represent an array of efficient solution strategies, including case-price strategies. Special care was taken to include problems that would be diagnostic of versatility as negative instances; that is, they could be solved more easily by unit than by case prices (e.g. 10 quarts). We expected that skill related to experience would be demonstrated by a flexible use of case- and unit-price strategies on problems where each was appropriate.

Quite aside from the great variety of techniques that skilled people used to optimize solutions, individuals could be readily classified in terms of whether or not they were flexible or inflexible (single algorithm) problem-solvers. All drivers except one were flexible problem-solvers; most of them used optimal strategies as well. Approximately one-third of the white-collar and icebox workers were flexible. Without exception the students were inflexible problem-solvers. Most of them tended to use the literal unit-price strategy throughout. The small number who took up on the case-price technique applied it indiscriminately to all problems, regardless of their numerical properties, including an order for 101 quarts which involved working with long division to find the number of cases and ending up with a fraction of a case.

We set up these group comparisons not so much to characterize

Table 1.4. Expert pricing strategies used by a veteran wholesale driver on his own and experimental delivery tickets.[a]

Solutions using unit price	Solutions using case price	Solutions using mixed case and unit prices
Multiples without overt multiplication 2 UP 3 UP 4 UP 5 UP 10 UP 100 UP	Single case CP Multiples without overt multiplication $CP \times C$ $\dfrac{U}{U/C} = C; CP \times C$ $UP \times U/C = CP; CP \times C$	CP + UP CP + 2 UP 2 CP + 2 UP CP − UP 2 CP − UP 10 CP − UP
Multiplication $U \times UP$ $UP \times U$	Factoring & addition 10 CP + CP	
Factoring & addition 10 UP + 2 UP 100 UP + 2 UP		
Factoring & multiplication Factored UP; $UP_1 \times U$; $UP_2 \times U$ Factored U; $UP \times U_1$; $UP \times U_2$		

a. UP = unit price; U = number of units; CP = case price; C = number of cases; U/C = number of units per case.

novice performance as to increase understanding of the characteristics of skilled cognitive activity. We are not implying that some special ability is involved in the use of a case-price technique. Obviously the situation could have been structured in such a way that everyone used case prices or, alternatively, everyone used unit prices, simply by being told to do so. But knowing to do something does not necessarily make for skilled performance. Skill requires knowing how to, sometimes referred to as procedural knowledge. In the pricing task, domain-specific subject knowledge (information about cases and prices) combined with procedural knowledge to produce flexible least-effort strategies. These could be raised to the level of a virtuoso performance, as shown by an experienced driver's repertoire of pricing strategies on our tasks (Table 1.4). In addition to straightforward multiplication using either unit price or case price, this driver converted many problems to subtraction and addition, factored some problems, and used combinations of case and unit prices to simplify others.

Conclusions

Let me now try to reestablish ties with the broader questions that motivated these studies of working intelligence. One motivation was a test of method. We wanted to determine if we could bring some rigor to the study of thinking as it functions in the world of purposeful activities in which people customarily engage. We are not prepared at this stage to offer a full assessment, but several observations about method seem warranted. Several bear on the technical problems of conducting basic cognitive research in a nonresearch setting; others have to do with broader methodological issues.

On the technical level these studies have demonstrated the usefulness of an industrial environment as a setting for research on practical thinking. At the present state of theorizing, categories such as "practice" and "goal-directed action" are insufficiently specified to guide research in many settings. In the industrial environment, these constructs could be translated into "occupation" and "task," naturalistic categories defined by the environment, which facilitated the selection of appropriate phenomena for study. Working within a single plant also proved advantageous. In both the product assembly and delivery ticket analyses, our access to materials and information was instrumental in minimizing random variation in both observational and experimental situations. Recall that we were able to determine the most frequent partial-case product assemblies from the complete set of load-out order forms, thus avoiding the problem of dealing with atypical or less familiar orders in the search for systematicity. Access to the company's price lists allowed assessment of each driver's knowledge of wholesale prices, a control lessening the risk of working with a small sample. The factory as a research site substituted in some respects for the school, an institution that for years has been exploited for experimental studies. However, in one important respect the factory does not substitute for a school: its population is not captive for purposes of research. While in these particular studies selection-biasing factors were held to a tolerable level, they could not be

avoided. Some individuals drawn at random declined to participate; others were discharged and lost motivation for participating;
two dropped out, finding the sessions difficult. This experience
indicates that studies of adult practical thinking are likely to benefit from methods which maximize the interpretability of individual
performance and draw on, but do not rest on, statistical comparison
between groups.

The research strategy in these studies combined laboratory
methods such as task analysis with observational methods characteristic of field work. In bringing task analysis to the field, we
reversed the typical laboratory paradigm. Most investigators begin
with a formal or rational decomposition of the task of interest and
then go on to refine their model by empiric or computer simulation
studies (Siegler, 1980; Resnick, 1976, is an exception). The dairy
research began with empirical observations, which were used to
generate a description of the task-in-context. We then refined this
description by considering it against laboratory models, such as
models of problem solving. The description was useful when it
guided us to significant knowledge and strategy components of the
task and suggested parameters to investigate in task simulations.

We have made some progress in analyzing skills involved in
performance of certain work tasks. To the extent these analyses
support the laboratory models, they increase the range and power
of these models. To the extent these analyses uncover characteristics not represented or inadequately represented in the models,
they contribute to the advancement of laboratory as well as naturalistic studies of thinking.

We were concerned to carry out these studies in such a way as to
achieve an account of the processes and knowledge underlying task
performance. However, limitations in time and level of specificity
of the data did not always support microanalysis. Laboratory examples of well-analyzed cognitive tasks have built on years of accumulated experience with particular tasks and paradigms (e.g. number series problems, conservation problems). As yet, there is no
such heritage of model tasks for the study of practical thinking.
Well-analyzed tasks require many interrelated studies spanning a
long time period. To determine, for example, whether mental
representations of product arrays change with increasing experience, specially designed studies are necessary, and these may well
benefit from the use of recording devices that are suitable to a

laboratory-like setting. It is questionable whether process models of practical problem-solving can be developed without reiterative cycles of both laboratory- and nonlaboratory-based studies.

What general problems arise with respect to the interpretation of these studies? Simon (1976) raised this question with respect to laboratory-based task analysis and specified key questions that a process-theory model must satisfy. These include the validity and uniqueness of the task description, generalizability, and usefulness for studies of transfer and learning. The problem of generalizability is especially important, and it has two aspects. The first is task generalizability: to what extent does the task selected for study share at least some characteristics with other tasks involving problem solving? Only the assumption of cross-task commonality of process can justify studies of performance on arbitrarily selected laboratory tasks. Similarly, laboratory investigations must assume some interindividual commonalities in strategy in order to make statements about "human problem-solving" on the basis of the small number of individuals whose performances are observed and analyzed. Recognition of these problems requires a long-range strategy of development and test of various problem-solving models.

Field-based cognitive analysis, such as that reported here, also encounters problems of validity and generalizability, but as the foregoing assessment makes clear, these problems do not reflect special liabilities inherent in field settings. Laboratory studies have no intrinsic methodological advantage. The advantage of relevance, however, remains on the side of field-based studies. In occupational or school settings, the researcher works with tasks whose requirements and conditions of performance reflect the demands that our society poses for intelligent performance.

Leaving aside questions of method, these naturalistic studies of problem solving lend support to a practice framework of cognition. We began with a functional theoretical orientation holding that cognitive skills take shape in the course of individual participation in socially organized practices. The dairy studies examined practices that involve neither esoteric bodies of knowledge nor highly technical skills. Yet the evidence suggests the fruitfulness of a practice-based approach.

In spite of the small number of people involved in the comparisons, the job-related nature of skilled performance is readily discernible. It is most evident in contrasts between dairy employees as a group and students. Although on some tasks employees and students achieved similar levels of accuracy, their strategies differed markedly. Students tended to treat problems according to their literal format and to handle the quantitative aspects of manual tasks, such as product assembly, by applying rules of procedure appropriate to paper-and-pencil arithmetic. These findings justify the continued exploration of the contrasting characteristics of academic and practical problem-solving (Scribner & Fahrmeier, 1982).

Differential patterns of skills appeared as well on an occupational basis. In each case, the occupation providing on-the-job experience also provided the greatest number of experts on the simulated tasks. While this finding may appear trivial, it goes beyond the common-sense observation that practice makes perfect. The issue is not accuracy or error but rather modes of solution. Strategy analysis demonstrated that experience makes for different ways of solving problems or, to put it another way, that the problem-solving process is restructured by the knowledge and strategy repertoire available to the expert in comparison to the novice. Other studies have amply demonstrated these effects of experience in pursuits such as chess and music (Bamberger & Schon, 1976), which require mastery of symbol and rule systems not encountered in everyday activities. The present studies suggest that a pattern of development from novice to expert performance may not be restricted to such specialized activities but may represent the course of adult skill acquisition in commonplace tasks as well.

The pattern of occupation-skill relations, while present, is mixed, and it would be an oversimplification to imply that the skills found in these studies are tied to particular jobs in any deterministic way. In each comparison, one or more individuals who apparently lacked on-the-job experience with the task showed the same fluency in optimizing solution strategies as practitioners. Conversely, in every case, one or more individuals from the occupation in question did not turn in a skilled performance. The probabilistic nature of experience-based skills poses problems that a functional approach to thinking must meet.

Although only a handful of tasks has been studied in depth, they reveal common features which offer interesting suggestions for a general theory of practical thinking. Variability was an outstanding characteristic of skilled performance on all tasks examined. Product assembly and pricing-out appear on first inspection as proto-typical examples of repetitive industrial work. They both present the worker with recurring problems of the same kind, often problems of an identical kind. A rational task analysis might not have revealed the diversity of operations hidden under these same-problem formats. In some approaches to problem solving, an individual's inconsistency in strategy and performance is troublesome to the model. Yet increasingly investigators are turning up such "inconsistencies." In almost every area of cognitive development, psychologists have discovered that subtle differences in task demands may lead to widely varied performance (Klahr, 1979). Controversies are keen. Why do versions A and B of task X lead to such wide differences in performance? Why do problem isomorphs — that is, problems designed to have an identical structure of solution moves — often fail to operate as isomorphs (Hayes & Simon, 1977)? Explanatory concepts are advanced, but many attempts to take account of situational changes in performance have the status of appendages to the theoretical machinery rather than of components integrated within it.

Bartlett's (1958) classic studies of thinking avoided this dilemma. He considered that problem solving has the same characteristics as skilled performance in other modalities and that a defining attribute of skill is variability. Moreover, he held that variability is rule-governed: "all forms of skill expertly carried out possess an outstanding characteristic of rapid adaptation . . . so what is called the same operation is done now in one way and now in another, but each way is, as we say, 'fitted to the occasion'" (p. 14). This is a fitting description of the kind of thinking we have seen in action at the dairy. The variability we observed was neither random nor arbitrary. It was sufficiently systematic to appear in analyses without benefit of statistical tests. Following Bartlett, we might consider these regularities as forms of adaptation. We can then put to future studies this proposition: skilled practical thinking is goal-directed and varies adaptively with the changing properties of problems and changing conditions in the task environment. In this respect, practical thinking contrasts with the kind of academic thinking exemplified in the use of a single algorithm to solve all problems of a given type.

The concept of adaptive thinking need not be left on an analogical level. The dairy research raises one line of speculation that would be intriguing to pursue: practical thinking becomes adaptive when it serves the interests of economy of effort. Product assembly provided a vivid example of thinking saving manual effort; pricing-out provided a parallel demonstration of thinking saving mental effort. Effort-saving functioned as a criterion distinguishing skilled from amateur performance, not only for the researchers but for dairy employees evaluating their own or others' work. We do not know how general a characteristic of working intelligence such effort-saving might be. It may be peculiar to the special environment of the industrial workplace, or it may be specific to Western culture with its emphasis on efficiency and time- and labor-saving devices. Alternatively effort-saving may be a general characteristic of practical thinking, conferring "elegance" on solutions to problems in mathematical theory as well as to those confronted on the shop floor. These speculations suggest possible common questions for future functional studies of thinking, wherever they take place.

2. Institutional Decision-Making

Hugh Mehan

Many of the decisions made in everyday life are complex and open. They are complex in that people must choose among several alternatives which differ in regard to several criteria, each with different and incommensurate value (Tversky, 1972; Quinn, 1976). Everyday decision-making is open in that the range of alternatives is not known in advance, the alternatives and criteria do not remain stable from the beginning to the end of the situation, and other alternatives and problems may emerge in the course of decision making (Bartlett, 1958; Schutz, 1962).

Decision making in institutional settings is a variety of everyday decision-making. Educators in school settings must routinely assess students' performance and determine which learning environments are appropriate for their education. Teachers make such determinations within classrooms when they make moment-to-moment decisions about students' performance during question-and-answer sequences or across lessons, or when they place students into ability groups. Educators make such decisions between classrooms when they decide to promote students to the next grade, retain, or demote them. This last kind of decision making, specifically as practiced by committees of educators in determining whether to place students in special education programs or to retain them in their regular classrooms, was the subject of the study reported here.

The Special Education Referral System

The special education referral system is a naturally occurring feature of schools. Through this system, students are identified, assessed, and often placed in special education programs. The operation of this referral system provided a routinized setting for a naturalistic study of everyday decision-making in institutional settings.

Under normal circumstances, students progress through school in a regular sequence. They enter school in kindergarten and, at the end of each year, are promoted to the next higher grade. Not all students, however, follow this routine career pattern through school. Under unusual circumstances, students are removed from their regular classroom during the school year and are placed in a variety of "special education" programs. These special career paths have been a long-standing feature of public schools in the United States. Recently, federal legislation formalized the procedures involved in placing students in special education programs. Public Law 94-142, "The Education for All Handicapped Students" Act, was enacted to integrate handicapped individuals into the mainstream of American life.

The process mandated by PL 94-142 to identify, assess, and eventually place students in special education programs is a rich source of naturally occurring, routine decision-making, instances of which are difficult to create in laboratory settings. The study reported here followed the progress of students' cases through that referral system. Materials for the investigation were gathered in many ways. Official school records were reviewed; educators were interviewed, classrooms and meetings were observed, and key events were videotaped.

A given case has the potential of progressing through a number of major decision-making points, including "referral," "appraisal," "assessment," "reappraisal," "evaluation," and "placement," along the various "career paths" in the system (Fig. 2.1). During the 1978–79 school year in which material for this study was gathered, a total of 141 first-time referrals were processed through the special education referral system (Table 2.1).

This information about the products of the referral system represents the educational "facts" of the referral process (Mehan, Meihls, Hertweck & Crowdes, 1981). To explore the institutional practices that constitute these educational facts, "constitutive" analyses were conducted of a number of key events at the referral, assessment, and placement phases of the referral system.

Since the referral process starts in the classroom, the study attempted to uncover the grounds of teachers' referrals and depict the

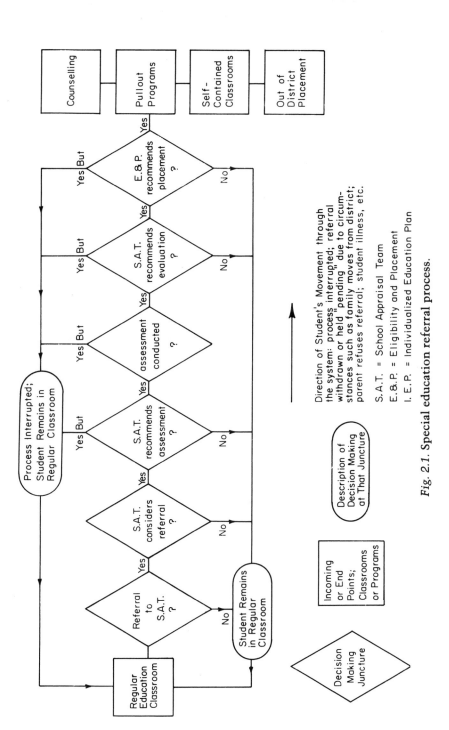

Fig. 2.1. Special education referral process.

Counselling

Pullout Programs

Self-Contained Classrooms

Out of District Placement

E.&P. recommends placement ?

S.A.T. recommends evaluation ?

assessment conducted ?

S.A.T. recommends assessment ?

S.A.T. considers referral ?

Referral to S.A.T. ?

Regular Education Classroom

Process Interrupted; Student Remains in Regular Classroom

Student Remains in Regular Classroom

Direction of Student's Movement through the system: process interrupted; referral withdrawn or held "pending" due to circumstances such as family moves from district; parent refuses referral; student illness, etc.

S.A.T. = School Appraisal Team
E.&P. = Eligibility and Placement
I.E.P. = Individualized Education Plan

Description of Decision Making at That Juncture

Incoming or End Points; Classrooms or Programs

Decision Making Juncture

Table 2.1. Career paths through the referral system

Career Path	Description	No.	%
1	Child referred, case never considered by School Appraisal Team (SAT); child remains in classroom	1	0.7
2	SAT considers case, no assessment recommended; child remains in classroom	19	13.6
3	Process interrupted at appraisal phase; child remains in classroom	24	17.1
4	SAT considers case at reappraisal phase, makes direct placement (Adaptive (PE) = 1; Bilingual = 3; Reading = 1; Counseling = 6)	11	7.9
5	SAT considers case, recommends assessment; assessment conducted, no evaluation recommended; child remains in classroom	28	20.0
6	Process interrupted at assessment or reappraisal phase; child remains in classroom	4	·2.8
7	Eligibility and Placement (E&P) Committee considers case, no placement recommended; child remains in classroom	1	0.7
8	Process interrupted at evaluation phase; child remains in classroom	1	0.7
9	E&P considers case; recommends placement in educationally handicapped classroom	7	5.0
10	E&P considers case; recommends placement in learning disabilities group	36	25.7
11	E&P considers case; recommends placement in severe language handicapped classroom	3	2.1
12	E&P considers case; recommends placement in multiple handicapped classroom	2	1.4
13	E&P considers case; recommends placement in speech therapy	3	2.1
14	E&P considers case; recommends placement outside of district	0	0
	Total	140	99.8

relations between teachers' accounts and students' behavior. To do so, teachers provided accounts of students' behavior during video-taped lessons. These accounts show that teachers do not perceive students' behavior directly. Their judgments about referrals are mediated by culturally and experientially provided categories that bear little relation to students' actual classroom behavior (Mehan, Hertweck, Combs & Flynn, 1982).

When the referral process involved psychological assessment, the study examined the procedures for assembling test results and reaching a diagnosis that was then used at later stages in the referral system. Videotapes of actual educational testing situations and the test results and reports produced from them formed the important data sources for this part of the overall study. Meihls (1981) found that test results are constructed jointly by teachers and students rather than being solely students' productions. Diagnoses by school psychologists are informed by test results, to be sure, but in impor-tant ways they are also influenced by teachers' informal opinions and by students' behavior in the informal aspects of testing situa-tions.

Mehan (1983) similarly analyzed the language of placement committee meetings. Reports made by psychologists and nurses during the "information presentation" phase of the meeting were treated differently from reports made by parents and teachers. Despite the fact that the reports by the professionals on the com-mittee employed a highly technical vocabulary, they were accepted without challenge or question, while the reports by parents and teachers were continually interrupted by requests for information and further clarification.

This differential treatment is explained by the authority that reports gain by their mode of presentation. The "professional report" gains its status and authority because it is obscure, difficult to understand, and embedded in the institutional trappings of the committee meeting. This authority contributes to the assembly of a "presentational" mode of making decisions, in which decisions are presented, not discussed; credentialed, not negotiated.

The Rational Model of Decision Making

The prevailing view in the social sciences literature, as well as in the federal law that governs the education of all handicapped students, is that social organizations, such as school systems, and the actors within them behave according to rational rules or criteria in reaching decisions. The origins of this "rational model" (Allison, 1971; Benson, 1977) lie in the Hobbsean concept of actors as utilitarian and value maximizing (Schutz, 1943; Weber, 1947; Simon, 1949; Schelling, 1950; Garfinkel, 1967). Parsons' (1932) delineation of the theory of action in terms of the means-end schema particularly influenced the development of this model.

The four primary elements of the models of rational action are: goals and objectives, alternatives, consequences, and choice (Allison, 1971). The goals and objectives are the "payoffs" or ends that the actors wish to reach. The actors must choose among a set of alternatives displayed before them in a particular situation. To each alternative is attached a set of consequences, or outcomes, which will ensue if that particular goal or objective is chosen. Choice consists simply of selecting that alternative whose consequences rank highest in the decision maker's payoff function.

This characterization is little more than an elaboration of the pervasive everyday assumption that people's actions are goal directed, or intentional. To conceive of action as rational is to do more than treat choices as merely calculated, purposive, or strategic. What rationality adds to the concept of purpose is consistency: consistency among goals and objectives and their relation to a particular actor, and consistency in the application of principles to select optimal behavior (Allison, 1971:28–29). The element of consistency, which gives action its decidedly rational character, is handled in one of two ways in prevailing theories: as "comprehensive" rationality or as "bounded" rationality.

According to Allison (1971), most theories of individual and organizational choice employ a concept of comprehensive rationality whereby individuals and organizations choose the best alternative, taking account of its consequences, probabilities, and utilities. Such choices require the consideration of all possible alternatives, an assessment of the probability of each one, and an evaluation of each set of consequences for all relevant goals. In this formulation, the alternatives refer to all alternatives; the consequences mean all consequences that will result from the choice of any one alternative. As Watkins (1970:206) notes, such "a decision scheme should consist of a complete specification of the possible outcomes, a complete preference map, or a complete allocation of payoff values to the outcomes, and (where appropriate) a comprehensive analysis for dealing with risks and uncertainties" (cf. Schutz, 1943; Janis & Mann, 1978).

Inherent in the rational model is an "optimizing" principle (Simon, 1949; March & Olsen, 1976). It has the goal of making the best decisions by maximizing the positive consequences and minimizing the negative consequences. The description of Benjamin Franklin's method for making systematic use of available information before rendering a practical judgment is a prime example of this optimizing principle (Elstein et al., 1978:25). Franklin apparently listed all the factors supporting or militating against a course of action, summed all the values in the pro and con columns, and made his judgment. However, in naturally occurring decision-making situations it is not clear just what the variables are that need to be weighed, or whether people employ such an algebra in actual practice.

There is a remarkable similarity between descriptions of comprehensive rational action within economics and sociology and descriptions of formal operational thinking within developmental psychology. Both treat the actors as "scientific reasoners." Piaget depicts the development of thinking as progressing through a fixed sequence of stages: from sensori-motor, through preoperational concrete operational, to formal operational thinking (Inhelder & Piaget, 1958). Formal operational thinking is the pinnacle of this developmental sequence. While the concrete operational child reasons from one element to another, with no overall structure for representing relationships, formal operational thinkers are able to coordinate the functioning of parts into an integrated structure. The coordination involves the ability to construct the combinatorial of all possibilities, to manipulate one variable at a time while holding everything else constant, and to deal with possibilities that are not actually observed. That is, formal operational thinking is assumed to entail a cognitive structure that is fully describable in terms of the logic of the propositional calculus (Wason, 1977).

In short, the reasoning of the actor in the rational model of formal organizations and the reasoning of the problem solver in the Piagetian model of cognitive development have analogous characteristics. Both the rational bureaucrat in a social organization and the formal operational thinker test hypotheses by gathering all the relevant information, considering all possibilities in their entirety, and varying one factor at a time while holding all other variables constant. That is, they employ "scientifically rational" forms of reasoning, solving problems in accordance with the canons of formal propositional logic.

Comprehensive rationality is sometimes employed essentially as a norm. Actual events are explained or criticized as approximations to the choices made by the comprehensive model. Use of the comprehensive model as a normative ideal invites invidious distinction between the decision making that transpires in naturally occurring situations and that which transpires in the so-called rational models of decision making (Parsons, 1932) or in formal operational thinking (Inhelder & Piaget, 1958). As a result, everyday decision makers are said either to employ "imperfect rationality" (Watkins, 1970) or to be characterized as "reluctant decision makers" (Janis & Mann, 1978).

While comprehensive rationality with its optimizing principle seems to epitomize fair judgment, it is often not clear whether the conditions necessary for making comprehensive decisions can be met in everyday and institutional decision-making situations. A number of theorists (e.g. Simon, 1949; Watkins, 1970) restrict their claims concerning optimal choice by focusing on the limits of human information-processing capacity in comparison with the complexities of problems that decision makers face. People do not make decisions by maximizing the positive consequences and minimizing the negative consequences, because "determining all the potentially favorable and unfavorable aspects of all feasible courses of action would require the decision maker to process so much information that impossible demands would be placed on his resources and mental capacities." While attempting to acquire the degree of knowledge needed to anticipate alternative outcomes, the decision maker is likely to be overwhelmed with information: "So many relevant variables may have to be taken into account that they can not all be kept in mind at the same time. The number of crucially relevant categories needed for rational decision making usually exceeds the capacity for processing in immediate memory. Handicapped by the shortcomings of the human mind, the decision maker's attention, asserts Simon, shifts from one value to another with consequent shifts in preference" (Janis & Mann, 1978:22).

People's performance on formal operational tasks leads Shweder (1977) to the further conclusion that the reasoning of well-educated

Western adults is no different from that used by Zande oracle readers and other so-called primitive thinkers. Both ignore correlation-relevant information. This "magical thinking" is said to be an expression of a universal cognitive-processing limitation of the human mind.

In sum, the social, ecological, and psychological limits of a person's capacity as alternative generator, information processor, and problem solver can strain the decision-making process such that conformance with the comprehensive or scientific ideal is difficult, if not impossible. The gap between the ideal model and actual practice is a matter of cognitive limitation; it is a failure, really, of the individual decision-maker. Decision makers make mistakes and errors because they cannot keep enough information in their heads or because they are inundated with too much information. Because of these bounds, intendedly rational action requires simplified models that extract the main features of a problem without capturing all its complexity.

As is the case with other concepts that structure everyday human activities, rational models of decision making in both comprehensive and bounded forms have an underlying or root metaphor (Pepper, 1944; Lakoff & Johnson, 1980). This metaphor is composed of a set of terms, which gain their meaning from their participation in a conceptual web (Allison, 1971):

1. The rational model implies that events have causes.
2. Decisions presuppose a decider and a choice among alternatives with reference to some goal.
3. Actions are taken by purposeful agents.
4. What is to be explained is the action, which is behavior that reflects purpose or intention.
5. An action is explained by reference to the aims of a unitary actor and his or her goals and objectives.

While the individual actor in a situation of choice, such as chess or prisoner's dilemma, is usually the unit of analysis, the rational model of action metaphor has been recapitulated at the organizational level. In such studies, the organization is equated with a person. As in everyday life, persons take actions that have causes; so, too, must organizations. An attempt is made to explain organizational events recounting the aims and calculations of organizations. Researchers studying organizational behavior see actions; they look for motives behind them.

Examination of various analyses of organizational and governmental actions (e.g. the Cuban missile crisis, the origins of World War I, Pearl Harbor) showed that each analysis assumes that what must be explained is an action or behavior that reflects purpose or intention: "the actor is a national government. The action chosen is a calculated solution to a strategic problem. Each explanation consists of showing what goal the organization was pursuing when it acted, and how the action was a reasonable choice, given the nation's objectives." The concept of rationality is important in organizational studies because it enables theorists to structure problems of choice. If the theorists know the ends of a decision maker, then they can predict what actions will be taken to achieve those ends. They do so by calculating the most reasonable way for the decision maker to achieve the goals, on the assumption that this is the way that will actually be taken, "because the decision maker is rational" (Allison, 1971:13, 50). The concept of rationality is also important because, if people act rationally, their behavior can be fully explained by reference to unitary actors and in terms of the goals they are trying to achieve.

The federal law that governs special education is based on the comprehensive version of the rational model of decision making. The major purpose of this law is "to assure that all handicapped children have available to them a free appropriate public education which emphasizes special education and related services designated to meet those needs" (Sec. 601c).

The handicapped students' needs are to be met by developing an individualized educational plan (IEP). The plan is developed by:

1. Documenting the student's current level of performance
2. Stating the goals to be obtained by the end of the school year
3. Stating the short-term, intermediate steps leading to the annual goals
4. Documenting the particular special education and related services which will be provided to the student

That is, the needs of the student are to be matched to the characteristics of a special education program. The student's needs are the first, foremost, and primary basis upon which the educational decision-making concerning placement is to be made.

The Decision-Making Process

The special education study was motivated by the belief that in order to understand decision making, the process must be explored as it unfolds in naturally occurring situations. Videotapes of the placement meetings were made for analysis, as well as documents used in and produced during the placement meetings. These materials and the information gained about the placement process from observations in the district afforded an unusual opportunity to examine educational decision making *in situ.*

Decisions to place students into special education programs were made by the eligibility and placement (E&P) committee, a team at the district level composed of the referred student's parent or parents, the school administrator in charge of special education, the school nurse, the district psychologist, the referring teacher, and a special education teacher. This committee had a number of placement options. It could recommend that the student be retained in the regular classroom, be placed in a number of special education programs, receive counseling, or be entered in a program outside the school district at district expense. Special education programs within the district can be grouped into "whole day" or "self-contained" programs and "pullout" programs. Self-contained programs (career paths 9, 11-12, Table 2.1) are considered more severe placements, because the student is removed from the regular classroom on a permanent basis. In pullout programs, such as the learning disabilities program, the student spends part of the school day in the regular classroom and part of the day in a special classroom.

E&P committees considered 53 cases during the course of this study. The great majority of the students (74%) were placed into pullout programs (career paths 10 and 13, Table 2.1), while 23% were placed into self-contained classrooms (career paths 9, 11-12, Table 2.1) by these committees. No students were placed in special education programs outside the district (career path 14, Table 2.1).

The committee meetings that were observed in the district during the year of the study followed a regular pattern. The meeting was convened by either the district representative or the school psychologist in charge of the case. Then each of the committee members who had information about the student under consideration for placement made a report. Immediately after these reports, the student's placement was determined. Then, parents were told of their rights to private schooling, and the goals and objectives for the educational placement were discussed. Hence, committee meetings routinely had the following "phases," which took place in a regular temporal sequence:

1. Information presentation phase
2. Decision phase
3. Parents rights' phase
4. Goals and objectives phase

There are a number of striking features about the interaction among the committee members concerning the placement of students. Placement decisions were made quickly. After the school psychologist, classroom teacher, nurse, and parents provided information about the student (phase one), the student's placement was determined. The following exchanges are representative of the interaction in the second or "decision" phase of the meeting:

Psychologist: Does the, uh, committee agree that the, uh, learning disability placement is one that might benefit him?
Principal: I think we agree.
Psychologist: We're not considering, then, a special day class at all for him?
Special Education Teacher (SET): I wouldn't at this point.
Others: No.

· · · · ·

Psychologist: Okay, in light of all the data that we have, I think that the program we want to recommend is the learning disability group pullout program.
Mother: Pullout — I don't understand that.
Psychologist: For Tracy. You know, that's the program we sort of talked about that day, where he would be pulled out of the classroom for specific work on the areas that he needs, that, you know, are identified today.

· · · · ·

Psychologist: Okay. Now, okay, now then, let's, why don't we take a vote, um, for the learning disabilities group pullout program. Um, is there anyone, anyone who does not agree? Okay. I think that was unanimous. *(Soft laughter.)* All right. Then what we have to do now is sign. But, um, before we sign, I'd like to have uh, Suzanna, um, talk about the rights to private schooling and talk about your rights as parents.

District Representative (DR): I think you probably have these two forms, but they talk about your rights as parents. I'm going to give you a copy anyway so, um, you are aware.

Psychologist: I think you received it in the mail before.

DR: Yeah. You probably did. I'd also like to inform you of your rights as parents to private schooling for Ricardo *if* the district should not have an appropriate program for the child. Uh, this is the law. However, under the same law, we feel that we *do* have a program for your child that would meet his needs. Okay? So I'm going to ask you to sign this form, and you'll keep a copy, and I'll sign the form too. And this is just only to inform you of your rights. Okay?

Parent (inaudible. Signs form.)

These exchanges do not have all the features routinely associated with rational decision-making in either its comprehensive or its bounded forms, which assume the presentation of a range of alternatives and the consideration of consequences of any choice singly and in combination with others. One of the significant ways in which these activities differed from current theories of decision making concerns the range of alternatives. The entire range of possible placements was not discussed during these placement meetings. At most the possibility of placement in one or two closely related programs was considered, such as an educationally handicapped classroom or a learning disability program. And these possibilities were seldom debated or discussed. An alternative was presented to the committee by the school psychologist without question or challenge by other members of the committee, including the parents.

These observations point to a gap between the rational model as conceived in the ideal and the real decisions observed in actual practice. We seek to understand this manner of reaching educational decisions. While we may agree that these committee members are not reasoning like scientists, or even like Ben Franklin, there is considerably less agreement about why this is so. It is important to avoid disparaging everyday decision-making by comparing it to rational models and formal logic. Instead, institutional decision-making should be defined in its own terms, consistent with the participants' practices. The present inquiry is therefore recollective. It aims to recollect what is known by participants in their practical activity, albeit tacitly known by them (Mehan, 1979; Heap, 1980). It does not want to impose schemas from experimental situations on everyday life situations, because the principles that organize experimental situations vary in significant ways from the principles that organize everyday life situations: "There is a danger . . . in applying the language developed for the psychology of the individual to describe the functioning of the social system. When we speak of organizational goals, organizational choice, organizational language, and decision making, we must restrict our reference to certain leaders and subgroups and not regard the organization as a person. If we do not we will oversimplify organizational behavior" (Katz & Kahn, 1978:480–481).

Practical Circumstances of Institutional Decision-Making

Study of the circumstances of decision making about special education, which includes the organization of both the immediate problem-solving situation and the school system as a social institution, turns up "good organizational reasons," to borrow a phrase from Garfinkel (1967), for decision making in placement meetings to be structured in the way that it is. Decision-making in institutional settings confronts people with a number of economic, legal, and practical considerations that constrain placement decisions and the processes by which such decisions are reached. For example, the public law governing special education indicates that 12% of the school-aged population are to be served by special education programs. The compulsory thrust of this law provides an incentive to search for, identify, and place students into special education programs in order to meet mandated quotas.

The legal incentive to search for special education students is reinforced by financial incentives. School districts are provided funds from state and federal sources for each student in regular school classrooms and a greater amount of money for students in special education classrooms. They receive more money for students in pullout special education programs, and still more money on a sliding scale for students in whole day and more severe placement programs. This additional source of revenue serves as an incentive to search for students to place in special education.

Just as there are incentives to locate and place students in special education programs in order to receive the maximum state and federal support, so there are disincentives to find too many special students. Funds for special programs are not unlimited. A funding ceiling is reached when a certain number of students are placed in one classroom for the educationally handicapped or in one learning disability group, etc. No additional money is provided if more students than the quota are assigned to particular programs. These financial and legal considerations constrain placement decisions and reduce the number of options available to the committee.

The potential range of placement options available to the placement committee is manifold. Yet the comittee in this study gave no evidence of considering the entire range of alternatives in their meeting. A much smaller range of closely related placement possibilities was considered. A number of organizational practices operate to reduce the number of alternatives considered by the committee in its final placement meeting. Like Goffman's (1961) and Garfinkel's (1967) "management practices," many of these practices operate before a formal meeting is convened.

Certain placement options, while logically possible, are for all practical purposes not available to the decision makers during committee meetings. The option to place students in programs outside the district at district expense is one such option that is simply not available to the committee. That placement possibility was eliminated from consideration by administrative fiat long before placement committees met because of the inordinate expense involved in out-of-district placements. A separate program for mentally retarded students is another placement option not available to the committee as a consequence of prior administrative decisions. The district did not establish separate classrooms for these students. Instead, they are distributed to other programs, such as severe language handicapped (career path 11, Table 2.1). Given these institutional arrangements, it is not surprising that the out-of-district placement options were not considered by the committee during the year of this study.

The number of students already assigned to special education programs eliminates other options from consideration prior to an eligibility and placement committee meeting. Programs that are "full," having reached the funding ceiling, are eliminated from consideration, while programs that have not reached the legally mandated quota remain subject to consideration.

Vagaries in the school calendar also influence the consideration

of placement options. The district operates on a year-round schedule. Instead of conducting classes from September to June and
designating the summer months as vacation, a staggered schedule
of classes and vacations is maintained. Because of this staggered
schedule, regular and special education teachers who are to cooperate in the education of certain students often find themselves on
incompatible track schedules. This incompatibility of schedules
eliminates certain placement options from consideration by the
committee. One consequence of these legal, financial, and practical
constraints is that the designation "handicapped student" is as
much a function of the school calendar, the demographic characteristics of the student population, and other features of the social
organization of the school as it is a function of some inherent
characteristics of the student.

Once the list of logically possible placement choices has been
reduced to a smaller number of actually possible choices by the host
of practical circumstances constraining decision making, the committee decides on a placement for the student. The actions of the
E&P committee members suggest that the final placement decisions are made in terms of a number of factors, including the
educational programs that are available, the funds that are available, the teacher's schedules, and the legal requirements, rather
than solely in terms of the student's "disability." More specifically,
the committee first determined which placement categories were
available and then chose a placement for the student. The committee did not first assess the student, design a program, and then
search for an educational plan which matched that assessment in
each and every detail.

This practice of making placements by available category contrasts sharply with the theory of decision making inherent in special education law and rational models of action. The construction
of an individualized education plan for students with special needs
is envisioned in theory by some special educators, advocates (e.g.
the Council for Exceptional Children), and parents as a sequential
process in which the goals and objectives for the child's education are agreed upon, the services to be provided to the child are
spelled out, educational criteria are specified, and a written plan
is prepared, which is then signed by the parent. Thus, the law
implies a certain temporal order for the conduct of the placement
meetings:

1. Determination of child's present level of performance
2. Writing of goals and objectives based on the discrepancy between the child's actual and expected levels of performance
3. Explanation of parents' rights to educational services and the range of available services
4. Reaching a decision about the appropriate placement for the child based on those goals and objectives

This sequence of events was not followed in practice. The district's E&P meetings did not have that temporal order. The actual order of events was:

1. Presentation of information by committee members (same as #1 in the law)
2. Placement decision (#4)
3. Explanation of parents' rights (#3)
4. Writing of goals and objectives (#2)

The variation between the expected and the actual order of events in placement meetings demonstrates that the goals and objectives for the individual child were not written first, and then the services suggested to meet these goals. Instead, placement was selected in the context of available services.

The explanation of the parents' rights after the placement decision but before the goals and objectives were written is particularly telling in this regard. Typical of the statements read to parents during placement meetings is: "Mrs. Ladd, if we, um, after evaluating Shane, find that, um, we don't have the proper placement, the classroom available, appropriate placement for Shane, then you can request, or you have rights to private school, and you can request that. We've made the decision that we do have a class available for Shane to go into."

This statement indicates that the availability of an educational program had been determined before the goals and objectives for the student were determined. This practice effectively forecloses discussion of educational alternatives.

The organization of the information presentation phase of the E&P meetings is another indication that placement decisions are made in terms of available categories. Following is a typical presentation of a referral student's case by a school psychologist:

Psychologist: Um. What we're going to do is, I'm going to have a brief, an overview of the testing, because the rest of, of the, the committee has not, uh, has not an, uh, been aware of that yet. And, uh, then each of us will share whatever, whatever we feel we need to share.

Principal: Right.

Psychologist: And then we will make a decision on what we feel is a good, oh, placement for, ah, Shane. Shane is, ah, nine years old, and he's in fourth grade. Uh, he, uh, was referred because of low academic performance, and he has difficulty applying himself to his daily class work. Um, Shane attended the Montesorri School in kindergarten and first grade, and then he entered Carlsberg-bad in, um, September of 1976 and, uh, entered our district in, uh, '78. He seems to have very good peer relationships, but, uh, the teachers, uh, continually say that he has difficulty with handwriting. 'Kay. He enjoys music and sports. I gave him a complete battery, and, um, I found that, uh, he had a verbal I.Q. of 115, performance of 111, and a full scale of 115, so he's a bright child. Uh, he had very high scores in, uh, information which is his long-term memory. Ah, vocabulary was, ah, also, ah, considerably over average, good detail awareness, and his, um, picture arrangement scores, he had a seventeen, which is very high —

SET: Mmmm.

Psychologist: — very superior rating, so he, his visual sequencing seems to be good, and also he has a good grasp of anticipation and awareness of social situations. Um, he (*scanning her notes*) scored in reading at 4.1, spelling 3.5, and arithmetic 3.0, which gave him a standard score of 100 in, uh, reading, 95 in spelling, and 90 in arithmetic. When compared with his overall score, it does put him somewhat, ah, below his, you know, his capabilities. I gave him the Bender Gestalt (*clears throat*), and he had six errors. And his test age was 7–0 to 7–5, and his actual age is nine, so it, uh, he was considerably beneath his, uh, his, uh, age level. His — I gave him the, uh, VADS, and his, um (*looking through notes*), both the oral-aural and the visual-written modes of communication were high but the visual oral and the oral written are low, so he, uh, cannot switch channels. His expressive vocabulary was in the superior range. Uh, visual perception falls above age level, so he's fine in that area. And fine motor skills appear to be slightly lower than, uh, average (*voice trails off slightly*). I saw them. He read words very quickly when he was doing the academics, but I didn't see any reversals in his written work. Uh, I gave him several projective tests, and, um, the things that I picked up there is that, um, he does possibly have some fears and anxieties, uh. So I had felt, ah, that perhaps he might, uh, uh, benefit, um, from special help. He also was tested, um, in 1976, and at that time he was given the WISC-R, and his I.Q. was slightly lower, full scale of a 93. His, um, summary of that evaluation, uh, was, uh, he was given the ITPA and he had high auditory reception, auditory association, auditory memory. So his auditory skills are good. He was given another psychol — psychological evaluation in 1977. He was given the Leiter, and he had an I.Q. of 96. And, um, they concluded that he had a poor mediate recall, but they felt that was due to an emotional overlay and they felt that some emotional conflicts were, uh, interfering with his ability to concentrate. That's about all I have, Kitty. Would you like to share with us.

The organization of the E&P meetings complements the interactional work of educators earlier in the referral process. Placement outcomes are not so much decisions reached in the meetings as they are ratifications of actions that took place at previous stages of the decision-making process.

Considerable preplacement planning precedes the formal placement meeting. The reappraisal meetings often serve this purpose. They are occasions to prepare the paperwork needed in the placement meeting. The preplanning saves considerable time during placement meetings, which are attended by several highly paid professionals with busy schedules. The reappraisal meetings are also viewed as an opportunity for the staff to reach a consensus before meeting with parents. The consensus can be either a gentle way of informing the parent of the child's problem or a defensive strategy for dealing with a parent aggressively seeking expensive service outside the district.

This is not to say that the E&P committee is simply applying a rubber stamp to decisions made surreptitiously (Becker, 1963) or performing a public ritual to parade decisions made behind the scenes (Goffman, 1961). The distinction between conspiracy and ratification is similar to the organizational differences between the problems posed to subjects in experiments and those organized by participants in naturally occurring situations.

In an experimental situation, a finite number of variables is presented to the subject. The subject's job is to sort out this small number of variables. Thus, the problem is under the control of a single person or can be managed by that person. The information available to the committee is not of the same sort. The number of variables that the committee has to consider is large, much larger than that which is presented to the subjects of an experiment. The scope and complexity of the variables is so great, in fact, that each single member of the committee does not know them all, or even what they are. In fact, part of the project of the committee is first to find out what the relevant variables are and then to sort them out. By contrast, the subjects in experiments have only the sorting operation to perform, because the variables have been isolated and presented to them.

The problem-solving situation for the placement committee is like other naturally occurring situations and is unlike experimental situations by virtue of the presence of other people who serve as social resources (Lave, 1979; Cole & Traupmann, 1981; Levin & Kareev, 1980). The committee members are knowledgeable not only in the general sense of being highly trained and experienced educators but in the specific sense of each committee member being a repository of information about the particular student discussed. Each person comes to the meeting as an "informed citizen" (Schutz, 1964:120–134) about the student. Each has a memory of similar committee meetings held in the past as part of this stock of knowledge. As a consequence of this social distribution of knowledge, the information upon which decisions are reached is not any one individual person's memory; it is in the collective memory of the group.

Therefore, it is more productive to think of the E&P committee meeting as a culmination, a formalization, of a lengthy process that originates in the classroom. The construction of an educationally handicapped student's career or educational biography starts when the teacher makes the initial referral. Often, the teacher has only a general notion that a student "is in trouble" or "needs help." This initial, rather general attribution establishes the presumption of a handicap. This attribution becomes refined as more and more institutional machinery (e.g. tests, committee meetings, home visits) is applied to the case, until finally, by the placement meeting, only a parent's refusal to sign the documents during the placement meeting would be likely to change the assumed placement. The fact that all but one of the cases brought before E&P committees resulted in special education placement is further evidence that early actions were being ratified at this stage in the process.

This ratification of actions reached at earlier stages or events in the referral process is similar to the process by which a person becomes transformed from a "normal person" to a "mentally ill patient" (Goffman, 1961; Scheff, 1966; Rosenhan, 1973). The process of the construction of mental illness starts when a person is presented to a public health official. The entrance of a specialist into a situation that has been defined as "something wrong with someone here" establishes the presumption of a defect within the individual. This presumption is reaffirmed as the person, now a patient, goes through successive stages of the psychiatric intake process until, finally, the staff and patient alike accept the definition.

Conclusions

This investigation of the organizational practices of decision making in educational placement shows that there is no need to disparage everyday decision-making by comparing it with rational models, formal reasoning, or scientific thinking. Sir Cyril Burt observed about the use of the predicate calculus, which is at the heart of scientific reasoning, as a model for everyday reasoning: "Logic . . . used as a method of analysis would be both inappropriate and illuminating but used as a standard for critical evaluation it would not only be inappropriate but highly misleading. Piaget seems to have fallen into the trap thus indicated. After a series of ingenious experiments and valuable psychological observations, he suddenly assumes the Cambridge logician's academic gown, and judges the children's performance in terms of the continental version of the Russell-Whitehead symbolism. I am thinking of the ideal adolescent who is supposed to perform a combinatorial analysis yielding 16 alternatives and to test them systematically. He forgets that this logic is modelled on the mathematician's ideal: it is not the logic of everyday life" (Wason, 1977:112).

When describing the way in which everyday decisions are reached in institutional settings, one need not posit a gap between some ideal model and actual practice. Instead, it seems more appropriate to call into question the efficacy of scientific reasoning as a model of everyday reasoning, because there are good organizational reasons why institutional decision-making occurs in the way that it does. The decision-making circumstances assumed to exist by the rational model are not available to problem solvers in formal organizations like schools, hospitals, and businesses (March & Olsen, 1976; Weick, 1976; Bensen, 1977). Decision makers simply do not have the unlimited access to unlimited resources presupposed by rational decision-making models.

Furthermore, the rational model assumes that all factors being considered in the decision-making calculus have an equal weight. But in the complexity of institutional settings not all factors necessarily do have an equal weight. A certain fastidiousness is required when considering all the alternatives, which can blind the decision maker to an appreciation for the most important factors that need to be taken into account. As Watkins (1970:206) noted: "A well known obstacle to computerizing chess is the lack of any known way to program a computer to concentrate on *interesting* developments: like the ideal decision maker of normative theory, the computer surveys the entire board and takes every possibility into account."

In the case of the school district, fiscal, legal, and practical circumstances constrain the process by which decisions are reached. For example, when the placement of a student into a special education program is being considered, the student's age, gender, and IQ scores and the space available in a program may all be factors to weigh. But the space available in the program may be the overwhelmingly important factor, outweighing all others in its consequences for the decision makers. That is, in dealing with comparable problems, decision makers may know from prior experience that it is best to be highly selective and pay attention to a few salient alternatives that they know well in advance, instead of painstakingly computing the combination of all possibilities. These organizational constraints and this prior knowledge lead educational decision-makers to reduce the range of alternatives, make educational placements by available category, and ratify actions taken earlier.

Cognitive psychologists have described a number of heuristics that individual problem-solvers use to cope with information overload, limitations of short-term memory, and other information-processing limitations. Some of these heuristics include the "salience heuristic" (used to select information), the "availability heuristic" (to recall information), the "representativeness heuristic" (to classify information), and the "anchoring heuristic" (to retrieve initial judgments — Tversky & Kahneman, 1974; Norman & Bobrow, 1975). Some of the institutional practices that groups of people working in social organizations have devised to cope with the practical, legal, and fiscal constraints on decision making are part and parcel of an institutionally arranged system for making frequently recurring decisions (Quinn, 1976).

Problem-solving heuristics and institutional practices are similar processes, although their locus of operation seems different. Problem-solving heuristics are thought of as operating "between the ears" of individuals; institutional practices operate "between the people" in an organization. Thus, similar cognitive processes are recapitulated at different levels of social structure. While the psychological and social operations are similar, one does not reduce to the other. Decision making at the institutional level cannot be described simply by adding a few more factors to a psychological model (Simon, 1976), nor vice versa. A complete cognitive theory needs to include a description of both psychological and social cognitive operations, as well as a description of their articulation together (Cicourel, 1980; D'Andrade, in press; Laboratory of Comparative Human Cognition, 1981), in order to account for how both sets of processes are made manifest in the interaction between people.

A number of important psychological theories incorporate a "central processing" feature (Inhelder & Piaget, 1958; Witkin & Berry, 1975; Simon, 1976; Laboratory of Comparative Human Cognition, 1981). Central processing in this context implies a universal set of cognitive operations, internal to the individual, which operate in a centralized fashion to control how the world is interpreted and acted upon. Central processing is also a feature of the rational model of decision making, in both its comprehensive and its bounded forms. Central processing in the psychological context implies the operation of a unitary actor. Individual problem-solvers or large-scale organizations make choices by considering payoff functions, generating possible alternatives, and assessing consequences of probabilities, and they do so in centralized, controlled ways on particular occasions.

The decision making observed in this institutional context does not have the features associated with central processing. Instead, decision making seems to be "socially distributed." The decision making is distributed in two senses of the term: across participants and through time.

The decision making is distributed across participants in that information about the case is not under the control of any one committee member. Various members of the committee have information about certain aspects of the case (the teacher knows about the student's classroom activities, the psychologist knows about the student's test performance, the nurse has made a home visit). Decision making is distributed through time in that bits and pieces of the final decision are made at various stages in the referral process. The process starts in the classroom; information is added in the appraisal, assessment, and reappraisal phases. Meetings with parents provide still more information to some, but not all, of the committee members.

Thus, information is gathered at different points in time and is scattered across various committee members. The first time that the committee hears all the particulars of a case is in the E&P meeting. At this time the complete picture of the student emerges from the particulars previously distributed across the temporal phases of the referral process and the separate committee members.

The decision-making situation in which the variables or information are not under the control of any one person is an example of what Schutz (1964) called the "social distribution of knowledge" and what cognitive psychologists call "distributed processing" (Laboratory of Comparative Human Cognition, 1981; Levin, 1981). In socially distributed processing, the information upon which decisions are made is in the collective memory of the group, not in any one individual's memory.

This distinction between central and socially distributed processing enables the logical status of the committee's actions to be reconsidered. Looked at from the point of view of a group of people deciding an educational placement based on a student's needs, the committee seems illogical and irrational, because it is not considering the full range of possible placements, not considering one variable at a time, and not reviewing the complete means-ends matrix. But this interpretation dissolves when a socially distributed view of decision making is taken into account. The actions of the committee look more rational when the many other factors, including money available, space available, teachers' schedules and compatibility, and legal constraints, as well as the students' needs, are entered into the equation. Moreover, although the combination of all possible placement categories is not considered in any one committee meeting, the full range is distributed across the referral, appraisal, and evaluation phases of the referral process. Watkins (1970:206) exactly captured this aspect of everyday decision-making practices: "An ideal decision scheme is pictured as being present to the agent's mind in its entirety, a completed whole in which the several components simultaneously play their dual role. An actual decision scheme is usually built up bit by bit, so that the arrival of an isolated bit of situational information may have a disproportionate influence. And even when all the evidence is in, the practical significance of different parts of it may wax and wane as the decision maker attends now to this factor, now to that."

The rational model of decision making implies that events have causes and that bureaucracies perform large actions for large reasons. For some purposes, organizational behavior can be usefully summarized as action chosen by a rational decision-maker, centrally controlled, completely informed, and value maximizing. However, the present study and other work (Allison, 1971; March & Olsen, 1976) suggests that such a view must be balanced by the appreciation that large organizations are highly differentiated decision-making structures. By this "organizational process" view, large acts emerge from many smaller actions, socially distributed across many levels of an organization. These small acts are the consequence of regular procedures. Standard operating procedures constitute routines for dealing with standard situations. Routines allow large numbers of ordinary people to deal with numerous instances day after day. In the school district under study such routines include directives written to enact the provisions of special education federal law, directives written about special education students and off-campus placements, the sequence of decision making, and the temporal order in the conduct of business at a given E&P meeting. Such organizational routines and institutional practices structure the decision-making situations and narrow the possibilities in terms of which decision makers can make decisions about students' placement.

Furthermore, the project before the committee is preeminently a practical one. The decision-making task is a part of the educators' job, a routine event in the course of their daily, institutional lives. This practical concern makes the committee sensitive to the nature of the particular case before them and to its particular outcome. The committee is faced with a specific problem that demands an immediate, concrete solution, and demands it now. They are concerned with this student, this placement, at this time. They are not concerned with generating the range of all possible actions that exist in the abstract for the sake of doing so. Thus, the members of the committee have a pragmatic not a theoretical motive for their actions (Schutz, 1964; Scribner, 1977). Their project is to get this work done, to settle this case, so that they can get back to other practical projects that are piling up on their desks or that await them in their classrooms.

In this respect, the decision-making action of the committee is submerged in the other practical activities confronting the committee members during the course of their daily, institutional lives. What appears to be the project from the point of view of rational action (making decisions) turns out to be a component part of more inclusive practical projects. The manifest cognitive task is embedded in an ongoing project of action.

What occurs here is a shift in perspective — really a shift in metaphor — for viewing organizational behavior. When organizational behavior is examined from the perspective of the rational model, one sees "acts" and "choices," and searches for "reasons" and "motives." When organizational behavior is examined from the perspective of the organizational process perspective, one sees end results, and looks for the routine practices that constitute them. As a consequence of this shift in perspective, organizational behavior can be understood less as deliberate choice and more as end results, or as consequences of organizations functioning according to standard operating procedures. For this case study, the shift in metaphor means that the placement of a student is more a function of organizational procedure than of organizational choice. The placement of a student in a special education program is not so much a decision made as it is an enactment of routines.

3. The Dialectic of Arithmetic in Grocery Shopping

Jean Lave

Michael Murtaugh

Olivia de la Rocha

The ubiquity and unremarkable character of routine activities such as grocery shopping qualify them as apt targets for the study of thought in its customary haunts. For the same reasons, these activities are difficult to analyze. Such an enterprise faces thorny theoretical as well as methodological problems, for it depends on an integrated approach to everyday activities in context (Lave, in preparation). We address these general problems here mainly by example, focusing specifically on a familiar social institution, the supermarket, which is a highly structured environment for the exercise of a clearly defined activity, grocery shopping.

In recent years there has been increasing concern about the ecological validity of experimental research within cognitive and developmental psychology (e.g. Bronfenbrenner & Mahoney, 1975; Neisser, 1976; Cole, Hood & McDermott, 1978; Bronfenbrenner, 1979). There is speculation that the circumstances that govern problem solving in situations which are not prefabricated and minimally negotiable differ from those that can be examined in experimental situations. The fundamental questions raised by such speculation demand a more radical change in the nature and scope of theoretical and empirical research than has, perhaps, been generally recognized.

However, in an attempt to develop an adequate perspective from which to consider cognition in context, the analysis of data on supermarket arithmetic has been initiated as simply as possible, with a series of five common-sense propositions about the contextualized nature of human activity. These have provided guidelines for the empirical study, which in turn suggested more strongly the outlines of a systematic theoretical position. First, arithmetic activity has formal properties which make it identifiable in the flow of experience in many different situations. Second, the enormous productivity of script theory (Schank & Abelson, 1977) and the organization of environments in relation to scripted activities (e.g. the drugstore, fourth grade classroom) suggest that the human organization of activity gives primacy to segments on the order of ten minutes to two hours. Arithmetic problem-solving is thus smaller in scope than the units of activity in which people organize and think about their activities as wholes. It follows from these two assumptions that arithmetic activity should be strongly shaped in form, outcome, and meaning by the broader scope of activity and setting within which it occurs. It should also be shaped by the past experience and beliefs of the problem solver about what that individual is doing, what should happen in the course of doing it, and what the setting is in which it is taking place. Finally, an "integrated" approach to arithmetic activity in context has two meanings: the integral nature of activity in relation with contexts, and the mutual interdependence of mental and physical activity. Both meanings of *integration* prescribe a research methodology whereby data should be gathered directly about people-doing-in-their-usual-contexts.

These propositions do not constitute a theory of activity-in-setting, for they do not specify relations between activity and setting or between the individual and the social order within which the world is actively experienced. In their present form, however, they suggest a series of analytic steps for the elucidation of the case study. Grocery shopping was selected because it is an activity which occurs in a setting specialized to support it: the supermarket. Taking the supermarket as the arena for grocery-shopping activity, the analysis focused on the question: What is it about grocery shopping in supermarkets that might create the effective context for what is construed by shoppers as "problem-solving activity"? What are the general characteristics of problem solving when something happens in the course of shopping that appears problematic to the shopper? And how does the character of problem solving within grocery shopping specifically affect the nature of arithmetic activity?

To answer these questions, the Adult Math Skills Project was designed to investigate arithmetic decision-making processes during grocery shopping. This involved extensive interviewing, observation, and experimental work with twenty-five adult, expert grocery shoppers in Orange County, California. Detailed, transcribed observations of shopping preparation, a major shopping trip, and storage and use of the purchased foodstuffs over a period of weeks represented one dimension of the work. A comparative dimension involved a sampling of arithmetic practices in several settings by these same individuals. The Orange County residents varied in age from twenty-one to eighty, in income from $8,000 per family to $100,000, and in education from eighth grade to an M.A. degree. Twenty-two were female, and all were native speakers of English whose schooling took place in United States public schools.

The data were obtained through participant observation. Before entering the supermarket, shoppers strapped a tape recorder over their shoulder and were asked to "think out loud" while proceeding through the store, because the two anthropologists accompanying them were interested in learning about their shopping procedures, whatever they might be. As a shopper walked through the store, one researcher maintained a running conversation with the shopper. This approach grew out of pilot work using both more and less active methods, which indicated that shoppers feel more comfortable describing their behavior as part of a conversation than simply as a monologue. The conversational approach also made it possible to clarify many of the shoppers' comments and other aspects of the shopping environment that would otherwise not be clear in a taped recording.

The researchers also sought information about influences on the shopping decisions that the shoppers themselves might not volunteer. Once an item was selected, the shopper was asked about other items present which had not been mentioned. These questions generated much additional information. In all cases the researcher was careful not to interpret the situation for the shopper but rather to clarify the shopper's behavior for the record. Since the attempt to exercise high ethnographic standards could not eliminate the interaction between actor and observer, rather than ignoring it, the analysis takes it into account.

The Constructs of Setting, Arena, and Context

The conceptualization of setting derived from Barker's view that "the environment of behavior is a relatively unstructured, passive, probabilistic arena of objects and events upon which man behaves in accordance with the programming he carries about within himself. . . But when we look at the environment of behavior as a phenomenon worthy of investigation for itself, and not as an instrument for unraveling the behavior-relevant programming within persons, the situation is quite different. From this viewpoint the environment is seen to consist of highly structured, improbable arrangements of objects and events which coerce behavior in accordance with their own dynamic patterning" (1968:4).

For Barker, a segment of the environment is sufficiently coherent to be identified as a behavior setting if little of the behavior found in the setting extends into another setting, if there is sufficient sharing of personnel within that setting but limited sharing with related settings, if behaviors in the setting are closer to each other in time and space than to behaviors outside the setting, and if there is greater sharing of objects and modes of behavior in subparts of the setting than between this setting and related ones. Barker and Wright (1954) operationalized these criteria in undertaking to describe all of the settings of a year's behavior in a small town in Kansas. The goal of their monumental effort was not to produce an ecological description of a town but to account for the behavior of its inhabitants. They argued that for each setting there is a standing pattern of behavior, which can be thought of as a set of norms prescribing appropriate behavior. They often referred to these literally as "rules of the game." Further, the setting and the patterned sequence of behavior taking place in the setting are similar in structure, or "synomorphic."

This conceptualization of setting, with its ideal of structural fit, or synomorphy, provides a promising beginning for theorizing about activity, setting, and their interrelations. But it assumes a unidirectional, setting-driven relation between activity and setting, which reduces activity to a passive response to the setting. Correspondingly, analysis of the internal organization of activity becomes impossible. Barker's conceptualization also precludes analysis of the relation between behavior and setting, because only one of the two poles of this relation is available for analysis in its own right. He recognized the existence of a more complicated state of affairs than his model can encompass, remarking that "a great amount of behavior in Midwest is concerned with creating new milieu arrangements to support new standing patterns of behavior, or altering old milieu features to conform to changes in old patterns of behavior" (1968: 32). But his model has no mechanism in it that would account for these possibilities.

The obvious way to reject the view that settings are objective entities, independent of observer and participant alike, is to place new emphasis on Barker's view that the elements which create behavior settings change from setting to setting, and to reinterpret settings in phenomenological terms as the constructions of participants (cf. Laboratory of Comparative Human Cognition, 1981). But if setting is not an objective phenomenon, it is hard to account for Barker's enumeration and description of behavior settings in a town in Kansas. This impressive empirical evidence supports the theory of settings as objective entities and casts doubt on the feasibility of a strictly phenomenological alternative. This poses a dilemma, for which the time-honored solution is appropriate: both views are partially correct, though neither is complete.

Certain aspects of behavior settings have durable and public properties. The supermarket is such a durable entity — a physically, economically, politically, and socially organized space-in-time. In this aspect it may be called an "arena" within which activity takes place. The supermarket as arena is the product of patterns of capital formation and political economy. It is not negotiable directly by the individual. It is outside of, yet encompasses the individual, providing a higher-order institutional framework within which setting is constituted. At the same time, for individual shoppers the supermarket is a repeatedly experienced, personally ordered and edited version of the arena. In this aspect it may be termed a "setting" for activity. Some aisles in the supermarket do not exist for a given shopper as part of his setting, while other aisles are multifeatured areas to the shopper who routinely seeks a particular familiar product.

The relationship between these newly differentiated units of analysis, "arena" and "setting," is reflected in the ordinary use of the term *context*. What appear to be contradictory features of meaning may be accounted for by recognizing that context refers to a relationship rather than to a single entity. For on the one hand, context connotes an identifiable, durable framework for activity, with properties that transcend the experience of individuals, exist prior to them, and are entirely beyond their control. On the other hand, context is experienced differently by different individuals.

The supermarket study distinguished between the imposed constraints of the supermarket as arena and the constructable, malleable nature of the setting in relation with the activity of particular shoppers. Because a social order and the experience of it mutually entail one another, there are limits on both the obdurate and malleable aspects of every context.

The Construct of Activity

In dealing with the active individual in interaction with her context, the study drew on the concept of activity that has been developed in Soviet psychology. Activity theory, in contrast with the setting-dominated view of interaction, addresses the organization intrinsic to activity. According to Leontiev, activity "is not a reaction or aggregate of reactions, but a system with its own structure, its own internal transformations and its own development" (Wertsch, 1981:255).

Leontiev defined three levels of activity. The highest level is that activity which occurs in relation to motive, or "energizing force" (e.g. play, work, formal instruction). Leontiev gave hunger as an example of a motive: "This provides the energizing force behind an organism's activity, but at this level of abstraction nothing is said about the goals or ends toward which the organism is directed." This level appears too abstract to relate to the person-acting-in-context approach of the supermarket study. Moreover, work and play refer to cultural categories of activity rather than to specific activities in context. The remaining levels in the theory of activity fit more easily with the units of analysis in the study. The second level is an action defined by its goal (e.g. solving an arithmetic problem, finding the shelf in the supermarket with olives on it). The third level is that of operations, which contrasts with the action level since "certain conditions in the environment influence the way an action is carried out without giving rise to consciously recognized goals or subgoals" (Wertsch, 1979:86–87). Examples include shifting car gears or putting a can of olives in the grocery cart.

The wholistic nature of activity in context is shown in Leontiev's strong emphasis on the derivation of meaning by actors from the multilevel activity context. Meaning is located in relations between the levels of activity and action, on the one hand, and action and operation, on the other. Sense and meaning are distinguished, which parallels the distinction between personal setting and public arena in the supermarket study. For Leontiev, sense designates personal intent, as opposed to meaning, which is public, explicit, and literal. Sense derives from the relations of actions and goals to motivated (higher order) activities of which they are a particular realization. Furthermore, "the goal of one and the same action can be consciously realized in different ways, depending on the connections it has with the motive of the activity" (Wertsch, 1981:264–265).

This same relational emphasis operates "downward" as well in the system of activity, at the action/operation interface. Zinchenko, for example, designed tasks so that the "same" arithmetic problems were treated as conscious actions in one experimental session and as operations in the course of inventing math problems in another session. The arithmetic stayed the same in formal mathematical terms, while its role in the subject's activity changed. This change, according to Zinchenko, had clear effects on the subjects' memory of the arithmetic: "Material that is the immediate goal of an action is remembered concretely, accurately, more effectively, more durably. When related to the means of an action (to operations) the same material is remembered in a generalized way, schematically, less effectively, and less durably" (Wertsch, 1981:272). These results support the view that to comprehend the nature of arithmetic activity as a whole requires a contextualized understanding of its role within that activity. Indeed, they provide a strong argument for the necessity of analyzing any segment of activity in relation to the flow of activity of which it is a part.

But neither Soviet psychology nor Barker's functionalist brand of setting determinism addresses the nature of the articulation between activity and setting. The supermarket study distinguished between a supermarket as an arena, which is a non-negotiable, concrete realization of a political economy in place, and as a personal setting of grocery-shopping activity. The setting both is generated out of grocery-shopping activity and at the same time generates that activity. In short, activity is dialectically constituted in relation with the setting. For example, suppose a shopper pauses for the first time in front of the generic products section of the market, noting both the peculiarly plain appearance of the products, divested of brand names and other information to which the shopper is accustomed, and the relatively low prices of these products. This information provides a potential new category of money-saving strategies, which may be added to an existing repertoire of such strategies. This in turn leads the shopper to attend to the generic products on subsequent shopping trips. The setting for these future trips, within the supermarket as arena, is thereby transformed. And any change in the setting within the arena transforms the activity of grocery shopping. Neither setting nor activity exists in realized form, except in relation with each other; this principle is general, applying to all levels of activity-setting relations.

The Supermarket as Arena and Setting

The arena of grocery shopping is the supermarket, an institution at the interface between consumers and suppliers of grocery commodities. Many of these commodities are characterized in consumer ideology as basic necessities, and the supermarket is the only avenue routinely open for acquiring them. Typical supermarkets keep a constant stock of about seven thousand items. The arena is arranged so that grocery items remain stationary, in locations assigned by suppliers and store management, while shoppers move through the store, pushing a cart, searching for the fifty or so items they buy on a weekly basis. The arena may be conceived of as an icon of the ultimate grocery list: it is filled with partially ordered sequences of independently obtainable objects, laid out so that a physical progression through the entire store would bring the shopper past all seven thousand items.

A shopper's progress through the arena, however, never takes this form. The supermarket as "list" and the shopper's list are of such different orders of magnitude that the fashioning of a particular route through the market is inevitable. Part of what makes personal navigation of the arena feasible is the ordered arrangement of items in the market and the structured nature of purchase intentions of the shopper. The setting of grocery-shopping activity is one way of conceptualizing relations between these two kinds of structure. It may be thought of as the locus of articulation between the structured arena and the structured activity.

For example, the arrangement of the arena shapes the setting, in that the order in which items are put into the cart reflects their location in the supermarket rather than their location in any of the activities from which shoppers routinely generate their lists (e.g. meal planning, cupboard inventory). Yet the setting is also shaped by the activity of the shopper. Without babies and dogs, a shopper may routinely bypass the aisles where diapers and dogfood are located. Expectations that the chore ought not take more than an hour shape the amount of time that shoppers allocate to each item and hence the degree of effort and structure to their search. These searches in turn have articulatory implications for the arena, which is created, as in packaging design and display of products, in response to the character of individual search structures.

The character of the resulting synomorphy is part of what is meant by "setting." The articulatory nature of setting is to be stressed. A setting is not simply a mental map in the mind of the shopper. Instead, it has simultaneously an independent, physical character and a potential for realization only in relation to shoppers' activity. All of this together constitutes its essential character.

An example from the supermarket illustrates the mutual relations between setting and activity, such that each creates the other, both coming into being at the same time. A shopper and the observer walk toward the frozen enchilada case. Until the shopper arrives in front of the enchilada display, it is as if she were at not just a physical but a cognitive distance from the enchiladas. In contrast, she and the enchiladas, in each other's presence, bring into being an entirely different quality to the activity:

Shopper (speaking hesitantly, eyes searching the shelves to find the enchiladas): Now these enchiladas, they're around 55 cents. They were the last time I bought them, but now every time I come . . . a higher price.

Observer: Is there a particular kind of enchilada you like?

Shopper: Well, they come in a, I don't know, I don't remember who puts them out. They move things around too. I don't know.

Observer: What is the kind you're looking for?

Shopper: Well, I don't know what brand it is. They're just enchiladas. They're put out by, I don't know. *(Discovers the display of frozen Mexican dinners.)* Here they are! *(Speaking vigorously and firmly.)* They were 65 the last time I bought them. Now they're 69. Isn't that awful?

Here the shopper's demeanor before and after she locates the enchiladas points to the relevant contrast. There is, on the one hand, her vague characterization of the product she intends to purchase before she locates it and, on the other hand, her precise description and vigorous tone once she has it in sight. This difference — between activity and setting caught in transit (before she finds the enchiladas) and activity in setting (as she finds them) — is ubiquitous in the data, and it illustrates what is meant by the integral and specific character of particular activities in particular settings.

Grocery-Shopping Activity

Grocery-shopping activity is made up of relatively discrete segments, such as the enchilada purchase. The shopper stops in front of one display after another and goes through a process of deciding which item to transfer from shelf to cart. In most cases it is possible to face the display, locate an item, and take it from the shelf without moving more than a foot or two from the initial position.

Within a particular shopping activity segment, size and brand are taken into account, in that order, in making decisions, while price and quantity are considered at the end of decision processes (Murtaugh, 1983). But the complexity of the search process varies a great deal across items. Many selections are made without apparent consideration, as part of the routine of replenishing supplies. More often than not, however, shoppers produce an account for why they routinely purchase a particular item rather than an available alternative. This use of "old results" suggests that part of the move from novice to expert grocery shopper involves complex decision processes, a few at a time, across many trips through the market.

Much of the decision making which occurs as shoppers place themselves in physical relation with one display after another is of a qualitative nature. Shoppers care about the taste, nutritional value, dietary implications, and aesthetics of particular groceries. In relation to this qualitative decision-making, commodity suppliers and store management respond with large amounts of persuasive information about products, much of it adhering to the item itself. Shoppers face overwhelming amounts of information, only a small part of which they treat as relevant. Even this information is brought into play only when a shopper establishes a new choice or updates an old result. In general, through time, the experienced shopper transforms an information-rich arena into an information-specific setting. These transformations of past experience, taking place in the appropriate setting, form an integrated whole that is the basis of what appear to be habitual, mechanical-looking procedures for collecting items purchased regularly.

The integration of activity-in-setting is not limited to repeated purchases. Nor is setting merely a stage within which action occurs. The setting imposes shape on potential solution procedures even in new cases of search or problem solving. Indeed, the setting often serves as a calculating device. One shopper found an unusually high-priced package of cheese in a bin. He suspected an error. To solve the problem, he searched through the bin for a package weighing the same amount and inferred from the discrepancy between prices that one was in error. His comparison to other packages established which was the errant package. Had he not transferred the calculation to the environment, he would have had to divide weight into price, mentally, and compare the result with the price per pound printed on the label, a much more effortful and less reliable procedure. Calculation of weight/price relations devolved on the structured relations between packages of cheese (whose weight varied within only a small range; weight, price per pound, and price were printed on each package but not the steps in the calculation of price per pound) and the activity of the shopper (who searched among them for an instructive comparison). In another case, a shopper exploited the fact that chicken thighs come in packages of six. She compared package prices and chose a cheap one to ensure small size, explaining that she would select a moderate-priced package when she wanted larger serving portions. In this case also, weight/price relations were enacted in the setting.

Shoppers describe themselves as engaged in a routine chore, making habitual purchases. But their description must be addressed as data, not as part of the analysis. "Habit" and "routine" should be treated not as empirical descriptions of repeated episodes of the same activity in the same setting but as statements of an ideological order. For the arena and the general intentions of the shopper ("doing weekly chores"; "grocery shopping, again") come into juxtaposition repeatedly in such a way as to make it both customary and useful for the shopper to claim that shopping is "the same" from one occasion to the next.

The similarity is not a matter of mechanical reproduction, however. Grocery lists almost always include nonspecific categories such as "treats" for children. The category is reproduced from week to week, but the specific treats vary, often in response to features of the setting (e.g. a candy sale, a new fruit in season). Indeed, as the fruit example indicates, the setting generates activity as well. Consider also the experience of walking past a display and having a delayed reaction, which leads to a backtrack and consideration of a needed but forgotten item. Since activity and setting, as well as relations between them are highly structured, shoppers have many alternative ways to generate a path through the store. Thus the sequence of choices of grocery items as the shopper moves through the aisles, is not all that heavily constrained. What the shopper learns from past experience is not a fixed path through the setting but numerous short-run structuring devices that can be played end to end, to produce one path this time, a different but structurally related path another time.

For instance, shoppers generally do not order their physical activity to conform to the order of their private grocery lists, which would involve much greater physical effort than ordering their activity to conform to the market layout. This is confirmed by a shopper: "Well, let's see if I've got anything over in this . . . I usually look and see if I've got anything in these, yeah, I need some potatoes. I usually shop in the department that I happen to be in. I check my list to see if I have anything on the list, to save me from running all over the store."

Saving physical effort is a useful rationale for using setting to organize the sequence of shopping activity. But a more general—and generative—principle is at work. Personal grocery lists order items differently than these same items are organized in the supermarket arena. Partial orderings of related items are often found on grocery lists, reflecting the manner in which the list was generated. It is still the case, however, that lists are fundamentally collections of discrete, independent items. Within grocery shopping the segments of activity are relatively independent, and hence one segment is rarely a sequentially ordered condition for another one. Almost by default, then, the structure in the setting—the shoppers' version of the layout of goods on the shelves and aisles—is what they utilize to order their activity. This gives the appearance of a choice between mental and physical effort, when the choice is in fact between a more or a less compellingly structured component of the whole activity-in-setting, any structure being available for use in sequencing the activity. Thus, when shoppers' lists involve item interdependence (e.g. buy eggs only if the ham looks good), the source of sequencing might just as well be the lists instead of the market layout, or some mix of the two.

In sum, an activity-in-setting that is labeled by its practitioners as a routine chore is in fact a complex and generative task. Descriptions of the activity as "habitual" and "routine" are ideological in nature, leading shoppers to interpret their own activity as repetitive and highly similar across episodes, rather than to treat its nonmechanical, generative variability as normative. These considerations must surely affect the manner in which shoppers come to see certain parts of activity-in-setting as smoothly repetitious and other parts as problematic.

Arithmetic Activity in Grocery Shopping

Grocery shopping activity in the supermarket setting provides the context that determines which events shoppers will experience as problematic, and in what respects. These particular features of grocery shopping "problems" in turn give specific shape to arithmetic problem-solving. Arithmetic in the market is strongly marked, for instance, by shoppers' views that shopping is a routine activity. In the dialectical relation between grocery shopping and the supermarket setting, repeated interactions produce a smooth "fit" between activity and setting, streamlining each in relation to the other, and generating expectations about how the activity will proceed. A "routine" episode is expected to unfold unproblematically and effortlessly, as if ideally the whole enterprise had the status of an operation, in activity theory terms. It is in relation to this expectation that "problems" take on meaning; they are viewed as snags or interruptions in the smooth process of shopping. Further, where both expectations and practice lead to relatively unproblematic activity, snags and interruptions will be recognized, indeed generated, so as to be limited in scope — small-scale relative to the activity as a whole.

Another determinant of the character of problem solving in grocery shopping is the nature of choices to be made by the shopper. The supermarket is thought of by consumers as a locus of abundant choices, for which the stock of thousands of items constitutes apparent evidence. But contradicting this view is a different order of circumstances: the shopper cannot provide food for the family if he leaves the supermarket empty-handed, due to attacks of indecision. That is, the shopper, faced with abundant alternatives, nonetheless cannot avoid making choices. Conversely, because the making of choices cannot be avoided, it is to the seller's advantage to proliferate decision criteria in the shopping setting. This contributes to the shopper's experience of abundant choices, helping to maintain the contradiction between choice and the necessity of choosing. This contradiction is not itself generally recognized, much less viewed as problematic, by shoppers. But in conjunction with the routine and dialectical character of shopping it contributes to the structuring of arithmetic activity.

These characteristics — the generative routine, the contradictory quality of routine choices, and the dialectical form of activity-in-setting — together shape the rationalizing character of arithmetic calculation in the supermarket. The term *rationalization* has been proposed as a hallmark of everyday decision-making (e.g. Bartlett, 1958). It is used in common parlance to refer to after-the-fact justification of an action or opinion. The term contrasts sharply with folk characterizations of rational decision-making, in which evidence should provide logical motivation for a conclusion. Without the contradiction, the production of a rational account of choices would not be construed by the observer as rationalization. Activity-in-setting is complex enough that a description of the activity as "marshaling the evidence after the fact" does not take into account contradictory, multiple relations between evidence and conclusions. For in decision processes such as those in grocery shopping, it is impossible to specify whether a rational account of choice is constructed before or after the fact. It occurs both before and after different orders of fact — before a unique item is chosen but after the determination that a choice must be made. The rationalizing relation of evidence to conclusion is not, then, a matter of "everyday thinking" or "unscientific use of evidence" but is an unavoidable characteristic of the dialectical constitution of grocery-shopping activity. The relations between evidence and conclusion are an inevitable outcome of the organization of the activity-in-setting rather than of the mode of operation of the everyday mind.

Although arithmetic problem-solving plays various roles in grocery shopping, its preponderant use is for price comparison. This kind of calculation occurs at the end of largely qualitative decision-making processes which smoothly reduce numerous possibilities on the shelf to single items in the cart. A snag occurs when the elimination of alternatives comes to a halt before a choice has been made. Arithmetic problem-solving is both an expression of and a medium for dealing with these stalled decision processes. It is, among other things, a move outside the qualitative characteristics of a product to its characterization in terms of a standard of value, money.

That arithmetic is a prevalent medium of problem solving among shoppers is itself an interesting problem. Certainly the terms in which it is used to justify choice are symbolically powerful in this society, being mathematical, "objective," and monetary. In the supermarket, calculation may be the most immediate means of rational account construction in response to interruption because of its condensed symbolic connections to both mathematics and money, that is, its position in folk theory about the meaning of rationality. Indeed, a good case can be made that shoppers' ideological commitment to rational decision-making is evidenced by their justificatory calculations and explanations, for the alternative is to declare that choices as constrained as those for which price arithmetic is invoked are arbitrary and hence not worth effort to explain. One shopper, referring to a television commercial in which an animated package of margarine gets in an argument at the dinner table, selects this brand and comments ironically:

Shopper: I'll get the one that talks back.
Observer: Why?
Shopper: Others would have been more trouble.

Support for the interpretation of price arithmetic as rational accounting, in both senses of that term, comes from research on the decision processes used by shoppers in choosing grocery items (Murtaugh, 1984), which showed that if arithmetic is utilized, it is employed near the end of the process, when the number of choices still under consideration is not greater than three and rarely greater than two. Of 803 grocery items purchased by 24 shoppers, 312 involved explicit problem solving through consideration of alternative brands and sizes. Of these 312 cases, 125 involved some arithmetic calculation; this represented about 16% of the total items purchased. Most of these cases — 77 in all — involved price comparisons among different brands within the same product-class. Since data were recorded on the prices and quantities of each grocery item mentioned by a shopper, it was possible to test objectively the shopper's claim that one item was less expensive than another. In only four of the 77 cases did the shopper proceed to select the more expensive alternative.

This finding indicates that shoppers are not comparing prices merely to gain information that will then be weighted appropriately with respect to other information, such as other features of competing brands. Rather, shoppers explicitly compare prices only when they have no strong preference among brands. In the light of these data, it would be difficult to picture arithmetic as a major motivation "driving" shopping activity. Justifying choices, just before and after the fact, is a more appropriate description of its typical character.

Dialectically Constituted Problem-Solving

If activity-in-setting as a whole is crucial in shaping problem solving, the character of problem-solving activity should vary from setting to setting. The supermarket data supported this view (see also Barker & Wright, 1954; Barker, 1963). We compared shoppers' arithmetic in the supermarket with their performance on an extensive paper-and-pencil arithmetic test, covering integer, decimal, and fraction arithmetic, and using addition, subtraction, multiplication, and division operations, based on a test from the Torque Project at MIT. The twenty-five shoppers varied in the amount of their schooling and in the time since their schooling was completed. Their scores averaged 59% on the arithmetic test, compared with a startling 98% — virtually error free — arithmetic in the supermarket. The subtest scores on the arithmetic test correlated highly and significantly with each other (from .72 to .84, at .001), but not with the frequency of arithmetic problem-solving in the supermarket. The frequency variable was employed after the problem-solving success variable in shopping showed no variance. Willingness to engage in arithmetic activity provides an alternative index of facility with arithmetic. Number of years of schooling correlated highly with performance on the arithmetic test ($r = .47$, $p = .003$) but not with frequency of calculation in the supermarket. Years since completion of schooling likewise correlated significantly with arithmetic test performance ($r = -.53$, $p = .001$) but not with frequency of grocery-shopping arithmetic ($r = .12$, n.s.). In short, to the extent that correlational evidence provides clues, arithmetic problem-solving in test and grocery shopping situations appears quite different, or at least bears different relations with shoppers' demographic characteristics. Analysis of the specific procedures utilized in doing arithmetic in the supermarket lends substance to this conclusion, besides illustrating the dialectical form of arithmetic problem-solving.

A successful account of problem-solving procedures in the supermarket must explain two puzzles uncovered in the grocery-shopping data. The first puzzle is the virtually error-free arithmetic performance by shoppers who made frequent errors in parallel problems in the formal testing situation. The other puzzle is the frequent occurrence of more than one attempt to calculate in the course of buying a single item. Shoppers carried out 2.5 calculations, on average, for each grocery item that served as an occasion for arithmetic. Further, while the nearly error-free character of ultimate problem-solutions is a remarkably clear finding, intermediate calculations in a sequence when more than one occurred, were often in error. This must be accounted for as well.

The routine nature of grocery-shopping activity and the location of price arithmetic at the end of decision-making processes suggest that the shopper must already assign rich content and shape to a problem solution by the time arithmetic becomes an obvious next step. Problem solving under these circumstances is an iterative process. It involves, on the one hand, what the shopper knows and what the setting holds that might help and, on the other hand, what the solution looks like. The activity of finding something problematic subsumes a good deal of knowledge about what would constitute a solution. In the course of grocery shopping many of a problem solution's parameters are marshaled into place as part of the process of deciding, up to a point, what to purchase. Consider the shopper who knew which cheese package was inconsistent with others before he established whether there was really an inconsistency or not. The dialectical process is one of "gap closing," to adapt Bartlett's (1958) term, between strongly specified solution characteristics and information and procedural possibilities for solving the problem.

Thus a change in either solution shape or resources of information leads to a reconstitution of the other: the solution shape is generated out of the decision process up to an interruption or snag. But the act of identifying a problem changes the salience of setting characteristics. These in turn suggest, more powerfully than before, procedures for generating a specific solution. Information and procedural knowledge accessed by eye, hand, or mental transformations thereof make possible a move toward the solution or suggest a change in the solution shape that draws it closer to the information at hand.

One segment of a grocery-shopping expedition illustrates the dialectical nature of gap-closing arithmetic problem-solving processes and, more specifically, makes it possible to typify some of the parts of such processes. However, in view of the contradiction inherent in the enterprise of observing "the ordinary," caution is appropriate about the relevance of this example to the interpretation of price arithmetic as rational account-production activity. For it seems probable that interaction between the shopper and the observer in the example has given a special character to the activity segment, perhaps not a difference in kind of activity so much as in emphasis. The shopper may well think of the observer as the embodiment and arbiter of normative shopping practices; while the observer believes his own role is to investigate empirically the appropriateness of normative models of rational problem solving. The combined effect of the assumptions each has about the observer's role is to intensify the focus on rational accounting, in terms common to folk ideology and much of consumer economics, at the expense of the qualitative character of decision making which in fact leads to most purchase selections in the supermarket, even in the data.

In the shopping transcript, a forty-three-year-old woman with four children discusses the price of noodles while taking a few steps toward the noodle display:

Shopper: Let me show you something, if I can find it. I mean talk about price. Last week they had that on sale I think for 59 cents.
Observer: Spaghetti?
Shopper (with the vagueness associated with imminent arrival): Yeah, or 40 — I can't remember . . . That's not the one.

The shopper then puts an old result into practice, taking a package of elbow noodles from the shelf and putting it in her cart. It is a

32-ounce package of Perfection brand noodles, costing $1.12. This decision prefigures and shapes the course of the subsequent conversation and calculations. The latter are best-buy problems, comparing price per unit of weight for pairs of packages. The other three packages weigh 24 ounces, 48 ounces, and 64 ounces. The difference in price per unit is not a linear function of size:

American Beauty noodles	24 oz. for $1.02	68¢/lb
Perfection noodles	32 oz. for $1.12	56¢/lb
American Beauty noodles	48 oz. for $1.79	59½¢/lb
American Beauty noodles	64 oz. for $1.98	49¼¢/lb

The 64-ounce package is clearly the best buy.

Observer (acknowledging the shopper's choice of the 32-ounce package): Perfection.

Shopper: Yeah, this is what I usually buy. It's less expensive than — is that American Beauty?

Observer: Yeah.

Shopper: That, what I need right now is the elbow macaroni. And I always buy it in two-pound . . . [packages]. I'm out of this.

The statement, "It's less expensive than . . . American Beauty," is the choice that establishes the point of reference for comparative calculations. The statement, "I always buy it in two-pound packages," establishes an initial solution shape. This statement also provides evidence both that the choice is an old result and that numerical simplification work has occurred, since the weight on the package is expressed as "32 ounces" rather than as "2 pounds." The shopper expands on the qualitative choice criteria that have shaped her purchases in the past:

Observer: This seems like a big package of elbow noodles, and you add these to the macaroni?

Shopper: I add some, I just take a handful and add it to the rest, to the other packaged macaroni, 'cause I add macaroni to it. Plus I use that for my goulash.

Observer: For the goulash. O.K. And you like this particular kind? Are there other alternatives here?

Shopper: Yeah. There's large elbow. This is really the too-large economy bag. I don't know if I, probably take me about six months to use this one. And I just, I don't have the storage room for that kind of stuff. I guess if I rearranged my cupboards, maybe I could, but it's a hassle. . . . I don't know, I just never bought that huge size like that. I never checked the price though on it. But being American Beauty, it probably costs more even in that large size.

The nature of the decision-making problem is shown here in integral relation with the particulars of interaction between the shopper and the observer. For qualitative reasons (e.g. standard meals, storage capacity) the shopper has previously avoided purchase of the large size. But she is caught in a public situation in a discussion in which she would like to display her shrewdness as a shopper. And best-buy purchases are the best evidence of rational frugality in this setting, even though qualitative criteria take precedence for her, as for most shoppers, most of the time.

The next interchange starts a process of simplification of the arithmetic comparison. The shopper transforms large numbers of ounces into a small number of pounds:

Observer: That's what, that's six — *(Probably he is starting to say "64 ounces.")*
Shopper: It's four pounds, and what did I buy? Two? Oh, there is a big savings. Hmmm, I might think about that next time, figure out where I can keep it. I actually try to look for better prices. I used — I guess I used to, and I was such in the habit of it that some of the products I'm buying now are leftovers from when I was cutting costs. And I usually look. If they have something on sale, you know, a larger package of macaroni or spaghetti or something, I'll buy it.

If the preemptive character of financial evidence as a means of demonstrating utilitarian rationality requires illustration, this segment provides it. The shopper's clearly stated earlier decision to reject the large-size package on the basis of kitchen storage capacity is not sufficient, when challenged, to override the opposite choice on monetary criteria. She places a general value on price as a criterion for choice and correspondingly emphasizes that her current financial state does not require such choices. This has the effect of emphasizing the absolute nature of the value. It produces a half-commitment to future action, which does not seem likely to occur once the pressure of observer demand on the production of rational accounting is removed. She also adopts a strategy of, "If I can't be right, at least I can demonstrate my objectivity," both by admitting she is wrong and by accepting quantitative, symbolically objective criteria as overridingly legitimate. Meanwhile she has made a calculation, correctly, that four pounds of American Beauty noodles would be cheaper than two pounds of Perfection noodles. It is not possible to infer what calculation took place, only that she arrived at a correct solution.

The next segment follows almost immediately in the transcript. The shopper sees what appears to be a comparison of packages which offers a counterexample to the conclusion that the large size is a best buy. If correct, it would soften the impression that she has violated a general principle ("bigger is cheaper") in her shopping strategy:

Shopper: But this one, you don't save a thing. Here's three pounds for a dollar 79, and there's one pound for 59.

She is comparing two packages of American Beauty spaghetti noodles. But what she believes to be a one-pound bag weighs only twelve ounces. She quickly notices the weight printed on the package and corrects herself:

Shopper: No, I'm sorry, that's 12 ounces. No, it's a savings.

These two statements involve two calculations. In some form (there are adequate alternatives) the first calculation was probably $1 \times 60 = 60$ and $3 \times 60 = 180$, and thus there is no difference between the items in price per pound. If the weight of the smaller bag is less than one pound, then the equations are no longer equivalent, and the three-pound bag is the better buy. Only a "less than" relation would be required to arrive at this conclusion.

The problem-solving procedures used by the shopper follow a pattern. She starts with a probable solution, but inspection of the evidence and comparison with the expected conclusion cause her to reject it. "No, I'm sorry," is her acknowledgment that the initial problem solution is in error. Pulled up short by the weight information from the package, she recalculates and obtains a new conclusion. This pattern is an example of gap-closing, dialectical movement between the expected shape of the solution and the information and calculation devices at hand, all in pursuit of a solution that is germane to the activity that gave it shape in the first place. The arithmetic is not simple in terms of the paper-and-pencil conventions used to represent it: $1.79/3 = .59$. It requires an active process of simplification to transform it into the form the shopper used.

Once the shopper has concluded that the large bag of noodles is a better buy than the small one, she comments:

Shopper: They had some on sale there one day, and the large package was like 69 for two pounds, and it was 59 for one pound. And it was just such a difference, I, you know, it was almost an insult to the shopper to have the two on the same shelf side by side

She concludes with another two-round calculation in gap-closing form. This episode is initiated by the observer, who addresses not the size difference but the monetary one, emphasizing its magnitude. The observer may be trying to acknowledge the shopper's amended views, for he repeats her previous conclusion:

Observer: Well, you seem to think this was a real big difference, then, this four pounds of —
Shopper: Yeah, that is. That's two dollars for four pounds *(referring to the American Beauty elbow noodles).* This is a dollar *(referring to the Perfection elbow noodles in her cart).* That's 50 cents a pound, and I just bought two pounds for a dollar 12, which is 60. So there is a difference.

The shopper begins by simplifying $1.98 to two dollars and $1.12 to one dollar. But the calculation leads to the conclusion that both are 50 cents per pound. This conclusion does not fit the established solution shape, "a big difference" between the smaller and larger bags of noodles. The current problem, as simplified, produces the intermediate solution that four pounds of noodles for two dollars is 50 cents per pound. This move serves two purposes: it is a means to recheck information simplified from that printed on the package, and it is the first item in the next round of calculation. The second round is a similar price comparison, but with a "more than" relation: $1.12 is more than one dollar. It would be consistent with a desire to appear objective and to meet the norms of the observer that the shopper would round up from 56¢/pound to 60¢. She thereby reiterates the earlier conclusion about the direction of difference in price.

One characteristic of gap-closing arithmetic procedures is the need to assign multiple functions to individual moves. Dialectically ordered problem-solving processes pose this problem. It may be necessary to give up the goal of assigning arithmetic problems to unique locations — in the head or on the shelf — or labeling one element in a problem-solving process as a "calculation procedure," another as a "checking procedure." It may be difficult even to distinguish the problem from its solution.

Research on the acquisition of arithmetic skills by new members of Weight Watchers (de la Rocha, in preparation) posed the problem of food portion control: "Suppose your allotment of cottage cheese for the meal is three-quarters of the two-thirds cup the program allows?" The problem solver in this example began the task muttering that he had had calculus in college and then, after a long pause, suddenly announced that he had "got it!" From then on he appeared certain he was correct, even before carrying out the procedure. He filled a measuring cup two-thirds full of cottage cheese, dumped it out on a cutting board, patted it into a circle, marked a cross on it, scooped away one quadrant, and served the rest. Thus, "take three-quarters of two-thirds of a cup of cottage cheese" is not just the problem statement but also the solution to the problem and the procedure for solving it. Since the environment was used as a calculating device, the solution was simply the problem statement, enacted. At no time did the Weight Watcher check his procedure against a paper and pencil algorithm, which would have produced $\frac{3}{4}$ cup $\times$ $\frac{2}{3}$ cup $=$ $\frac{1}{2}$ cup. Instead, the coincidence of problem, procedure, and enactment is the means by which checking takes place. This implies that there is a strong monitoring potential in gap-closing procedures, when various aspects of problem solving are juxtaposed.

The calculations made by the shopper in the supermarket were possible because of her active construction of simplified versions of them. In order to do the complex work of simplifying problems, she needed a clear grasp of "what she was doing." "Knowing what one is doing" means generating a process oneself, in context (e.g. decision making in the supermarket). Then, when faced with a snag, one has already produced a partial form of the solution.

Checking procedures, in this analysis of gap-closing arithmetic, consist of an ongoing process of comparing the current state of knowledge of the problem and the current definition of the solution. The intention is to check the plausibility of both procedure and solution in relation to previously recognized constraints on answer characteristics rather than by comparison of two linear problem-solving procedures without reference to such constraints (the convention in pencil-and-paper arithmetic-checking procedures).

In supermarket arithmetic, an alternative to arithmetic problem-solving is abandonment of the arithmetic and resolution of snags through exercise of other options. Abandonment of a calculation may occur when it becomes too complicated for solution within grocery-shopping activity in the supermarket setting. Abandonment, like a high level of success at calculation, supports the view that the juxtaposition of various aspects of problem solving makes monitoring of the process exceptionally productive. In one example, a forty-five-year-old mother of five children and her fifteen-year-old daughter are shopping, together with the observer. The mother is interested in ketchup but turns to the barbecue sauce, next to the ketchup, when her daughter calls attention to it:

Daughter: Do you want some Chris and Pits barbecue sauce? We're almost out.

Shopper (to the observer): Heinz has a special *(on ketchup).* I have a coupon in here for that. And I was going to make spareribs one night this week, which I didn't mention to you, but that was in my mind now that she mentions the sauce. *(Examines her coupons.)* I want to see if their price on their barbecue sauce is going to be as — we usually buy Chris and Pits. *(Notices a Heinz ketchup coupon.)* Now see, this is the one that I was telling you about. But they don't have the 44-ounce ketchup here. *(Continues searching through the coupons until she finds the one for the barbecue sauce.)* Okay, 25 cents off any size flavor of Kraft Barbecue Sauce, including the new Sweet and Sour, which I would like to try because I'm going to have spareribs. But if you notice they don't have it — Oh, here they do. Hickory.

Observer: Kraft Hickory Smoked.

Shopper: Yeah, but they don't have the Sweet and Sour. *(To her daughter.)* You see it, D? Nope. Okay, see now, in a situation like this it's difficult to figure out which is the better buy. Because this is — I don't have my glasses on, how many ounces is that, D? *(Refers to Kraft Hickory Smoked.)*

Daughter: Eighteen.

Shopper: Eighteen ounces for 89, and this is? *(Refers to Chris and Pits.)*

Daughter: One pound, seven ounces —

Shopper: Twenty-three ounces for a dollar 17. *(Speaks ironically.)* That's when I whip out my calculator and see which is the better buy.

The comparison to be made is simplified by putting both weights into the same units. But it is difficult to simplify further: 18 ounces for 89 cents must be compared with 23 ounces for a dollar and 17 cents. The comment about using a calculator can be interpreted, solely on the basis of its tone, as a move to abandon the calculation. More convincing evidence of this intent is the fact that the shopper has a calculator in her purse, which she previously told the observer she uses rather frequently in the supermarket, yet on this occasion, as in the purchase of all but one grocery item, she makes no effort to get it out and suit her action to her words. She makes one more attempt to solve the problem and then abandons it even more definitively:

Observer: So what are you going to do in this case?

Shopper: In this case what have we got here? I'll try to do it quickly in my head . . . They don't have the large, um —

Daughter: Kraft Barbecue Sauce?

Shopper: Yeah, so what I'm going to do is, I'm going to wait and go to another store, when I'm at one of the other stores, because I'd like to try this.

One choice open to shoppers is to abandon a calculation, in the course of which they choose an option other than calculation as a basis for completing the decision process. Supermarket settings and grocery-shopping activity are rich in options for completing decision processes, and this circumstance adds support to what already appears to be a low penalty level for abandoning calculation in favor of some other criterion of choice. This contrasts with other activities-in-setting in which problem generation, and hence constraints on problem solution, are furnished to the problem solver in an asymmetrically structured sequence of interaction in which the problem solver has little to say about the terms. In those circumstances the only "option" other than success is failure, as in school tests and many problem-solving experiments.

The dialectical approach to problem solving explains the multiple-calculation and ultimately error-free arithmetic practiced in the supermarket setting. Multiple calculations cannot be easily accounted for in the linear progression models assumed in conventional algorithm-based arithmetic procedures. But the theory of gap-closing, dialectically constituted, arithmetic procedures predicts that calculating will occur in several stages or "rounds," which the supermarket study demonstrated in practice. Multiple calculational rounds are possible because of the initial conditions by which something becomes problematic in the course of activity-in-setting. The problem solver generates problem and solution shape at the same time; each entails the other. Procedures which operate on both problem and solution shape stand in juxtaposition to one another. Errors, which are frequent in early rounds, can therefore be recognized and instruct.

The end product of supermarket calculation is so accurate for two reasons. First, dialectical processes of problem solving make powerful monitoring possible because of the juxtaposition of problem, solution, and checking activities. When properties of the setting join in as calculating devices, they add another factor to those already juxtaposed: the enactment of problem solving. Second, any circumstance that makes abandonment of a calculation a feasible alternative leads to fewer completed calculations, but more correct ones, than if options were not available. If the process of problem generation is under the control of the problem solver, the solution shape is generated at the same time; alternatively, the problem solver may exercise options other than calculation.

Arithmetic practice may change over time within grocery shopping activity-in-setting. The effortful process of snag repair leads to a choice — to the moving of an item from shelf to shopping cart and the resumption of the rhythm of routine activity. The snag has been transformed into a rationally accountable choice. That choice replaces both problem and solution effort in future grocery-shopping episodes. But such a choice creates the terms for the occurrence of new snags, either as the choice becomes a baseline for new comparisons or as the criteria invoked in a rational account are violated (e.g. by rising prices, changes in relations of price and quantity, changes in family composition or food preferences).

As a whole, grocery-shopping activity changes over time, in a changing arena, in relation to changing activities-in-other-settings, and as a result of the activity taking place across repeated episodes. Shoppers marshal ideological efficiencies partially to domesticate this variability; but if they are to shape activity effectively, there must be scope within it for investigating, checking, updating, and reflecting changes occurring in this setting and elsewhere. To be effective over time requires smooth routines partly because this enables shopper-setting interaction focused about instructive novelties.

Snag repair contrasts with a routine choice when it becomes, for the moment, an activity-setting relation at its simplest. Think of the shopper's daughter in the last example as part of the setting. The daughter pointed out the barbecue sauce. The shopper did not go through a choice process initially. Instead, she and the setting brought a choice into being. She reflected this in her comment, "That was in my mind, now that she mentions the sauce." The relevant aspect of the setting need not be a person: replace the daughter with a bottle of sauce on the shelf, and an equivalent event would be the shopper who does a double-take as he passes this display and backtracks slightly to transfer the "forgotten" item from shelf to cart. Each may be thought of as a moment in the dialectical constitution of activity and setting.

Conclusions

The defining characteristics of arithmetic problem-solving in supermarkets must be sought in the dialectical constitution of grocery-shopping activity in the supermarket setting. Thus, in relation to the routine character assigned grocery-shopping activity, problems impinge on the consciousness of shoppers as small snags to be repaired. Given this ideology of routine and the complex structure of choice in the supermarket setting, arithmetic is used to produce rational accounts of choice. Procedures for solving problems are dialectically constituted, in the sense that setting and activity mutually create and change each other; in the process, "problems" are generated and resolved. These characteristics emerged from analysis of arena, setting, and activity. Had the template instead been the school ideology concerning linear algorithms for problem solving, analyzing the arithmetic practices would have been impossible. This demonstrates the value of analyzing both the context of activity and the activity in context.

This analytic principle has made it possible to account for price arithmetic in dialectical terms, as a process of gap closing. This process draws problems and solution shapes closer together, through operations whose juxtaposition gives them multiple functions and creates circumstances for powerful monitoring of solution processes. Successful monitoring, in turn, provides an explanation for the extraordinarily high level of successful problem-solving observed in the supermarket. There are specific ways in which the supermarket setting stores and displays information, offers means for organizing sequences of activity, acts as a calculating device, and shapes the way in which problem solving is construed by shoppers. These characteristics are not confined to supermarkets. Most, if not all, settings store information, offer a calculating potential, and provide means of structuring sequences of activity. These are general principles of the nature of settings. Likewise, gap-closing arithmetic (the simultaneous generation of problem and solution shape and the process of bringing them into coincidence), the production of rational accounts in complex choice situations, the abandonment of calculations, and use of other options are all at work in other settings; they form a general class of arithmetic procedures, with implications extending far beyond the supermarket.

The analysis of gap-closing arithmetic, indeed the very conceptualization of practical arithmetic as a gap-closing process, has implications for theories of cognitive processing as well. *Problem solving* is unfortunately a term often used synonymously with *cognition*, to describe, but not to contextualize, such activities as arithmetic practices. The assignment of unwarranted theoretical centrality to problem solving reflects a failure to comprehend these activities as practices *sui generis*. This conventional theoretical framework views a problem as "given," the generic "independent variable" in the situation. The effort, the solving of the problem, is correspondingly characterized as disembodied mental activity. But the reduction of cognition to problem solving *per se* simply cannot grasp the generative nature of arithmetic practice as cognitive activity. In dialectical terms, people and settings together create problems and solution shapes, and moreover, they do so simultaneously. Very often a process of solution occurs in the setting, with the enactment of the problem, and may transform the problem for the solver. Indeed, activity-setting relations are integral, generative, and finally dialectical in nature. This lesson applies to grocery shopping and to experience-generating segments thereof; it may be usefully applied to other, more inclusive systems of activity as well.

4. Adult Guidance of Cognitive Development

Barbara Rogoff
William Gardner

The search for influences on cognitive development has for some time focused on social interaction as an arena in which individuals encounter intellectual challenges and are guided by family and peers in learning to master them. A study of mothers assisting their children in preparing for a memory test on the categorization of objects illustrates adult guidance of children's cognitive activities. In this study instruction is conceived of as a joint problem-solving event in which a more expert individual (the mother) and a novice (the child) structure their interaction so as to transmit information from the expert to the novice. The cognitive activity that occurs in the interaction is apparent in the adaptations made by the participants as the novice gains greater understanding of the problem and as the expert evaluates the novice's readiness to take greater responsibility for the cognitive work.

Generalizing Skills and Information across Contexts

The importance of considering the context in which cognitive development occurs has been supported by research demonstrating a lack of generality of stages or capacities across situations (Brainerd, 1978; DeLoache & Brown, 1979; Feldman, 1980; Siegler, 1981; Rogoff, 1982a). Nevertheless, people are clearly able to generalize some aspects of existing knowledge and skills to new situations. Knowledge and skills have more general applicability than the specific episode in which they were originally learned or applied. Yet little is known about how people transfer skills from one problem to another or how they form a schema which includes several related but nonidentical problems.

We suggest that generalization from one problem to another is a function of the individual searching for similarities between new problems and old ones, guided by previous experience with similar problems and by instruction in how to interpret and solve such problems. Bartlett asserted that generalization "is not in the least likely to occur . . . unless there is active exploration of the situation that offers it an opportunity (1958:95)." Gick and Holyoak (1980) demonstrated that with logically isomorphic problems differing in context, subjects do not transfer relevant information from one problem to another unless they first notice the underlying similarity, though the transfer is relatively simple once the similarity is suggested. (An example of underlying similarity that goes unnoticed is the use of a single melody in "Twinkle Twinkle Little Star" and "The Alphabet Song.")

The similarity between problems is not given but is rather obtained through a process of problem solving. When faced with a new problem, individuals weave what they know about solving other problems and information about the new problem into a coherent approach which transforms the novel problem into a more familiar problem. The thinker makes use of whatever is familiar in the context of the new problem to apply information and skills available from familiar problems in bridging a solution to the novel problem (Petrie, 1979; Burstein, 1981). Aspects of the particular problem context are thus important in facilitating or blocking the individual's application of skills developed in one context to the new situation. Children need to learn skills in finding or creating similarity across contexts. An important function of adult-child interaction may be to provide guidance in creating links between the context of a novel problem and more familiar problem contexts, allowing the application of available skills and information.

Children may seldom be independently responsible for discovering the connections between problems or transforming available knowledge to fit new problems (D'Andrade, 1981). Adults arrange the occurrence of cognitive tasks for children and facilitate the children's learning by regulating the difficulty of the task, providing well-placed pointers, and by modeling mature performance (Laboratory of Comparative Human Cognition, 1980). Formal instruction and informal social interaction provide the child with a model of an expert applying appropriate background information to a new problem, thereby giving the child experience in the skillful generalization of knowledge to new problems.

In formal and informal instruction, information regarding cultural tools and practices (such as use of calculators, mathematics and writing systems, event scripts, and mnemonic strategies) is transmitted from experienced members of society to inexperienced members (Vygotsky, 1962, 1978). Vygotsky proposed that the higher mental functions appear first on the social level, between people, and later on the individual level, inside the child. "Human learning presupposes a specific social nature and a process by which children grow into the intellectual life of those around them" (1978:88). This growth occurs in the "zone of proximal development," that phase in the development of a cognitive skill where a child has only partially mastered the skill but can successfully employ it and eventually internalize it with the assistance and supervision of an adult. The adult structures and models the appropriate solution to the problem, engaging the child in this solution, as the adult monitors the child's current level of skill and supports or "scaffolds" the child's extension of current skills and knowledge to a higher level of competence (Wertsch, 1979; Wood, 1980). Social interaction with people who are more expert in the use of the material and conceptual tools of the society is thus an important "cultural amplifier" to extend children's cognitive processes (Cole & Griffin, 1980).

Instruction as Guidance in Transfer

Inasmuch as instruction provides training in the transfer of existing knowledge and skills to a new problem, people who are concerned with jointly accomplishing a cognitive performance must possess or create a common framework for the coordination of information. In an instructional situation, the establishment of an intelligible context of interaction by the participants is essential, since the learner's assimilation of new information depends on its compatibility with the learner's existing knowledge. Inherent in instruction is the construction of a context in which the new information is made compatible with the learner's current knowledge and skills. Brown called this "headfitting": "the distance between the child's existing knowledge and the new information he or she must acquire is a critical determinant of how successful training will be" (1979:251). Ochs (1979) pointed out that in early language learning, caregivers make the context of statements explicit by clarifying their own and the child's intentions and specifying the referents of a statement. Such a display of essential background knowledge is reduced as the child gains language facility.

Without the creation of a context for interaction which is intelligible to the learner, given his or her current knowledge and skills, the dyad cannot communicate, and the teacher will not be able to lead the learner toward an understanding of the new information. The structuring of the instruction serves as a scaffold for the learner, providing a framework for the solution to the problem. The learner can use this scaffold to support performance of new task components which he or she might not be capable of handling alone. In making new information compatible with the learner's current knowledge and skills, the teacher is guiding the learner in generalization to the new problem.

These arguments regarding guidance in cognitive development are illustrated with data from a study of thirty-two middle-class mothers preparing their 6- to 9-year-old children for a memory test on the classification of objects in tasks resembling home and school activities. The tasks were developed to simulate everyday teaching situations. The home task involved putting grocery items on shelves in a mock kitchen; the school task involved sorting photographs of common household objects into a tray divided into boxes. In both tasks the mother taught the location of eighteen items which were grouped into six categories. Both tasks took place in a room designed to look like an actual kitchen, with appliances and cupboards, kitchen curtains and decorations.

The mother was asked to view the items, either groceries or photographs, in their locations until she felt that she knew their organization, and during the instructional phase she was provided with a cue sheet illustrating the items in their locations for use whenever she needed it. The mother was told to use whatever teaching methods she liked, except revealing the cue sheet, to help the child learn the locations of the items. She was encouraged to teach as she would at home when organizing the kitchen after a shopping trip or when assisting her child on a homework problem. Both mother and child were informed that it was important for the child to know the organization of the items because after a short delay the child would return to the kitchen to place some of the old items and some new items in their proper locations.

The creation of a familiar problem context to guide the transfer of skills and information is illustrated by the instructional interaction between a mother and her 8-year-old son in the kitchen task. The mother begins, as the experimenters suggested, by relating the experimental task to the more familiar task of organizing a kitchen after returning from the store:

Mother: This should be fun. (*Stands and looks into the grocery bag containing items.*) Okay, now we just got home from the store, okay?
Child: Yeah.
Mother: And we want to have everything in a certain place, so everyone knows where it goes. Okay, first of all, let's start with this one. (*Points to shelf 1.*) Okay, let's pretend we're going on a picnic (*points again to shelf 1*), and we'll think: what do we need on a picnic?

Transfer of information from the kitchen context is useful in the learner's performance since the categorization of kitchen items is quasi-normative and the child may be expected to be somewhat familiar with this order. The mother's reference to the need "to have everything in a certain place, so everyone knows where it goes," provides task-relevant information regarding the need both to classify the items and to remember their organization. The child can interpret the mother's instructions relevant to the laboratory task according to the sequence of actions implied by the evocation of the familiar context.

After they have completed placement of all three items on the first shelf, the mother uses the everyday kitchen context to prepare the child for the upcoming memory test:

Mother: You just glance at that. (*Points to shelf 1.*)
(*Child turns and looks at shelf 1.*)
Mother: If I brought all these things (*gestures toward grocery bags*) and I wasn't home, that you'd put them right back there. (*Points to shelf 1.*) Okay? So there's olives, pickles, and ketchup just for picnics.
(*Child asks unintelligible question.*)
Mother: No, that's just where you're going to put 'em back when you come back and I'm not here. Okay?
(*Child nods.*)

The mother prompts the child to study the grouping of items: "You just glance at that." Two sentences later, she provides an example of rehearsal: "So there's olives, pickles, and ketchup just for picnics." Perhaps to motivate the study she has just prompted, between that prompting and the modeled rehearsal the mother asks, "If I brought all these things and I wasn't home, that you'd put them right back there. Okay?" The mother provides information about the memory test in familiar terms, in order to make the child sensitive to the need to prepare for future retrieval. The child is indeed sensitive, asking an apparently clarifying question, and in response the mother translates her description of the upcoming memory test out of the grocery-sorting context into the context of the experiment itself. The mother thereby indicates that the goal framework of the grocery-sorting context is interchangeable with that of the experimental context.

A similar example appears with a mother instructing her 9-year-old daughter. The mother introduces the task by drawing parallels between the laboratory kitchen and their own kitchen at home:

Mother: Okay, now, this is going to be a very organized kitchen. *(Child gives a bright look with a nervous smile.)*
Mother: Okay, just like ours, right? "House Beautiful." So we're going to organize things by categories. You know, just like we don't put the spoons in the pan drawer and all that stuff. So we're going to organize the groceries by categories, okay?
Child: Yeah.

This mother concludes the instructional session by referring explicitly to similarities of the experimental task with their kitchen at home. She points out the relevance of transferring information from the familiar setting to the novel one for successful test performance: "See, it's the same idea."

Mother: You think you can remember? I think you can. Okay. That's . . . *(Word unclear. Gestures toward one of the cabinets.)* See, that's the same way we do at home, isn't it?
Child (nodding): Kind of. *(Giggles.)*
Mother: Yeah, but we have all the baking supplies and stuff in one area, don't we?
Child: Yeah.
Mother: We have all the fruits in one area. I mean, we don't have applesauce cans and applesauce fruits over in the turnaround with the flour, do we?

Child: No. *(Shakes head.)*

Mother: See, it's the same idea. That's how you organize a kitchen. *(Looks at the shelves and gestures toward them.)* Okay, can you remember which is on which shelf?

Child: Yeah, I think.

Mother (walking toward kitchen door): Super smart kid. See, now you can go home and clean up our kitchen, right?

(Child walks toward kitchen door.)

These interactions illustrate how the mother guides the child in transferring relevant concepts from more familiar settings to the relatively novel laboratory task. In instruction using the zone of proximal development, the adult oversees the construction of an instructional context by establishing references to what the child already knows. This context allows the child to build new information or skills into the existing knowledge structure. The zone of proximal development is thus a dynamic "region of sensitivity to instruction" (Wood, Bruner & Ross, 1976; Wood, Wood & Middleton, 1978), which reflects not only the learner's capabilities but also the properties of the task context in which the instructional communication occurs.

Participation in the Problem's Solution

In successful instruction the adult must determine the child's region of sensitivity to instruction and adjust the scaffolding to support the child's developing capabilities in that context. However, the adult must involve the child in the solution of the problem rather than simply solving the problem and reporting the solution to the child. Effective instruction may require the teacher to lead the learner through the process, with both involved in the activity. A novice often learns information and skills in formal or informal instruction by observing an expert while participating at a comfortable but slightly challenging level, the zone of proximal development, in the problem's solution. Wertsch and Stone (1979) referred to such teaching and learning as "proleptic instruction." In this process a novice carries out simple aspects of the task as directed by the expert. By actually performing the task under expert guidance, the novice participates in creating the relevant contextual knowledge for the task and acquires some of the expert's understanding of the problem and its solution. Proleptic teaching contrasts both with explanation, where the adult talks about a task rather than guiding the child through the task, and with demonstration, where the teacher carries out the task rather than involving the child in action. Proleptic instruction integrates explanation and demonstration with an emphasis on the learner's participation in the instructional activity.

The concept of proleptic instruction illuminates the form of instruction employed in formal instructional settings, such as school, and informal instructional settings, such as home or apprenticeship training. Formal school instruction has been regarded as relying primarily on explanation, the provision of rules in the verbal mode; informal or out-of-school instruction has been seen as proceeding through demonstration, the provision of examples largely in the nonverbal mode (Scribner & Cole, 1973; Greenfield & Lave, 1982; Rogoff, 1982b). But while differences in instruction in different settings are likely to occur, the concept of proleptic instruction applies equally to the teaching and learning that occur in both formal school and informal everyday situations. Mehan and Riel (in press) challenged the view that verbal explanation used out of the context of a practical activity is the primary means of exchanging information in the school situation, when they showed that most messages in the classroom rely on both verbal and nonverbal modes of communication as the teacher guides the students through tasks. In the literature on the relative merits of teaching by rules versus examples, rules and examples are regarded as alternate methods of instruction (e.g. Dunkin & Biddle, 1974). It would be more productive, however, to examine their integration as the teacher guides the learner through provision of both explanation and examples, constructing a shared understanding of the material.

Similarly, informal instruction may often be better characterized as careful guidance and graduated participation in the task rather than as nonverbal demonstration. One example is the educational process used by the Guareños of the Orinoco delta of Venezuela to teach cultivation, animal husbandry, hunting, and fishing:

> The traditional vocational education system of the Guareños is highly structured and systematic, with either individual or small group instruction. Guareños feel that a knowledge of the intricate flora, fauna, and landforms of their island home, as well as the skill required to manipulate the implements used to exploit their habitat, can only be

gained through repeated physical practice. Hence, emphasis is placed on "learning by doing" through repeated practice over time rather than by simple watching and copying. Regardless of the complex of tasks to be taught, a teacher's first step is to familiarize his student verbally and visually with the physical elements of the appropriate location. The entire complex is demonstrated over a period of time; proceeding from simple to complicated steps, the complex is divided into individual tasks. Instruction is not only sequential but additive, so that at each succeeding step, tasks learned earlier are repeated. Finally, an entire task complex is learned, with only occasional verbal or physical correction needed. When competent, the learner is allowed to help the teacher and to experiment and use his own initiative, and the teacher eventually eliminates his need to fill that role (Ruddle & Chesterfield, 1978:393).

This same training process is used by Guareño adults in preparing 12- to 13-year-olds to train their younger siblings.

Similar technical training takes place in Wogeo, New Guinea:

The various skills are acquired mainly through direct participation in everyday tasks. The child may watch the adults for a time and then, without any encouragement imitate them as best it can, but more usually a demonstration is given as soon as it displays a marked willingness to assist. The explanations are so detailed that the need for seeking additional information seldom arises.

For example,

Karui, aged not quite eight, was already taking his labours seriously, and I one day heard him asking his step-father to allow him to plant some banana trees. The man stood behind him the whole time, telling him when the holes were deep enough and how far apart they ought to be, but did not handle either the trees or the digging stick himself. At last, when the job was completed, he asked whether the boy could manage in future by himself. "Yes indeed; I know already," was the reply. "Good! You have done well," the step-father returned (Hogbin, 1970:147-149).

Proleptic instruction functions as a deliberate but tacit process which the participants construct in the course of communication. They proceed opportunistically in the transfer of information and skills in a purposeful, flexible way, making use of pragmatic aspects of the context to develop the means of instruction. Instruction can be conceived as a complex, tacit process developed in the particular problem situation (Turvey, 1974; Glick, 1978; Kuipers, 1979), rather than as an explicit recipe for problem solution that is available out of the context of action. The parent or other expert is available to mark the crucial actions, provide guidance at choice points, and indicate important variations. This tacit process is illustrated in the role adults play in the development of children's narrative skills:

> When thinking about the task of narrating a story it becomes clear that it is not something that we learn through direct teaching. A child does not receive such directions as these: (a) think of what the story is about, (b) think of the characters in the story, (c) think about their goals and motives, (d) reconstruct story events in line with people's goals and motives, (e) talk about the events in your own words and do not worry about remembering every last detail verbatim. Yet we all can think of times when adults say to children, "What did you do in school today?" or "What did you see at the movies?" or "What was the story about that you watched on TV last night?" When our first question does not elicit very much we might say, "Well, who was in the story?" "What happened?" "Where did she go?" Implicitly, our questions demonstrate those we would ask ourselves if we were trying to recount a set of events. [We "teach"] children in this less conscious way as we [help] them through the narration tasks with our spontaneous questions (McNamee, 1980:19).

While the information and skills are conveyed through the shared construction of a solution to the cognitive problem rather than through explicit free-standing directions for how to solve such a problem, the development of the structure for communication of the information may proceed quite deliberately. Deliberate action can be observed as a person persists in efforts to reach a goal in the face of interruptions or problems that arise during the process of implementation of the means to that goal (Glick, 1978; Greenfield, 1980).

An example of such deliberateness appears in the study as one mother discovers an error in placement which interrupts the development of her transition from two sorted groups (which she calls "lunch" and "fruit") to a new group of items ("snacks"):

> *Mother (after completing placement and rehearsal of items in the fruit category):* Okay, that'll be an easy way to remember. Here's lunch. *(Points to shelf 4.)* Here's fruit. *(Points to shelf 5 then walks toward grocery bags.)* Okay, you've eaten a good lunch, right?
> *Child:* Mhmm. *(Walks toward grocery bags.)*
> *Mother:* Now you can have a snack —

At this point the mother notices that an item on an earlier shelf has been misplaced. She interrupts herself, and an exchange concerning its correct placement ensues. Twenty-two transcript lines later she resumes the shift to the snack shelf exactly where she had left the matter earlier:

Mother: Cancel the cookies on that shelf, okay? And there's that blueberry muffin mix. (*Shuts cupboard doors, covering shelves 2 and 3 where the misplacement of items was repaired.*) Okay, so now you've eaten lunch, and you say, "Mom, may I have a snack?" So let's keep the snacks on the bottom shelf.

That the mother marks the transition to the snack shelf in essentially the same way despite a substantial interruption exemplifies the planful, deliberate character of her role in the instruction.

In common use as well as in social science, the term *instruction* seems to be used primarily to refer to situations in which an expert deliberately and explicitly attempts to increase the knowledge and skills of a novice. This may be a function of a bias toward regarding school teaching as the epitome of teaching — witness the interchangeable use of the term *schooling* for *education* in the psychological literature. However, even in social interaction that is not conceived of as instructional, scaffolding and proleptic instruction are pervasive when a person who is relatively expert communicates with another who is relatively novice. This may be clearest in infancy, where adults rarely regard themselves as "teaching" the infant but they routinely adjust their interaction in ways consistent with providing support for the child's learning.

This adjustment is apparent in the development of conversation between mothers and their 3- to 18-month-old babies: "The mothers work to maintain a conversation despite the inadequacies of their conversational partners. At first they accept burps, yawns, and coughs as well as laughs and coos — but not arm-waving or head movements — as the baby's turn. They fill in for the babies by asking and answering their own questions, and by phrasing questions so that a minimal response can be treated as a reply. Then by seven months the babies become considerably more active partners, and the mothers no longer accept all the baby's vocalizations, only vocalic or consonantal babbles. As the mother raises the ante, the child's development proceeds" (Cazden, 1979:11).

The mother has a similar role in "bookreading" interactions, in which mother and infant apply labels to pictures:

The mother's (often quite unconscious) approach is exquisitely tuned. When the child responds to her "Look!" by looking, she follows immediately with a query. When the child responds to the query with a gesture or a smile, she supplies a label. But as soon as the child shows the ability to vocalize in a way that might indicate a label, she raises the ante. She withholds the label and repeats the query until the child vocalizes, and then she gives the label if the child does not have it fully or correctly.

Later, when the child has learned to respond with shorter vocalizations that correspond to words, she no longer accepts an indifferent vocalization. When the child begins producing a recognizable, constant label for an object, she holds out for it. Finally, the child produces appropriate words at the appropriate place in the dialogue. Even then the mother remains tuned to the developing pattern, helping her child recognize labels and make them increasingly accurate (Bruner, 1981:49).

The modification of maternal discourse by adults and children speaking to infants (Snow, 1977; Messer, 1980; Zukow, Reilly & Greenfield, 1982) may be an example of the advanced speaker functioning in the zone of proximal development and providing supports for the conversation of the novice. Caregivers repeat and expand upon the infant's contribution and provide visual supports and redundant information on their referents and intentions in order to aid the infant's learning of language. The structure of mother-child discourse allows the child to participate in conversations that may extend the child's competence in discourse: "A critical developmental function of dialogue is to provide the child with opportunities to participate in creating linguistic relationships of which she/he would be incapable alone" (Bernstein, 1981:117).

Infants are expert observers, and their parents may be expert instructors providing structure to the infants' learning without focusing on their role as instructors. Infants' propensity to seek proximity with their caregivers assists them in acquiring information about their environment and about the activities of the person who is followed (Hay, 1980). During times of cognitive uncertainty, one-year-old infants make use of and actively request "maternal referencing," turning to the mother and attempting to benefit from her appraisal of the situation to guide their exploration and learning (Sorce, Emde & Klinnert, 1981). If she seems to be interested in and enjoying a situation, the infant proceeds to approach and explore. If the mother signals fear or anger, the infant terminates exploration and retreats or avoids the situation.

Such referencing is facilitated by the child's ability to obtain information from the caregiver's points and direction of gaze (Butterworth & Cochran, 1980). By 12 months of age most infants are able to comprehend another person's point and to tell where another person is looking. If, however, infants appear not to understand a pointing gesture, mothers frequently simplify the task by touching the indicated object (Lempers, 1979). The adult increases the scaffolding to ensure understanding by the child but is unlikely to consider herself to be explicitly teaching. Much of parent-child interaction may be subtly structured in ways that promote the child's development of social and cognitive skills, without the explicit aim of instruction foremost in the adult's mind.

The Transfer of Responsibility

A crucial feature of proleptic instruction is the transfer of responsibility for the management of their joint problem-solving from the expert to the novice. This can be a subtle process involving successive attempts by the participants to assay the novice's readiness for greater responsibility and negotiations of the division of labor. The transfer of responsibility appeared in several aspects of the preparation of the mothers and children for the memory test. In some cases, the responsibility for placing the items was the mother's at the beginning of the classification of items and shifted to the child by the end. Toward the beginning, in placing the first few items, the mother was likely to take major responsibility for decisions regarding item placement and for providing the rationale for each sorting decision. However, as the instruction proceeded through the eighteen items, the child might take increasing responsibility for pieces of the sorting routine until he or she was independently determining the location of the item and the rationale for its association with other items in the same location. In this way, the mother began the instruction with highly supportive scaffolding for the sorting and gradually over the session permitted or encouraged greater participation by the child.

One example of scaffolding and of the child's increasing participation is taken from the school task, where the mother is asked to assist the child in learning the organization of pictures of common household objects to be sorted into colored boxes on a table. In this case, the mother and her 6-year-old son have completed the sorting of items and are reviewing where the items are placed:

Mother: Just look at it again, and see if we can see any similarities that'll help you remember. Maybe — first you — oh, first you get up in the morning. *(Points at the box containing grooming items and looks at child.)* Then you get ready —

Child (interrupting): Brush your teeth.

Mother: Yeah, brush your teeth. *(Touches items in the box containing grooming items)* So we'll remember those things go there. Then you eat your breakfast. *(Touches items in the box containing tableware items and looks at child.)* Then maybe after breakfast, maybe *(gesturing toward child)* you went to mow the lawn or something like — we'll make a little story. *(Touches items in grooming box.)* Like you got up in the morning *(looking at child)*, and got ready. *(Touches items in tableware box.)* Then we ate our breakfast. *(Touches items in the box containing cutting items.)* Then we went and mowed the lawn. *(Looks at child.)*

Child (nodding): And then we . . .

Mother: And then we *(pauses, touching items in the box containing cooking items)* went and cooked something *(pauses and looks at child)*.

Child: For lunch. And *(points in the box containing cleaning items)*.

Mother: And after lunch we *(pauses, pointing in the cleaning box)*.

Child: Cleaned up. *(Rocks forward in chair.)*

Mother: We cleaned up, and then we *(pauses, pointing in the box containing mechanical items, and looks at child)*. Maybe we went to the store to look at *(pauses, looking at the child and smiling)*.

Child: To look at things that have electricity in them. *(Looks at mother.)*

Mother: Okay. *(Gestures to all boxes, then sits back in chair.)* See if you can tell me the story. *(Touches child.)* Again, how did we do it? *(Points at grooming box.)*

The mother and child produced a mnemonic structure to facilitate the child's recall during the test. The mother managed their work so that by the end of the story construction the child was a major participant in the construction. At the beginning of the story mnemonic, the mother provided a great deal of the structure, but her attempts to involve the child were apparent as she paused, looked toward the child, and pointed toward the next box, all of which encouraged his filling in "blanks" in the story form.

One way to provide scaffolding is to make messages sufficiently redundant that if a child does not understand one aspect of the communication, other forms are available to make the meaning clear. As the child develops greater understanding, either over the course of ontogenetic development or in learning how to handle a problem over a shorter term of development, the adult can reduce the level of redundancy. Maternal discourse is organized in episodes referring to specific objects, and within the episodes the mothers provide great redundancy with regard to each object (Messer, 1980). For example, the organization of maternal speech into episodes providing great redundancy in referring to specific objects is greatest when mothers speak to very young children, suggesting that the structure of maternal communication provides a scaffold for learning (Messer, 1980).

A comparison of instruction with older and younger children in the school and home tasks also suggests that over the course of development mothers adjust the supports for learning (Rogoff, Ellis & Gardner, in press). When the 6- to 7-year-olds were contrasted with the 8- to 9-year-olds in performing the school task, which was perceived to be relatively difficult, the dyads involving younger children appeared to compensate for the difficulty of the task. Compared with young children in the home task or older children in either task, they produced more instructional communication: mothers provided more directives, open-ended questions, and non-verbal instruction; children were more involved in the instruction; and the dyad spent more time reviewing. In addition, the younger children in the school task showed slightly better recall and generalization of the organization of items in the memory test. The performance of the younger children would ordinarily be expected to be poorer than that of the older children in both tasks. However, with the dyads adjusting for the expected difficulty of the younger children learning the "harder" task, somewhat better performance was achieved by the younger group. The scaffolding for learning was adjusted to produce appropriate understanding of a particular problem for a learner at a particular level of ability.

This does not mean that scaffolding is adjusted perfectly to the task and ability of the learner. Errors are not only inevitable but also important for the calibration of the level of difficulty of the instruction and the transfer of responsibility from mother to child. At the beginning of the task session the mothers commonly provided redundant information to ensure correct performance (e.g. simultaneously pointing at the correct shelf, repeating the category label for the shelf, and looking toward the shelf). As the session proceeded, the redundancy was decreased, and when errors occurred the redundancy often reappeared. While the mothers and children often attempted to minimize errors and to downplay them when they occurred, errors in learning may nevertheless help the participants to adjust the rate at which responsibility is transferred to the child and to diagnose problems in the child's understanding. Instructors may prevent the development of skills for detecting and interpreting errors by intervening with the student's actions to prevent errors (Burton & Brown, 1979). In the study, the child's errors appeared to inform the participants regarding the appropriate level of responsibility for the child. The mother was often observed subtly testing the child's understanding by reducing the level of scaffolding and thereby allowing the child to participate to a greater extent. But if the child indicated lack of readiness or failed, the mother quickly re-erected the scaffolding which she had momentarily removed.

In many cases such negotiations of appropriate participation were managed through glances and other nonverbal cues. For instance, the mother might give the child a chance to indicate the location of the next item, and when the child hesitated, she might turn slightly toward the correct location. If the child still hesitated, she might glance at the correct location or move the item slightly toward its destination. She might begin rearranging other items in the correct group as the child was trying to determine where to place the item. When the child finally made the correct placement with this hint, the mother's assistance would be masked as a random rather than an instructional activity. Children also seek this kind of subtle hint when given standardized intelligence tests by strangers (Mehan, 1976).

An example of such adjustment in the supports for learning occurs in the exchange between a mother and her 6-year-old son sorting photographs of objects in the school task:

Mother (picking up picture of bucket and holding it in front of child): What's that?

Child: It's a bucket, and it helps you carry things and . . . *(Fidgets.)*

Mother: Yeah, and it helps you clean. *(Looks at child.)*

(Child nods.)

Mother: Okay, what else? Do you see something else that helps you clean? *(Adjusts broom in the cleaning box.)*

(Child watches mother's hand on bucket, then points to bucket, then to broom.)

Mother: The broom, so it should be put in here. *(Holds bucket in cleaning box.)*

Child (taking bucket from mother's hand and placing in correct box): Yeah.

It appears from both the child's response to his mother's first question requesting him to identify the item and from her reply to his attempt that she was searching for more than the name of the item. He provided the name of the item, but not the appropriate category label. She provided the category label and waited for him to place the item in the appropriate box. When action was not forthcoming from the child, the mother made his job more specific: to find another item in the same category. She took this a step further and offered him a candidate by adjusting the position of an item which would be an appropriate response to her latest question. He took the hint, indicated the item she had been adjusting, and they finally got the item placed. This process exemplifies the subtlety of feedback which commonly appears as the dyad establishes the appropriate level of scaffolding to ensure that the child takes responsibility for the cognitive activity to the best of his or her ability.

Another illustration of the give-and-take between mother and child as they negotiate the child's readiness to take on greater responsibility appears in the exchange between a mother and 7-year-old daughter organizing the grocery items. They begin on the thirteenth item, out of eighteen, at which point at least one grocery item had been placed on each shelf:

Mother (picking out margarine and handing it to child): This goes on bread.

(Child studies item.)

Mother: Where do you put that? *(Touches margarine, practically pushing it in correct direction as a hint.)*

Child: Ah. *(Makes unintelligible comment, then places margarine appropriately and returns to mother.)*

(Mother picks out can of pineapple, hands it to child, and smiles expectantly at child, hinting with her eyes moving pointedly toward the correct shelf.)

Child: Mm. The fruit goes here. *(Places item on appropriate shelf, perhaps without seeing mother's eye cues.)*

Mother (picking out rice and handing it to child): This is another starch. *(Pauses, turning and edging slightly toward the appropriate cabinet, then looks toward the cabinet, which contains two shelves.)*

Child: It goes over here. *(Stands poised by wrong shelf in correct cabinet, not placing item, apparently waiting for a more specific cue.)*

Mother: No. *(Points at correct shelf.)* It goes right down here.

(Child places item on correct shelf.)

Mother (picking out wheat thins and handing them to child): This is a snack.

(Child looks in carton, looks at mother, and grins without moving toward placement of item, apparently requesting more information.)

(Mother laughs and nudges child, apparently withholding further information.)

(Child places wheat thins correctly.)

Mother (picking out ketchup and holding it toward child): What is this?

Child: Ketchup. *(Moves to place it on incorrect shelf.)*

Mother: No.

(Child pauses in mid-step, waiting for more information.)

Mother (providing no cue): Where does it go? Think.

(Child backs up to center of room and appears to "think.")

Mother: Okay. *(Looks at appropriate shelf, capitulating in giving a cue.)*

(Child makes no move.)

Mother (pointing at correct shelf): It goes over here with the pickles and the olives. *(Points at pickles and at olives, making her cue quite explicit.)* Okay?

(Child nods and places item on correct shelf.)

The interaction of this dyad illustrates the adaptations that each participant makes in trying to establish the appropriate level of responsibility. The mother tried to establish a greater degree of independent action on the part of the child, and the child sought the information needed to complete placement of the items. This interaction also illustrates the involvement of both participants in structuring the cognitive task and influencing each other's actions and communication.

Social interaction is often conceived as the independent effects of one person on another, such as the mother's effect on the child, or as their reciprocal effects on each other. Viewing the actions of two people in an interactional context as separable events, at either end of a causal arrow, allows questions to be addressed regarding who is influencing whom and how. In contrast, one may focus on the joint participation of two people in the completion of the task and the negotiation of the transfer of information, as they work together in an interdependent fashion to construct the event. Teaching and learning rely on the creation of a shared context for instructional communication. The aim is not to separate the role of mother and child in order to examine their influence on each other, but rather to observe how either or both of them contribute to the communication of information and skills.

In the study, the mothers usually carried great responsibility for structuring the interaction. They generally had greater skill and authority, reinforced by the researchers asking them to take responsibility and giving them access to information to which the child did not have access. Nevertheless, instruction may also be effectively accomplished if the child takes responsibility for obtaining the information. The learner plays a critical role in instruction, in that it is the learner who is in the end responsible for figuring out the material (Kaye, 1979; Lave, ms.). In two examples from the study, children indicated a desire for more information and managed the interactions with their mothers so as to obtain it.

In the first example, the mother had become confused about the correct placements in the school task, and her 9-year-old son guided her in obtaining the needed information from the cue sheet, which indicated correct item placements, to which she had access and he did not:

Mother: Golly gee, between your mother and yourself we've got this in a big mess. I think we've got a couple of them where we haven't —

Child (interrupting, disgusted): Which ones are right so I don't change them?

Mother (touching items in grooming box): This one's right. Let's see . . .

Child (touching cutting box): Is this one right?

Mother: And that one's right.

Child (touching machines box): Is this one?

Mother: Nope.

Child (pointing at cleaning box): Is this one?

Mother: Is that one right? Yes, that one's right.

Child: Okay, these, these, and these. *(Points at the three correct boxes twice.)*

Mother: That's just about as good as it could be. *(Sighs.)* I think that's great.

Child: Look! *(Points at cue sheet.)*

Mother: Shall we find out if that's right? *(Checks cue sheet.)*

Child: Find out.

Mother: Find out? All right, I will. *(Checks cue sheet.)* Let's see . . .

Child (pointing at machines box): Is this one right?

While the mother acknowledged her confusion, the child instituted a checking routine: "Which ones are right so I don't change them?" He led his mother through a step-by-step check of the correctness of items in each box according to the cue sheet. When three of the six boxes had been checked, the child rehearsed them. The mother indicated that she was satisfied with the sorting of the items, sighing: "That's just about as good as it could be." The child was not yet satisfied, however, and compelled the mother to check the placement against the cue sheet provided by the experimenters for the mother's reference.

In the second example, a 9-year-old girl insisted on further preparation for the upcoming test, despite her mother's moves to terminate the instructional session:

Mother: Okay. Let's go. *(Flatly.)* That's it.*(Stands.)*

Child: We're done? *(Stands, incredulous.)*

Mother: Umhm.

(Child stays at table, making no move to leave.)

Mother (walking away from table): Now, do you need to sit and look at that a minute and see what's there?

(Child sits back down.)

Mother: Okay, you sit and look at that for just a minute then. *(Sits back down.)* Make sure everything —

Child (interrupting): But she's gonna change some of the things.

Mother: Well, that's true. *(Stands up).* But the . . . *(Word inaudible).*

Child: Okay, so this is the cleaning box. *(Points at it.)*

Mother: Umhm. *(Walks toward door.)* Okay. We're done.

(Child makes no move to stand and keeps finger in cleaning box.)

Mother (standing on exit side of table, and rehearsing grudgingly while pointing at each box): Cleaning box, appliance box, sharp, dishes, getting ready, cooking.

(Child studies array of boxes.)

Mother: Okay?

(Child studies array of boxes and gets up from chair slowly, nodding yes.)

Mother: Let's go.

(They leave room.)

The daughter questioned her mother's suggestion that the task was finished and ignored her mother's moves to leave. The daughter pointed out a difficulty of the test, that there will be some new items included in the test, but the mother again attempted to leave the work table. Rather than following, the child began to rehearse category names, finally enlisting her mother's assistance in studying. The mother grudgingly listed the category labels and continued to signal her desire to leave. But the child persisted in studying the material until finally she joined her mother in leaving the room.

Conclusions

In order to understand cognitive development, it is necessary to consider the everyday contexts in which children are provided guidance by adults in approaching and solving novel problems. Illustrations of mother-child instruction support the idea that adults assist children with new problems by guiding the transfer of knowledge and skills from more familiar contexts, thereby guiding the child in making connections.

Both the learner and the teacher are actively involved in such instruction. The child participates in problem solving with the adult, rather than listening to explicit explanation or watching demonstration by the adult. Information and skills are transmitted tacitly through pragmatic communication in the context of solving the problem, as the child's understanding is extended through participation in the problem's solution. The instruction occurs in the interaction between novice and expert, who together structure their communication so that the novice is brought into the expert's more mature understanding of the problem. They jointly manage the transfer of responsibility for the task so that the novice is participating at a comfortable yet challenging level in the problem's solution. The expert revises the scaffolding for learning as the novice's capabilities develop, adjusting the support for the novice's performance to a level just beyond that which the novice could independently manage. In this manner, adults routinely guide children's growth in understanding problems and ways to solve them.

5. A Theory of the Teacher in the Learning Activities of Everyday Life

Patricia Marks Greenfield

Any function in the child's cultural development appears on the stage twice, on two planes, first on the social plane and then on the psychological, first among people as an intermental category and then within the child as an intramental category. (Vygotsky, 1966:44)

This chapter will focus on the Vygotskian idea that intra-individual skills have their origin in interindividual activity. As Vygotsky put it, "the transformation of an interpersonal process into an intrapersonal one is the result of a long series of developmental events" (Vygotsky, 1978:57). This idea can be illustrated in diverse domains of informal learning, where individual skills originate in cooperative activity through a scaffolding process. Initially in the learning of language or other skills, the teacher carries the greatest responsibility in the activity, erecting a scaffold for the child's limited skills. As the child's learning and development progress in a given domain, the scaffold gradually diminishes, the roles of learner and teacher become increasingly equal, and the point is finally reached where the child or learner is able to do alone what formerly could be done only in collaboration with the teacher.

The data which will be used to illustrate this concept come from a study of the transition from nonverbal to linguistic communication in language acquisition carried out in Los Angeles with a middle-class sample (Reilly, Zukow & Greenfield, 1978; Zukow, Reilly & Greenfield, 1982), and from a study of the acquisition of weaving skills carried out in Chiapas, Mexico, with a sample of Zinacanteco women (Childs & Greenfield, 1980). The aim is to show that, although a learner's age, culture, native language, and skill are totally different, the same developmental and educational process from interindividual activity to individual accomplishment applies. Our evidence extends the work of Wertsch and colleagues who have intensively studied this process in informal situations where American mothers must teach their preschool children how to do a puzzle or build a model (Hickman & Wertsch, 1978; Wertsch, 1979a-b).

Scaffolding and the Zone of Proximal Development

The scaffold is a metaphor, originated by Wood, Bruner, and Ross (1976), to describe the ideal role of the teacher. This metaphor is the basis for a theoretical model of the teacher in informal education. The scaffold, as it is known in building construction, has five characteristics: it provides a support; it functions as a tool; it extends the range of the worker; it allows the worker to accomplish a task not otherwise possible; and it is used selectively to aid the worker where needed. To illustrate this last point, a scaffold would not be used, for example, when a carpenter is working five feet from the ground.

These characteristics also define the interactional scaffold provided by the teacher in an informal learning situation. That is, the teacher's selective intervention provides a supportive tool for the learner, which extends his or her skills, thereby allowing the learner successfully to accomplish a task not otherwise possible. Put another way, the teacher structures an interaction by building on what he or she knows the learner can do. Scaffolding thus closes the gap between task requirements and the skill level of the learner, creating what Hunt (1961) called "the match" between the cognitive level of the learner and the characteristics of instruction, or what Brown (1975, 1979) referred to as "headfitting."

When a teacher closes the gap between task requirements and what the learner can accomplish on his or her own, this process of collaborative work between teacher and learner often advances the learner's skills as well as accomplishing the task at hand. The reason for this effect lies in what Vygotsky conceptualized as the "zone of proximal development." This is "the distance between the actual developmental level as determined by independent problem solving and the level of potential development as determined through problem solving under adult guidance or in collaboration with more capable peers. . . . the zone of proximal development defines those functions that have not yet matured but are in the process of maturation, functions that will mature tomorrow, but are currently in an embryonic state" (1978:86). Thus, adult guidance, when it functions as a scaffold in the zone of proximal development, not only leads the child to solve problems collaboratively that could not be solved alone, but also moves the embryonic skill toward its full-blown manifestation.

This "region of sensitivity" to instruction lies in the gap between comprehension and production (Wood, Wood & Middleton, 1978). The new skill component must be comprehensible although it has not as yet been produced. This idea, applied to scaffolding, means that the teacher provides the minimum necessary scaffolding for the learner to produce new skill components that are understood but not yet performed. Wood, Wood, and Middleton have demonstrated experimentally that a scaffolding technique incorporating this pacing principle, which they call "contingent instruction," is more effective in teaching 3- and 4-year-old children a difficult construction task than pure demonstration, pure verbal instruction, or alternation of demonstration and verbalization without reference to the learner's current skill level.

Scaffolding resembles the concept of shaping from Skinnerian psychology (1938). Both create an environment which reduces both error and failure experiences at the early stages of learning a new skill. There is, however, a major difference between them. Shaping involves a series of successive approximations to the ultimate task goal. While the learner is successful at every point in the process, he or she starts with a simplified version of the ultimate task. Scaffolding, in contrast, does not involve simplifying the task during the period of learning. Instead, it holds the task constant, while simplifying the learner's role through the graduated intervention of the teacher. Although scaffolding is more important in both language acquisition and learning to weave, the gradation of task difficulty characteristic of shaping also plays a role in both informal learning situations.

These two learning situations are extremely far apart in type of skill, age of learner, and culture of participants, which illustrates the broad applicability of scaffolding and the zone of proximal development to understanding the nature of instructional interaction in situations of informal learning. In the first example, the beginnings of language learning (between the ages of one and two) were studied among middle-class children in the United States. In the second example, learning to weave was studied among 7- to 15-year-old members of a subsistence Indian culture in rural Mexico, the Zinacantecos. In both cases the research method involved video recording in naturally occurring situations of informal learning. This method permitted microanalysis of the social interaction through which instruction was taking place.

Language Learning in Los Angeles

The study sample was composed of six children at various stages in the one-word period of language development, that is, the stage at which children are mainly uttering one word at a time. In terms of age, the children ranged from 9 months to 22 months at the beginning of the study. Each child was observed twice; the two observation periods were four to six weeks apart. The focus of the study was the role of the caregiver in the development of comprehension. In other words, language acquisition was approached as a situation involving informal education. The study dealt with the comprehension of one class of message, the adult-initiated offer. It looked at the development of the response to verbally expressed offers and the role of the caregiver in this communication process (Reilly, Zukow, & Greenfield, 1978; Zukow, Reilly & Greenfield, 1982).

Two types of offer messages were identified: the offer of an object, and the offer of an activity. An example of the former would be, "Do you want a banana?" An example of the latter would be, "Do you want to go for a walk?" In terms of the caregiver's role, the study investigated how the mother uses nonverbal cues to help the baby respond to otherwise incomprehensible verbal messages and how the baby's need for such cues changes with development. More specifically, it looked at how the representation of the offer message on a nonverbal level and the manipulation of the baby's attention by the caregiver function as a scaffold to enable the baby to give a meaningful response to a verbal offer which he or she would not otherwise understand.

The children were divided into three language levels, all within the one-word period, on the basis of diary reports of language production. The levels were defined according to the complexity of the implied propositions which they communicate. Children at

Level 1 are limited to implied propositions involving a single entity, for example, pointing at an object and naming it. Children at Level 2 are able to communicate an implied proposition consisting of an entity and an action, for example, naming the action of an agent. At Level 3, children are able to communicate an implied proposition consisting of two entities, for example, naming the possessor of an object.

After the children were categorized by language level, the video-tapes were analyzed for meaningful responses to offers, with emphasis on the scaffolding required at each language level and the process by which it was constructed. Very often it was found that mothers do interactive work, creating additional scaffolding if the offer does not immediately elicit an acknowledgment. In this inter-active situation, the child's response plays a role. For example, if the child was not looking, the mother might tap on the table to get the child to turn toward the banana, or if the banana was lying on the table, she might pick it up and extend it toward the child with an offer gesture, thus completing the nonverbal representation of the offer. That is, the mother translates the offer on a sensorimotor level, the level of visible action. The term *sensorimotor* is used here in a general sense to refer to perception and action, so its scope is not limited to the specific tasks described by Piaget (1951, 1952, 1954).

In this way, the mother elicits a comprehending response through a sequence of interactional work in which she adds cues one at a time, gradually enlarging the scaffold until it is adequate for the task. This construction of a scaffold piece-by-piece constitutes an interactive situation in which the child's response plays a role in stimulating additional scaffolding by the mother. Hence, the scaffold results not simply from the mother's action but also from a process of interaction between mother and child. In this process, the child's responses play an active role in shaping the nature and extent of the scaffold. This interactive process of mutual influence between mother and child is the specific mechanism by which the match or headfitting comes about.

This type of interactive process was manifested in a large class of communications labeled "eventually successful." In an eventually successful offer the mother frequently creates a scaffold one step at a time. For example, one sequence contained an initial verbal offer, "D'ya wan call Daddy?" which was transformed into a successful communication through the gradual construction of a nonverbal scaffold.

Successful communication is operationally defined, in terms of the organizational structure of the offer. The study revealed the following organizational structure:

I. Offer establishment
    a. Offer presentation
    b. Offer acknowledgment
II. Offer consummation
    a. Offer realization
    b. Offer enactment

Ia and IIa are carried out by one participant (the mother in this corpus of adult-initiated offers), Ib and IIb by the other participant (here the child). Sometimes an object offer is nested in an activity offer. This occurs when, after offering an activity, the mother offers the child an object that is required to carry out the activity. Thus, a toy telephone is required by the offered activity of "calling Daddy." The embedded object offer can be denoted by superscripts corresponding to the parts of the offer structure (Ia', Ib').

Communicative success is defined by the acknowledgment of the offer on the part of the child (Ib). To be counted as an acknowledgment, the response must be specifically appropriate to a particular offer, and it must be interpreted as a specific response by the caregiver (IIa).

The following episode illustrates the step-by-step scaffolding process. The mother's initial offer presentation to Jeremy is, "Jeremy, d'ya wan call Daddy?" (Ia). Calling someone on the phone is a complex activity involving at least three component actions. The child must lift the receiver to his ear, dial the phone, and finally talk into the receiver.

When Jeremy's mother first makes the offer, they are both sitting on the floor, Jeremy's back is to his mother, and the telephone is on the floor between them. The question alone provokes no response, other than Jeremy crawling away from his mother toward the camera. The mother gains his attention by calling his name twice. He responds by turning around to look at her. She raises the receiver to her own shoulder and proceeds to dial, demonstrating the first two component actions and the appropriate physical configuration for talking on the telephone. While dialing, she repeats the verbal offer, "D'ya wanna call Daddy? You wanna call Daddy?" Jeremy's gaze is still focused on his mother and the telephone. She then begins to talk into the receiver, demonstrating the final component, action, and thus completing a demonstration of the entire activity. The scaffold thus far has provided a nonverbal enactment of the activity initially offered on the verbal level. This enactment functions as a translation for the child who is in the process of acquiring language.

Jeremy continues to look at his mother as she holds the phone body and offers him the receiver, thus creating an object offer that is embedded in the activity offer (Ia'). His gaze continues to follow his mother's movements. She crawls closer to Jeremy to establish a more appropriate general configuration, which in this case is the orientation between Jeremy and the phone. She then asks, "You wanna talk?" This offer presentation simplifies the original offer presentation by making explicit one of the actions, talking, which is merely implied by the initial offer, "D'ya wan call Daddy?"

Jeremy acknowledges the embedded offer of the phone by lifting his chin into position to have the receiver next to his ear (Ib'). His mother then extends the receiver to Jeremy's ear, thus simultaneously realizing both the activity offer (IIa) and its embedded object offer (IIa'). This specific configuration then provides a scaffold for the third action, talking, which is the final enactment of the original offer (IIb). The mother uses an imperative form to induce Jeremy to participate and then models Jeremy's part, "Tell Daddy. Say hello," providing a demonstration of the final component. At this point, Jeremy finally produces some unintelligible sounds which the mother acknowledges as a partially satisfactory enactment (IIb) by saying, "Uh huh. Hello, Daddy. Hello, Daddy."

Although the telephone was initially present and Jeremy was looking at it, this situation is certainly not sufficient for the offer sequence to be consummated. In fact, before the offer sequence succeeded at all, the mother provided not only the configuration but all of the implied constituent components of the activity. All Jeremy does to acknowledge the offer presentation is to sit attentively and then attempt a repetition of his mother's utterance, very much like a routine.

The nonverbal scaffolding required for the comprehension of offers systematically decreases as language level increases. For example, the study showed that, at Level 1, which extended from 9 to 14 months of age, every element of an offer must be visibly present on the nonverbal level and the child's attention must be focused on the visual representation in order to give a comprehending response. As a hypothetical example, "Do you want a banana?" is a verbal offer of an object. If it is presented in this way to a Level 1 baby, there will be no specific response to the offer. What is required in addition is a complete nonverbal representation of the offer: a real banana must be offered by means of the appropriate gesture in the baby's usual location for eating, and the infant's attention must be focused on what is being offered. Once all these elements are present, a meaningful response in the form of an acknowledgment is possible. Such an acknowledgment may take the form of either a rejection (such as pushing away the banana) or an acceptance (such as opening the mouth to receive the banana). In the case of either positive or negative acknowledgment, the point is that effective communication of the offer has taken place and this has occurred through the use of a nonverbal scaffold. The example, "D'ya wan call Daddy?" illustrates the necessity of a complete nonverbal scaffold at Level 1 with an actual example from our data.

At Level 1, in short, a child is capable of responding to an offer sequence when all the relevant contextual and semantic information is present and attended to on the sensorimotor level. The responsibility for providing the elements and ensuring the child's attention rests with the mother. Note that successful activity offers require a demonstration of the activity, as well as the presence of the necessary objects and persons. Interactions that do not fulfill these requirements are not successful for the Level 1 child, who requires a complete nonverbal translation of the offer, that is, scaffolding to the maximum extent possible.

At the point where the child lacks the linguistic skills necessary to comprehend a given message, the scaffold is nonverbal. The mother presents word and sentence meanings that can be seen. This process gives the child an opportunity to learn new linguistic meanings which can then be internalized in the movement from inter- to intraindividual meaning.

At the stage of language development represented by the telephone example, the linguistic representation is irrelevant for communication, because the process is basically one of nonverbal communication. If this is the case, in what sense is it meaningful to speak of the mother's nonverbal representation as a scaffold for the successful accomplishment of linguistic communication? Looking at the situation from the adult's point of view, the mother may view herself as primarily attempting to communicate a linguistic message. So she may view the nonverbal representation as "cues" to the decoding of her linguistic message. This seems a particularly likely interpretation of the mother's point of view in those situations where a verbal offer is presented first and nonverbal elements are added only later when the verbal message fails to communicate. This is the situation in the telephone example.

More essential to the nature of the scaffold, however, is the situation from the child's point of view. I would argue that, at Level 1, the linguistic message is irrelevant to successful *communication*. It is not, however, irrelevant to *language learning*. Indeed, just because the nonverbal message is self-sufficient without language, it provides an opportunity to learn the meaning of the linguistic representation, which was heretofore an unknown quantity. The hypothesis is that the presence of both verbal and nonverbal representations provides an opportunity for a Level 1 child to form associations between words or phrases and their concrete referents. Thus, the nonverbal representation is a scaffold for the verbal in the sense that the former helps the child to learn the latter.

Developments in foreign language teaching utilize a nonverbal scaffold to "translate" or make manifest the meaning of unknown messages. For example, Kunihara and Asher (1965) found that methods involving the acting out of meanings by the teacher are more effective in teaching Japanese as a foreign language than are other methods of instruction involving hearing or seeing a verbal translation.

At this point, the analogy between informal learning and the scaffold breaks down, for the carpenter does not learn from his or her scaffold, but the informal learner does. That is, the scaffold not only helps successfully to accomplish the current task but also provides information which, as it becomes internalized, gradually eliminates the learner's need for the scaffold itself. A better analogy in this respect might be the labels on a typewriter keyboard. They provide a support for accurate typing while letter positions are being learned. However, in the acquisition of touch typing, the visual information provided by the keyboard ultimately becomes internalized, gradually eliminating the learner's very need for a visually labeled keyboard.

Evidence for this hypothetical process comes from the finding that children at the second linguistic level of the one-word period (between 15 and 17 months of age in our sample) need less scaffolding in the form of nonverbal representation in order to respond to verbally presented object offers. This developmental change suggests — although only longitudinal data can prove — that the means used to gain comprehension at Level 1 succeeded in teaching the child certain word or phrase meanings, and that at Level 2 the association between word and nonverbal referent has now been internalized so that the referent is no longer necessary for comprehension to occur.

Consider this example of comprehension by a Level 2 child in the absence of the referent: The mother and child are in the bedroom when the mother asks, "You wan some juice?" The child responds by leaving the room and running down the hall into the kitchen where the juice is kept. This mother's offer is presented on a purely linguistic level; that is, there is no object, gesture, or appropriate location to serve as a nonverbal scaffold. Yet the offer elicits a meaningful response. This older, more linguistically advanced child (although still in the one-word period) does not always need the nonverbal cues required by the less linguistically advanced and younger children. Because of its cross-sectional design, the language development study cannot prove that input at Level 1 caused improved linguistic comprehension at Level 2. However, it strongly suggests that the external scaffold used by the Level 1 child has now been internalized: the Level 2 child does not always need an externally situated translation of the verbal offer. He or she can perform the needed translation internally, representing the meaning of the utterance — the offer plus the specific object — in his or her mind.

The number of nonverbal cues required for meaningful response to a given type of offer substantially decreases as language level and age increase. At Level 1, offers are successful only if all elements are dramatized nonverbally, such as the objects or the activity being offered. At Level 2, in contrast, there are a number of examples of successfully communicated offers in which nonverbal dramatization is incomplete.

Whereas the mother of the Level 1 child constructs the referential meaning of her linguistic message for her child, the Level 2 child constructs the meaning for himself or herself. This developmental sequence toward comprehension of a linguistic message illustrates Vygotsky's (1978) idea that skills originate as interindividual collaborations which then become internalized, resulting in the intraindividual form, the capacity for independent accomplishment of the skill in question. This process of internalization also shifts the zone of proximal development, as yesterday's nascent skill becomes today's actual one. Thus, the mother or adult teacher is in the position of having to follow a moving zone of proximal development.

Mothers are sensitive to the match, for the input they provide correlates with the child's different needs at different points in development. For example, the modalities through which the mothers initiate their offers change with the child's development. The frequency of purely linguistic initiation, such as asking, "Do you want X?" without an accompanying initiation on the nonverbal level, increases steadily between Level 1 and Level 3 children. At Level 1, only 8% of all offers are initiated on the linguistic level alone. At Level 2, the percentage is 67%. At Level 3 it rises slightly to 75%.

Another aspect of this scaffolding process is that within a given language level more scaffolding is needed for a more difficult task. For example, children at Level 2, who can comprehend the absent object in a verbal object offer, as in the juice example, still invariably need an external representation of the activity in the more complex activity offers. An example of just such a complex activity offer follows.

The mother says, "Do ya wanna comb the baby's hair?" At that moment, several referential elements are missing on the sensorimotor level: the proper configuration, the objects, and the activity. Although one object, the doll, is visible, neither the comb nor the doll is in the child's possession. Without the necessary objects, no demonstration is possible. The mother then provides the objects and a demonstration of the specific activity. At this point the child acknowledges the offer by taking the doll, ultimately enacting the offer by combing the doll's hair.

The examples illustrate the symbolization capabilities of children at Level 2 and display the requirements for comprehension. At this level children are apparently able to represent symbolically the referent of a concrete noun, such as *juice* in the case where the child runs into the kitchen where the juice is kept. However, there is no evidence that the children are able internally to represent the referent of a verb or any linguistic representation of an entire complex activity. Thus, the mother of the Level 2 child has to demonstrate the activity of combing before her offer achieves communicative success.

These examples show that at Level 2 the child is now a more active participant in supplying the contextual and referential information. At Level 1, the mother is the sole provider of the structure, whereas at Level 2, the child assumes part of the responsibility, albeit enactively. Instances include the occasion when the child picks up the doll (object) in order to comb its hair, and the time when the child runs into the kitchen (location) for the juice (object). The fact that these children can supply missing sensorimotor contextual and referential information is evidence that at Level 2 children have at least partially internalized the sensorimotor structure of an offer sequence, the referential structure of a linguistic offer. Internalization of linguistic offers is complete at Level 3.

There is also a shaping aspect to the mother's developmentally graduated communication. Mothers not only make a given task easier by their collaborative intervention but also select simpler tasks. The ratio of the more complex activity offers to the simpler object offers rises steadily from Level 1 to Level 3. Thus, task difficulty as well as type of intervention is adjusted to the child's current level of development.

Other Examples of Movement from Interindividual to Intraindividual Activity in Language Acquisition

The research just described relates to development in the child's comprehension of linguistic messages. There is also a passage from interindividual to intraindividual forms on the production side of language development. A longitudinal study of productions from one-word utterances to early combinatorial speech traced most of the first two-word utterances independently produced by the children back to earlier dialogic forms (Greenfield & Smith, 1976). For example, Nicky, one of the children in the study, produced *want* plus an object for his first two-word sentences at 19 months, 27 days. One such example was "awada cacoo" (want record), uttered while the record player was turned off. About three weeks earlier, at 19 months, 4 days, similar linguistic propositions were produced cooperatively in question-answer dialogue with his mother. In these examples, the notion of 'want' is contained in the mother's question, while the object of 'want' is contained in Nicky's response.

Mother: What do you want?
Nicky: Showel (shovel).

In this question-answer sequence, the child makes use of a word, *want,* in his mother's question to convey the message 'want shovel.' Her question thus provides a scaffold for his message. Three weeks later, the scaffold has been internalized: the child can now provide both message elements himself, as in "awada cacoo" (want record).

Nicky's next step in syntactic development was the two-word pattern, *no* plus an object. This pattern could also be traced back to a dialogic form. Sometimes there was even microgenesis, or short-term development, from the interindividual to intraindividual forms within a given observation period. For example, Nicky's mother asked, "Do you want the dance record?" and Nicky answered, "No!" A few minutes later, his mother asked, "Do you want to listen to it?" referring to a record, and Nicky responded, "No record." His two-word utterance combines a propositional element, *record,* from his mother's earlier question, with his previous response, *no.* These examples strongly suggest a process in which both people's roles in the question-answer routine become internalized by the child, helping him progress from single-word utterances to two-word sentences.

Ochs, Schieffelin, and Platt (1979) provided other examples of a linguistic function being achieved interactionally in dialogue before being expressed syntactically by the child alone. Hatch, Peck, and Wagner-Gough (1979) have made parallel observations indicating that the internalization of dialogue plays a role in the second language acquisition of older children. Thus, the conversational partner provides a scaffold for the language learner's emerging capabilities.

Learning to Weave in Zinacantan, Chiapas, Mexico

The role of scaffolding in informal instruction was also illustrated in weaving in Zinacantan (Childs & Greenfield, 1980). Weaving is a skill that is not nearly as universal as talking, but it is nevertheless fundamental in the Zinacanteco culture. The Zinacantecos have a subsistence culture in the highlands of Chiapas in southern Mexico. Their native language is not Spanish but Tzotzil.

Fourteen girls were taped at various levels of learning to weave. Weaving level was measured by the amount of previous weaving experience, as shown by the number of articles woven. The girls ranged from first-time weavers to experts. They were videotaped in the most natural situation possible. At least one teacher was always present, except for the expert weavers. This teacher was always a close relative, usually the mother. The social situation was thus quite parallel to the situation of learning to talk. Unlike the middle-class California mothers, however, none of the weaving teachers (and only one of the learners) had any formal schooling at all. Another difference was that the principal teacher in the weaving situation was often aided by other closely related female onlookers.

The tapes were coded by means of a number of categories of action and interaction. As in the language study, the focus was on both verbal and nonverbal means of instruction.

Scaffolding was again an important theme of the results. First-time beginners produced woven material that was, to the eyes of the researchers, indistinguishable from that produced by the more experienced and expert weavers. This was made possible by the collaborative efforts of the teacher, who sensitively aided the learner wherever necessary to complete the task. First-time weavers clearly could not complete a piece of woven material on their own; yet they did so with the help of the teacher. By making this accomplishment possible through joint action, the teachers operated above what Vygotsky (1974) called the actual developmental level, in the learners' zone of proximal development.

For first-time beginners, the teachers' nonverbal involvement consisted primarily of taking over the weaving at the more technically difficult parts of the process. Thus, during two segments that were difficult because they involved a new process — selvaging and the first cycle of weaving — teachers took over the weaving 53% of the time. The teacher's heavy involvement at the more difficult parts of the process functions as a scaffold in making it possible for the learner to complete the piece of woven cloth. At the same time, this form of intervention provides a model for observation, thus supplying an opportunity for learning and ultimate internalization of the teacher's skill by the learner. The study indicated that the learners did in fact pay attention when the teachers took over: they watched the model 87% of the time, looking away only 13% of the time.

The basic idea that a scaffold functions to close the gap between learner abilities and task requirements implies that more scaffolding will be used in the harder parts of the task. To test this hypothesis, teacher intervention in the first cycle of weaving was compared with teacher intervention during a later cycle (a cycle consists of adding two weft threads to the weaving, thus passing both over and under every warp thread). The first cycle is intrinsically more difficult, because it constitutes a complete change from what has gone before and because special technical problems are associated with "getting started." For the completely inexperienced weaver the first cycle is also her introduction to weaving.

Comparison of overall teacher intervention in the weaving during the two cycles, excluding cases where there was no intervention during either cycle or where comparative data were not available, showed that every one of the eight teachers intervened more on the first cycle than on the later one. The size of the difference was dramatic: teachers participated in the weaving 65% of the time, on the average, in the first cycle, and only 16% of the time in a later one. This is clearcut evidence of more scaffolding in the harder parts of the task. Thus, the teachers' scaffold is sensitive to the level of task difficulty.

Equally fundamental to the scaffolding concept is sensitivity to the skill level of the learner and the idea that the scaffold supports what the learner can already do. Evidence for this notion was provided by the difference in amount and type of instructional techniques used with learners at different levels of experience. The more experienced the learner, the less frequently the teacher took over the weaving (Table 5.1). Thus, the teacher follows a moving zone of proximal development. The amount of time spent weaving independently also increased with experience (Table 5.1). This trend indicates that weaving knowledge is gradually being internalized by the learners.

Another change in type of teacher intervention as the learner's skill level increased was revealed by an analysis of teacher verbalization. The teacher's verbal aid, like her nonverbal aid, was graded according to the level of the weaver. Thus, beginners received

Table 5.1. Time teacher takes over weaving, works cooperatively with learner, and lets weaver work independently (%).

Teacher's degree of intervention	Previous weaving experience			
	None $(n = 2)$	1 piece of cloth $(n = 2)$	2–4 pieces of cloth $(n = 3)$	Expert $(n = 1)$
Teacher takes over	61	33	14	0
Teacher and learner work cooperatively	32	15	28	0
Weaver works independently of teacher	7	52	58	100
Total	100	100	100	100

mostly commands, the most direct form of verbal aid. As weaving experience increased, teachers used a higher proportion of statements, which are a more indirect form of verbal aid. Initially, commands constituted 91% of all verbalizations from teacher to learner, while statements constituted only 4%. By the time learners had from two to four woven articles behind them, teachers used commands only 53% of the time, while statements made up 40% of their verbalizations. This trend provides additional evidence of the internalization of the teacher's role. The decline of commands implies that the learners are becoming increasingly self-regulated with the development of skill. Extrapolation from Vygotsky's (1962) framework suggests that the teacher's overt command has been transformed into inner speech in the process of internalization.

Closely related is the finding that the frequency of multimodal instruction — verbal combined with nonverbal — declined as weaving experience increased. For the least experienced learners, the majority of the teacher-initiated interactions (68.4%) combined verbal and nonverbal elements. This figure declined steadily with increasing experience, reaching 33.6% for the girls who had previously woven from two to four articles. In a multimodal message, the nonverbal elements can provide cues as to the intended mean-

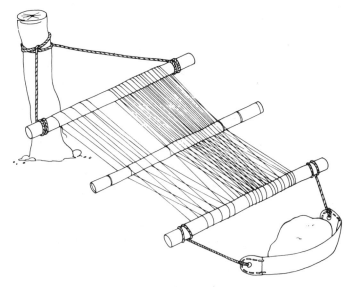

Fig. 5.1. Backstrap loom.

ing of the linguistic message, in weaving just as in learning to talk. Corresponding to this decrease in teachers' multimodal instructions was a steady increase in purely verbal messages as weavers became more skilled (from 17.4% among the rank beginners to 40.1% among the girls with two to four articles behind them). There is an interesting commonality here with the language learning process: the use of multiple and potentially redundant communication channels also decreased as the learner became competent in going from words to meaning.

As in the case of language learning, shaping has a role in weaving education. Girls with little weaving experience are given smaller items to weave. Smaller size makes the task easier by requiring less strength to maintain the tension in backstrap looms; in the actual situation a weaver leaning back would take the place of the rock pictured (Figure 5-1). Thus, shaping is integrated with scaffolding in the informal teaching of weaving in Zinacantan.

Comparison Between the Two Learning Situations

The main difference between language learning in Los Angeles and learning to weave in Zinacantan is that there are more failure

experiences in the language learning situation. The Los Angeles
mothers did not provide the necessary scaffold in about 15% of the
offers, and there the communication failed. In contrast, no weaving
failures, or even microfailures, were observed at any level of knowledge. This is because, in weaving instruction, the mother jumps in
as soon as she perceives the learner to have the slightest problem,
actual or potential. Errors may also be more difficult to control
between one and two years of age, the age of learning language,
than in middle or late childhood, the age of learning to weave.
Thus, age differences may contribute to this contrast.

There was an almost trial-and-error approach to the scaffolding
itself in the language learning situation, where a large class of
communications fell into the "eventually successful" category. In
these cases, the mother did not immediately provide all the scaffolding required for successful communication. She added piece by
piece in an almost trial-and-error way. She seemed, though not
consciously, to provide the absolute minimum information necessary for success, but was perhaps not quite sure what that minimum
was. In contrast, there was no evidence of this kind of trial-and-
error scaffolding process in Zinacantan. The teachers seemed to
provide exactly what was required from the very beginning. Consequently there were no observable weaving errors on the learner's
part in Zinacantan. From the learner's point of view, a trial-and-
error approach contrasts with scaffolding because a scaffold, designed for the current level of the learner, prevents error during the
course of learning a new skill.

In addition, as Barbara Rogoff pointed out, a teacher may find it
harder to prevent errors in a mental skill like language than in a
physical task like weaving, and harder to make a match between the
scaffold and the skill level of the learner. If so, the language teacher
would have a more challenging task than the weaving teacher. This
task difference is a possible explanation of the fact that learning to
weave in Zinacantan seems relatively error-free in comparison
with learning to understand language in Los Angeles, California.

Errors can be constructive in showing the limits of one's skill, as
Jean Lave has noted. However, this useful type of error mainly
occurs in a context where the teacher wants the learner's skill to
generalize to new situations never before encountered and the
learner has made an incorrect generalization. Such a context vio-
lates the Zinacanteco view of weaving. Zinacantecos want girls to
learn to weave a small set of specific patterns, not to transfer their

weaving skill to a wide variety of new patterns. This view serves the larger cultural goal of preserving tradition (Greenfield & Lave, 1982).

In the language learning situation, in contrast, generalization would have a definite value, for it enables the child to acquire linguistic knowledge that is not bound to the context in which the original learning took place. School learning also has generalization as an important goal. Hence, the use of error to show the limits in generality of current skills, thereby aiding the generalization process, can also contribute to an explanation of why errors would be more encouraged in school than out, more tolerated in learning to talk in general than in learning to weave in Zinacantan. Generalization is more valued and necessary in speech and schooling than in Zinacanteco weaving. Thus, task differences, age differences, and value differences are all possible factors in explaining the greater prevalence of error in the language learning situation than in the weaving situation.

Perhaps more interesting than the differences are the similarities across the two informal learning situations:

1. A scaffold adapted to the level of the learner in both cases ensures success at a task the child cannot do on his or her own.
2. The amount of scaffolding needed and provided decreases as the skill level of the learner increases. The teacher thus follows a moving zone of proximal development.
3. Ultimately, the scaffold becomes internalized, enabling independent accomplishment of the skill by the learner.
4. For a learner at a given level of skill, a greater scaffold is provided as task difficulty increases.
5. Scaffolding is integrated with shaping, the technique in which task difficulty is also varied as a function of learner skill.
6. In both situations, teachers appear unconscious of their methods or of the fact of teaching. For example, a Zinacanteco woman, interviewed about how girls learn to weave, said that they learn by themselves. The common belief in Western culture is that children also learn to talk by themselves (Chomsky, 1965).

Conclusions

In a general way this picture of the development of interaction in informal learning situations illustrates Vygotsky's point that a given activity is mastered interindividually before it is mastered intraindividually; that is, the learner first carries out an activity in cooperation with the teacher. The teacher's role is eventually internalized, and the child then proceeds on his or her own. These two very different examples of informal learning show that the phenomenon of scaffolding is a very general one that can illuminate instructional interaction in a wide range of learning situations.

The findings presented in this chapter touch base at several points with the other chapters in this book that deal with processes of informal instruction. One important commonality concerns the communication techniques used by mothers in informal learning situations. Rogoff and Gardner's results support ours in pointing to the use of high-redundancy messages early in an informal learning process, with a gradual reduction in redundancy as the task structure is internalized by the child. Rogoff and Gardner also found that the child's errors become a signal to the adult to upgrade the scaffolding. In early language learning, additional nonverbal cues, which are "redundant" from the adult's point of view but not from the child's, are provided when the child makes the "error" of not comprehending. In the case of learning to weave, the additional scaffolding placed at particularly difficult junctures in the task seems to *anticipate* rather than *respond* to errors, yielding a relatively error-free performance. Thus, while the frequency of observable errors may be quite different in the two situations, the underlying function of errors to guide instruction is the same. Errors, either anticipated or actual, are used as a signal to upgrade the scaffold, transferring responsibility from the learner to the teacher.

In comparison with out-of-school learning, in-school learning, where there is greater emphasis on independent work and trial-and-error learning, seems to apply the scaffolding principle less frequently. Teachers more than parents allow children to work independently, learning from their own mistakes. Scaffolding, in contrast, leads to relatively errorless learning because, in principle, just the right type and amount of help are provided at each point for the pupil to succeed. However, this distinction between home and school is certainly not absolute. Indeed, Mehan (1979) provided a few examples of verbal scaffolding by a teacher in a teacher-student dialogue in an elementary school classroom.

One reason why trial-and-error learning may be more prevalent at school and scaffolded learning at home is a difference of emphasis on learning versus getting the task done (Wertsch, this volume). School specializes in learning; outside-of-school activities usually give at least equal, if not greater importance to finishing the job. In the two learning studies the tasks were communication of an offer and weaving. In both cases the successful completion of the task at hand has a value in itself, independent of what the child learns from the process. An arithmetic problem, for example, does not have this same kind of intrinsic value. In the case of weaving, the cost of errors or failure is quite high in economic terms, for the Zinacantecos, a subsistence culture with scarce resources, cannot afford to waste weaving materials. Thus, the value of task accomplishment per se may explain why scaffolding is less prevalent in school than out, while the immediate cost of errors may explain why scaffolded interaction controls errors more in some learning situations than in others. For example, the high economic cost of errors in weaving versus the absence of a concretely apparent cost to communication failures in language learning may explain, to some extent, why error is more carefully controlled in the former situation than in the latter. An unanswered question is the extent to which school instruction could be improved by greater use of the principle of scaffolding, thus putting more emphasis on cooperative success in the early stages of learning and less emphasis on independent discovery through a process of trial-and-error.

Scaffolding is also related to the concept of cooperation. It can be conceived as an asymmetric type of cooperation where one person takes greater responsibility than the other for the successful accomplishment of a task by compensating for the other person's weaknesses. In a seminar, John Whiting and Beatrice Whiting pointed out that cooperation among pupils in school is called cheating. This observation illustrates the point that, in general, school traditionally values independent rather than cooperative learning. This contrast between the role of peer cooperation in and out of school is supported by Newman, Griffin, and Cole's observation (this volume) that cognitive tasks carried out individually in the classroom are often divided up among different children and approached cooperatively in the informal context of an afterschool club.

This concept of scaffolding and its potentially broad applicability to situations of everyday learning raises questions as to the cognitive skills required of the teacher. Usually the focus is on the cognitive development of the learner. Perhaps more important in real life is the cognitive development which allows a person to become an effective teacher. What are the cognitive skills involved in scaffolding? In England important individual differences were found in mothers' ability to use the technique of scaffolding (Wood, Wood & Middleton, 1978). What experiences or abilities produce these differences among mothers? What are the developmental stages which lead to a mastery of scaffolding? What are the component processes of scaffolding? These questions concerning the cognitive processes of the teacher would be interesting to pursue in the continuing investigation of learning experiences in the everyday world.

6.   Skiing as a Model of Instruction

Richard R. Burton
John Seely Brown
Gerhard Fischer

While some work has gone into developing specific learning environments, little has gone into clarifying the general issues that affect the acquisition of a complex skill, especially in a naturalistic setting. A study was made of an extremely complex skill, skiing, to determine why it has become so easy to learn. The goal was to analyze the features of a highly successful learning environment in order to articulate a general theory of learning environments.

Learning environments can be examined in terms of a paradigm called "increasingly complex microworlds" (ICM). In this paradigm, the student is exposed to a sequence of environments (microworlds) in which his tasks become increasingly complex. The purpose of an individual microworld is to provide the student with a task that he can perform successfully using a simplified version of the final skill that is the goal. This allows the student to focus on and master one aspect of the skill in a context that requires related subskills. As a result, the student learns when to use the skill as well as how to use it. The purpose of the sequence is to evolve the simplified skills toward the goal skill. The ICM framework focuses both on what is learned in any particular microworld and on how to choose the next microworld in the sequence.

A microworld is created by manipulating three elements: the equipment used in executing the skill, the physical setting in which the skill is executed, and the task specifications for the given equipment and physical setting. These manipulations allow the student to focus on the factors that are fundamental to learning a skill, rather than on factors that are not immediately relevant. A critical factor in determining appropriate microworlds is the process of debugging, or correction of systematic errors. The appropriate microworld can transform "nonconstructive bugs" into "constructive bugs," ones that can be readily learned from. Also, the role of coaching in the ICM paradigm increases in importance with the introduction of simplifications. Finally, the parallels to other learning environments, particularly computerized ones, make it possible to form a general theory of learning environments (Brown, 1982).

Why Skiing?

Skiing is an extremely complex skill to learn and to perform. It is representative of an important class of real-time control skills, or data-driven skills, where error correction is essential to cope with deviations and sudden changes in the environment. Additionally, skiing is of interest because highly successful methods have been developed to teach it. This is not true for most other complex skills. These methods suggest the criteria that are necessary to design successful learning environments for other complex skills. In addition, skiing provides an intuitively understandable domain, with which many people have personal experience. Even nonskiers can relate the examples used in learning to ski to other physical skills, such as bike riding or windsurfing.

Skiing is an instance of a success model (Papert 1976), being an example of the successful acquisition of a complex skill. In skiing, the conditions of learning are more important than the total time or the mere quantity of exposure. This implies that the teaching of skiing has evolved into a highly successful instructional process. The two main uses of a success model are to identify the features that make it successful, and to abstract these features and try to transfer them to less successful learning situations. There is no complete theory to explain why the learning process in skiing was so dramatically enhanced during the last twenty years, but four features are of great importance: redefinition of teaching goals, improved equipment, access to new environments, and better teaching methodologies and conceptualizations.

Factors besides the ones investigated in the study influence the learning process. Primary among these is the factor of motivation. The person learning to ski is highly motivated. This is so for many reasons. Skiing is fun. It provides a wide variety of experiences, since every run is different from the previous run. Skiing is good exercise. It provides a nice change in the life style of many people. Also the novice skier's motivation to improve remains high because ski areas have many expert skiers around. This also means that learning can take place according to the medieval craftsman model, in which the ability of the less experienced skier is enhanced through interaction with the more experienced one (Lave, 1977).

Motivation is an important consideration in the design of learning environments. Each environment in the sequence presented to new skiers maintains their motivation by allowing them to work on a functional set of subskills. The sequence can be arranged so that within each environment there is no focusing on particular subskills until the need for that subskill has been experienced.

There are also a few negative aspects of skiing. It is expensive, it is time consuming, and it can be dangerous. For these reasons, the task of identifying the aspects of skiing that make it a success model becomes even more interesting.

The ICM Paradigm

The acquisition of a complex skill is difficult when the starting state and the final state are far apart. Good learning environments, structured according to the ICM paradigm, provide stepping stones or intermediate levels of expertise, so that within each level the student can see a challenging but attainable goal (VanLehn & Brown, 1980). In skiing, technological advances and the methodologies built around these advances make it easy to get started. This means that practice, or a task within an intermediate level, is satisfying in itself and not just something that must be endured before the learner can enjoy excellence.

An example of the ICM paradigm is a novice learning to ski. The student begins on short skis over gentle terrain. The short skis make it easier to turn and therefore allow the student to work on higher-level tasks, such as developing a rhythm over a series of turns. Also, since it is easier to get up from a fall, short skis encourage a student to try more difficult maneuvers. The gentle terrain limits her speed and reduces the danger of injury. As the student gains ability within these constraints, she is given slightly longer skis and steeper, more complex slopes, until she is using full-length skis on uncontrolled slopes. At each step, the microworld in which she must perform is made increasingly complex.

The ICM paradigm may be applied to sports other than skiing. A large body of knowledge about skill acquisition is available in the literature of different sports. Textbooks for these sports supply a great deal of knowledge about the critical components and essential stepping stones for the complex skills they describe. They also identify the most common problems and suggest special exercises to eliminate those problems. However, these texts often lack a conceptual framework that would allow them to generalize their knowledge or to structure it according to different criteria. In this study, the process of learning to ski is analyzed within the framework of the ICM paradigm, with the goal of expanding the paradigm. Austin (1974), who analyzed the skill of juggling in terms of a computational metaphor, used the resulting analysis to develop novel methods of teaching juggling.

Manipulating the Learning Environment

One of the major design decisions within the ICM paradigm is choosing or generating appropriate microworlds. The primary method of generating alternative microworlds is the manipulation of equipment, physical setting, and task specifications. A taxonomy of knowledge, methods, and heuristics serves as a basis for evolving a theory of learning environments.

The equipment given a student is changed to create different microworlds. The best-known example of this in skiing is the variation of ski length. In the "graduated length method" a beginner skier is started on short skis. As the student becomes proficient, his skis are gradually lengthened to full-length skis. Short skis are used as transitional objects in the learning process. They make it easier to get started and make early success more likely. Short skis allow the student to focus on and learn the fundamental elements of skiing before going on to more difficult tasks. For example, short skis are easier than long skis to maneuver. Therefore, a student can try different maneuvering techniques to find out which ones are effective. At the next level, when the student has learned the fundamentals of maneuvering, he can go on to longer skis, which give him greater power and hence more speed.

An interesting perspective on the hand-held electronic calculator is to view it as a piece of equipment used as a transitional object in learning mathematics. It creates a microworld in which the student can focus on the concepts of a problem rather than on the calculation. The task of solving the problem is therefore simpler. The calculator also helps to avoid the discouragement of wrong answers due to calculational mistakes.

Why did it take so long for someone to think of using short skis in the learning process? For one thing, skiing itself changed. Twenty years ago people wanted to ski fast in straight lines, for which longer skis are better. Now the final state of expert skiing involves more turning, which is facilitated by short skis. For another thing, teaching by the graduated length method requires a different instructional organization. To be economically feasible, the new method needs large ski schools where students can rent short skis instead of buying them. The economic considerations that have hindered exploration of transitional objects in learning to ski will not be as important when they are employed in computer-based learning environments. In computerized environments, the transitional objects are symbolic structures rather than physical structures.

Short skis are not the only technological improvement in the equipment used in skiing. Safety bindings reduce the fear and eliminate the catastrophic consequences of wrong behavior, thereby supporting an active approach to mastering new challenges. In an interactive computer system, the "UNDO" command, which undoes the effects of the previous command, supports a similar type of exploration because it reduces the risk involved in making errors. Ski tows and gondolas provide access to new environments in the form of moderately steep and wide glaciers with snow conditions suited to the early phases of the learning process. In addition, they increase considerably the time that people can actually spend skiing.

Great care must be taken to choose a microworld in which the simplified skill is isomorphic in its most important components to the final form of the skill. In juggling, the skill of ball handling can be practiced with one or two balls. This develops the necessary subskills of tossing and catching, as well as hand-eye coordination. However, the easiest form of three-ball juggling, called cascade juggling, cannot be simplified to an isomorphic two-ball juggling (Austin, 1974).

Controlling the physical setting is another method for creating microworlds. Skiing is an integrated collection of subskills. A major aid in learning any complex collection of skills is the oppor-

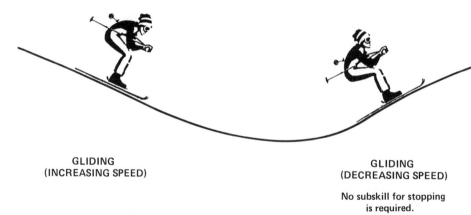

GLIDING
(INCREASING SPEED)

GLIDING
(DECREASING SPEED)

No subskill for stopping
is required.

Fig. 6.1. How physical environment can simplify the skill of skiing.

tunity to practice the subskills independently. Microworlds must be found or designed to allow a learner to exercise particular skills. For the beginner skier, gliding and stopping are two essential subskills that have to be learned. But stopping cannot be practiced without gliding, and gliding is dangerous unless one knows how to stop. In Simon's (1969) words, skiing is not decomposable, only "nearly decomposable." The problem can be solved by choosing the right setting. By the choice of a downhill slope that feeds into an uphill slope, the subskill of stopping is avoided (Fig. 6.1). This example leads to a rule: The decomposability of a skill is a function of the structure of the environment as well as of the skill itself.

Modern ski areas provide another manipulation of the environment that simplifies the skill of skiing. They provide the novice with constant snow conditions. A beginner can first learn to maneuver on packed slopes without having to worry about the variabilities of ice or deep powder. For one learning to play tennis, the ball-shooting machine provides a similar form of simplification. Receiving a stream of balls at the same velocity and in the same location removes some of the variables from the process of learning a stroke.

The wide variety of slopes in a large ski area has another important impact on learning. It allows the coach to choose a physical setting according to the needs of the learner and allows the sequence of microworlds to be tailored to the individual learner.

The manipulation of learning environments is a dynamic process. It is possible to alter the microworld by changing the task specification. The student may be asked to perform different tasks with the same equipment in the same setting. For example, a skier may be instructed either to traverse down a slope or to follow the fall line, the steepest way down, depending on what subskills are being perfected.

The manipulation of task specification is also used to teach higher-level skills. When a skier is presented with a gentle slope, she may be instructed to view turning simply as a means of going where she wants to go. Later, when presented with a steeper hill, she may be instructed to view turning as a means of controlling her speed. Task specification is a way to focus the student's attention on the important factors in a microworld.

Technological improvements have eliminated certain prerequisites for skiing. That is, they have simplified skiing by removing inessential parts. It is no longer necessary to spend a whole day of hard physical exercise to gain a thousand meters of elevation in order to ski one nice run. The goal of skiing is traversing slopes successfully, not developing stronger muscles and better physical condition by climbing uphill for several hours. If climbing were one of skiing's top-level goals, the use of gondolas and chair lifts would hardly be appropriate simplification. Clarifying the top-level goals may imply a different standard of measurement for the hierarchical ordering of the subskills and a corresponding change in the sequence of microworlds.

The importance of clarifying top-level goals can also be seen in programing. As computing becomes cheaper, concerns about computational efficiency will be replaced by concerns about cognitive efficiency, about how to facilitate the understanding and writing of programs. This change in perspective will require new conceptualizations and methodologies, which will lead to a new set of microworlds for the acquisition of the skills of programing and problem-solving (Fischer, 1977).

The range of possible microworlds that can be created using manipulations of a learning matrix is much larger than the range of useful ones. The designer of a learning environment must look carefully at what each microworld does for the overall goal. Four possible uses for a microworld come to mind. A microworld can provide:

1. The right entry points into an environment, making it easier to get started on a subskill

2. An environment in which the student feels safe, allowing him to focus his attention on learning skills
3. Intermediate goals or challenges that are, and seem to be, attainable
4. Practice of the important subskills in isolation, allowing the common "bugs" to occur one at a time instead of in bunches

A complicating factor in choosing microworlds is that nonmonotonic relationships often exist between manipulations of the microworld and the corresponding simplifications of the task. For example, skiing on a moderately sloping hill is a useful manipulation because the student can more easily maintain control of her speed. But the relationship between the slope of the hill and the nature of the task is nonmonotonic. That is, if the hill is too flat, it may be impossible to attain enough speed to turn. Another example of this sort is that skiing is difficult on a slope with big moguls, or mounds of snow, but when one is initiating turns, small moguls can be very helpful. Microworlds cannot be chosen simply by picking extremes in the factors involved.

Another concern in choosing a microworld is the danger of oversimplification. Skiing is representative of an important class of real-time, data-driven control skills. This means that a sudden, unexpected change in the environment requires high-order error-correcting and debugging skills to cope with the deviations. If the microworlds are too friendly, they may suppress the development of these high-order skills. The skier must learn to cope with deviations, such as icy spots or rocks that lie hidden under soft snow.

Developed ski areas simplify the task of skiing because their operators close avalanche areas and keep the skier away from crevices, pack down the slopes, and rescue people if they get hurt. This situation implies that people skiing only in these areas never acquire the planning and debugging knowledge they need to move around in more hostile environments.

One danger of task simplification is that it may lead to unjustified extrapolations. One of a coach's jobs is gradually to reduce the level of protectiveness, leading people to the right new challenges. A student should not be allowed to ski too long in an environment which does not require stopping, because there are very few runs with this characteristic. Another danger of simplification is that perfecting performance in one environment, such as packed slopes, may reduce the willingness of a skier to practice in another environment, such as powder, because the difference between his performance in the two environments may be too great.

Both of these dangers can be seen in efforts to teach computer programing that start with BASIC. The linear nature of a program in BASIC and the small size of solutions to typical introductory problems often lead students to develop debugging strategies that do not generalize to large programs. One such strategy is to trace through a program one statement at a time. Some students also resist leaving friendly, albeit limited, BASIC environments, in which they can adequately solve small problems, for the complexities of data declarations, functional decomposition, and advanced control-structure statements. These extrapolations are not ones intended by those who designed the learning environment. Rather, they arise from inappropriate generalizations made by the students using the microworlds in BASIC. Understanding the inappropriate generalizations that can develop in each microworld is one of the tasks facing a learning environment designer.

Debugging

Debugging plays a central role in the pedagogical underpinning of the ICM approach. As a student moves from one microworld to another at a higher level of complexity, she may need to modify her knowledge in several ways. New subskills may be introduced that must be mastered (e.g. skiing over moguls). Changes in the environment may require new interactions between skills (e.g. stopping and turning at the same time). And some skills that were idiosyncratic to a microworld may have to be unlearned (e.g. keeping the skis pigeon-toed during a snowplow has to be replaced with letting them run parallel).

While a designer should strive for simplifications that reduce the chances for incorrect generalizations, this is not always possible nor necessarily desirable. In skiing, an instructor has the problem of how to deal with the poles. Even though they are quite important for the advanced skier, the only major skill a beginner needs to learn is to carry them so that he will not hurt himself. While practice without poles would prevent formation of any inappropriate skills, empirical evidence suggests that eliminating the use of poles is not a useful simplification. Even if the poles are used incorrectly, they still support balance and mobility, and it is apparently easier to unlearn an incorrect use of poles than to incorporate the poles into a skill learned without using them from the beginning. The goal of a sequence of microworlds is not to remove all chances for misconceptions but, instead, to increase the possibility that a student will learn to recognize, learn from, and correct her own mistakes.

An important characteristic of a Piagetian environment (Papert, 1978) is the notion of a "constructive" bug. The learner gets enough feedback to recognize a bug, to determine its underlying causes, and on this basis to learn procedures to correct the bug. This notion contrasts sharply with the notion of a "nonconstructive" bug, where a student may recognize he is wrong but does not have the necessary information to understand why.

A critical design criterion for selecting the right microworld is finding one that transforms nonconstructive bugs into constructive ones. In the domain of skiing, there are several possible environmental supports for such a transformation. For example, if the skier leans too much into the hill with her upper body, a change to a steeper hill will indicate this to her because her skis will start to slide out from under her. Or if she holds her knees too stiffly, trying to stay on the ground while skiing over a bumpy slope will point out her inflexibility. Or if she does not ski enough on the edges of her skis or if she makes turns too sharply, a slope with soft snow, where she can observe her tracks, will indicate where each of these conditions is occurring. In all of these cases, the microworld is chosen to allow the student to use what she is currently experiencing to debug her technique.

A good coach knows a large number of specific exercises designed to transform nonconstructive bugs into constructive ones. These exercises are goal-directed toward certain bugs. His expertise must include the ability to distinguish the underlying causes, which may be hidden and indirect, from the surface manifestations of the bugs. To mention just one example: lifting up the back end of the inside ski in a turn provides the skier with the feedback that most of his weight is on the front end of his outside ski, where it should be. Exercises of this sort, which provide the basis for self-checking methods, are of vital interest and are essential in teaching and learning a physical skill (Carlo, 1974; DVSL, 1977), whereas in the cognitive sciences, research in self-checking methods is still in its infancy (Brown & Burton, 1978).

Another way to turn nonconstructive bugs into constructive ones is through the appropriate use of technology. The most obvious example is the use of a video camera, which helps the student to compare what she was doing to what she thought she was doing. Similarly, a computerized learning environment that records study sessions allows a student to review what she has done and perhaps to correct her own bugs.

Coaching

Acquiring a complex skill, even when supported by a good learning environment and the appropriate technology, does not eliminate the need for a good coach. The introduction of simplifications increases the importance of a coach. The coach must be able to accomplish four goals:

1. Make sure that within each microworld the right subskills are acquired, instead of ones that later have to be unlearned.
2. Design the right exercises, provide the right technology, and select the right microworlds to turn nonconstructive bugs into constructive ones.
3. Demonstrate a task the way a student did it in order to maximize the student's chances of recognizing his bugs.
4. Explicate knowledge in terms the student can understand and execute, that is, give good instructions.

The need for executable advice is illustrated by the many books that are written from the instructor's point of view. The student often receives advice, in the book or on the ski slope, that she cannot execute. An example of such advice is, "Put your weight forward," which is given to skiers who do not know where their weight is. The instructor tells the student the what without telling her the how and without providing her with knowledge or procedures to translate the what into the how.

Executable advice is distinguished from observable advice. For example, when the student is skiing in powder snow, the advice, "Your ski tips should look out of the snow," is observable by the student. That is, the student can see whether his ski tips stick out of the snow or whether they are buried below the surface. But the advice is not directly executable. The corresponding executable advice would be, "Lean back," or "Move your weight back" if the student knows how to shift his weight. This advice is not directly observable.

The interesting dependency relationship is that the what can be used to control the how. As a process becomes understood, the language of the process changes from how to what. This change has characterized the movement from machine language to higher-level programing languages in computer science. In a high-level language, the programer tells the computer what to do, leaving many low-level details that need to be expressed in machine language to the compiler.

There are other important aspects of coaching. The coach must:

1. Draw the borderline between free and guided exploration, for free exploration in a dangerous environment could end up with the student in a crevice or an avalanche.
2. Decide when to move on in order to avoid simplified versions of the skill that cause bad habits.
3. Be aware that coaching is more important at the beginning of the acquisition phase than later on. A conceptual model must be created, entry points must be provided, and self-checking methods must be learned, so that one can then self-coach.

Conclusions

The examination of skiing has clarified the relationship between holistic, activity-based learning and subskill or task analysis. Within each microworld that a beginning skier goes through, a particular aspect of the skill is focused on. But this skill is not executed in isolation. The student must still do simplified versions of many other skills required to ski. Simplifications of other interacting subskills let the student learn not only the particular subskill but also how it is used in the context of the entire skill. Focusing on a particular subskill allows important components of the skill to be easily learned, while simplifying the microworld ensures that the student learns how the subskill fits with other subskills without having complete mastery of those other skills as well. The analysis of skiing according to the ICM approach provides better insights into the complex issues of skill acquisition and design of learning environments.

7. The Creation of Context in Joint Problem-Solving

James V. Wertsch

Norris Minick

Flavio J. Arns

One of the most important points on which theories of cognitive development differ is how they view the role of social forces in the ontogenesis of psychological processes. No theory denies that social factors are part of the milieu in which humans develop, but some theories view these factors as relatively unimportant or as being subsumed under more inclusive theoretical categories, whereas others insist on their unique and primary role. This issue has great significance for formulating all other aspects of a theory of cognitive development.

Individual Versus Social Phenomena

Although there is a wide range of positions on this issue, developmental theories can roughly be divided into two categories. The distinguishing factor is whether a theory's explanation of ontogenesis begins with the individual or with social phenomena. By opting for an "individualistic" perspective, a theory views human experience and environmental forces strictly from the position of how they influence the individual's psychological development. This may involve borrowing from other disciplines, but such borrowing is in accordance with the individualistic perspective. For example, in its investigation of empirical issues raised by Chomskian or neo-Chomskian paradigms, cognitive psychology implicitly accepts the assumption that explanation begins by focusing on the individual. This point is applicable regardless of one's position on Chomsky's (1968) claims about innate structures.

In contrast, developmental theories that have grown out of traditions such as Marxian theory or symbolic interactionism assume that explanation of the individual's ontogenesis must begin with an examination of social phenomena. These "social perspective" theories differ among themselves in many respects, but they share at least two fundamental assumptions. First, they assume that social phenomena are governed by a unique set of explanatory principles. In consequence, social phenomena cannot be reduced to the sum of individual psychological phenomena. Marx (1977) made this assertion when he dealt with socioeconomic relations in a society, as did Mead (1934) when he spoke of the social act. Second, such theories assume that at least certain aspects of the individual's psychological functioning are determined by these social phenomena. The fact that the social phenomena are governed by an independent set of principles means that they can provide an "entry point" for the explanation of the individual's psychological processes, both cognitive and affective.

The most important individualistic theory in modern developmental cognitive psychology is that of Piaget. He examined social activity solely from the perspective of how it influences the individual's development. He assimilated it into the same equilibration model that accounts for other aspects of the individual's operative intelligence. For example, the notions of egocentrism and decentration were viewed as being equally relevant to the "mountains task" and to social interaction. Piaget assumed that no other principles than those that apply to the individual are needed to explain ontogenesis. To the extent that he analyzed social interaction and sociocultural factors, he did so in terms of the same explanatory principles, such as equilibration and adaptation, that apply to the individual.

The Social Perspective

An important example of a social perspective theory is that of Vygotsky (1956, 1978, 1981) or, more generally, the Vygotskian school of Soviet psychology. A fundamental claim of this school is that cognitive development is explained largely by what Leontiev (1972) termed the "appropriation" of socioculturally evolved means of mediation and modes of activity. This approach does not rule out biological growth and individual experience with physical reality as factors in the explanation of development. Indeed, one of Vygotsky's basic assumptions — an assumption that has often been misinterpreted or ignored — is that a major force in ontogenetic change is the dialectic that emerges when the "natural" line of development comes into contact with socioculturally defined tools and patterns of activity. But he considered social factors to play a central role in explaining ontogenetic change, and he recognized that the nature and evolution of these factors cannot be explained on the basis of a set of principles relating only to the individual. Luria summarized this position: "In order to explain the highly complex forms of human consciousness one must go beyond the human organism. One must seek the origins of conscious activity and 'categorical' behavior not in the recesses of the human brain or in the depths of the spirit, but in the external conditions of life. Above all, this means that one must seek these origins in the external processes of social life, in the social and historical forms of human existence" (1982:25). For the Marxian-inspired position of the Vygotskian school, the first step in explaining the development of the individual is thus to step outside of the psychology of the individual and to consider an independent set of principles which explain sociocultural evolution and social processes in general.

Our goal in this chapter is to explicate how this school attempts to deal with this issue and to illustrate the approach by using its constructs to analyze adult-child interaction data from a cross-cultural study. An assumption of our argument is that if an approach claims that social phenomena play a role in determining individual psychological phenomena, it is incumbent on that approach to specify what those social phenomena are and how they are governed by their own set of principles. For this reason much of our analysis will focus on social processes.

The first step in outlining the Vygotskian school's proposal is to recognize that it assumes a unique set of analytic units. Although Vygotsky focused primarily on the notions of human consciousness and the higher mental functions, such as voluntary memory, voluntary attention, perception, and thinking, which make up the intellectual side of consciousness, several of his Soviet followers (e.g. Davydov & Radzikhovskii, in press) argued that his ideas are best understood and integrated in a theoretical framework that takes different units as its object of study. Specifically, they posited "activity" (*deyatel'nost'*) as the basic analytic unit in psychology.

The major figure responsible for this reformulation was Leontiev (1972, 1975, 1981), whose theory of activity has provided the main focus for the Vygotskian school during the last thirty years. Although there is an ongoing debate in the Soviet Union about the extent to which an activity-based approach extends or even distorts Vygotsky's basic ideas, we will not go into the complexities of this argument here, nor will we attempt to provide a complete account of the theory of activity as it exists in contemporary Soviet psychology. Such accounts are available elsewhere (cf. Leontiev, 1972, 1975, 1981; Smirnov, 1975; Wertsch, 1981, in press). Instead, we will focus on those aspects of the theory that are relevant for interpreting the data on styles of adult-child interaction in rural Brazil.

Three distinct but interrelated units of analysis are defined by the theory of activity. The first and most global level of analysis is the "unit of an activity" (*deyatel'nost'*). As Leontiev (1975) pointed out, this use of the term *activity* must be distinguished from its use in the general "theory of activity." A unit of activity refers to an actual, identifiable activity as opposed to a generic notion of human activity, and a particular level of analysis as opposed to the more general theory that encompasses all levels of analysis. Leontiev defined an activity as "the nonadditive, molar unit of life for the material, corporeal subject. In a narrower sense (i.e., on the psychological level) it is the unit of life that is mediated by mental reflection. The real function of this unit is to orient the subject in the world of objects. In other words, activity is not a reaction or aggregate of reactions, but a system with its own structure, its own internal transformations, and its own development" (1981:46).

This level of analysis concerned with activities is seldom included in Western approaches to cognitive psychology. Perhaps the construct that is most like it in contemporary Western social science is the notion of "frame" as outlined by Goffman (1974). For the notion of an activity similarly focuses on the socioculturally defined context in which human functioning occurs. Among the activities mentioned by Vygotskian psychologists are play, instruction or formal education, and work.

In the empirical study reported in this chapter we will be concerned with two of these activities: formal schooling and household economic activity, which is a form of work or labor activity. The study focused on their implications for psychological processes. In particular, it examined how familiarity with one or the other of these two activity settings influences the subjects' interpretation and performance of a task. For example, the institution of formal schooling is organized in such a way that learning is the overriding "motive," to use Leontiev's term. This means that the students are encouraged to take over responsibility for tasks even when they are not yet able to perform them correctly. Because the emphasis on learning and independent functioning predominates over the emphasis on flawless task performance, errors are expected and sometimes even encouraged.

These expectations contrast with those in household economic activity, where the emphasis is on error-free performance since the tasks or chores involved contribute to the smooth functioning of the household economic system. If members of a household raise livestock to supply their own food, caring for this livestock is an activity in which flawless task performance is valued over learning for learning's sake. This does not mean that learning does not occur or is discouraged; it simply means that a learner's performance is monitored closely and that independent functioning is not encouraged until it is likely to be error-free. The overall activity setting is structured in such a way that learning may occur in a form similar to apprenticeship (Lave, 1980).

Whereas this first level of analysis concerned with activities provides a bridge to social institutional phenomena, the second level of analysis focuses on units that are psychological in a sense more familiar to Western cognitive and developmental psychology. This level is concerned with the "unit of a goal-directed action" (*deistvie*). To specify the nature of an activity is not to specify the particular means-ends relationships that it involves but simply to identify the socioculturally defined milieu in which it occurs. The best indication that these two levels of analysis are separate is that an action can vary independently of an activity. As Leontiev observed: "One and the same action can be instrumental in realizing different activities. It can be transferred from one activity to another thus revealing its relative independence. Let us turn . . . to a crude illustration. Assume that I have the goal of getting to point N, and I carry it out. It is clear that this action can have completely different motives, i.e., it can realize completely different activities. The converse is also obvious: one and the same motive can give rise to different goals and accordingly can produce different actions"

(1981:61). Hence, the goal-directed action of moving from one point to another can be executed while engaging in any one of several different activities, such as labor or instruction.

The empirical study of Brazilian adult-child interaction concerned the goal-directed action of arranging objects in accordance with a model. Specifically, it examined how subjects carried out the task of placing miniature farmyard objects (e.g. toy animals, gates) on a board so that the resulting array matched a model that was available to guide their action.

The third level of analysis in the theory of activity is concerned with the unit of an "operation" (*operatsiya*). Whereas an action is associated with a goal, an operation is associated with the conditions under which it is carried out. As Leontiev explained:

> [An] important aspect of the process of goal formation is making the goal concrete or selecting the conditions of its attainment . . . Any goal—even one such as "reaching point N"—exists objectively in some objective situation. Of course the goal can appear in the subject's consciousness in abstraction from this situation, but the same cannot be said for the *action*. Thus, apart from its intentional aspect (*what* must be done), the action has its operational aspect (*how* it can be done) which is defined not by the goal itself but by the objective circumstances under which it is carried out. In other words, the *performed* action is in response to a task. The task is the goal given in certain conditions . . . I shall label the means whereby an action is carried out its *operations* . . . If we imagine a case in which the goal remains the same and the conditions in which it is given change, then only the operational composition of the action changes" (1981:63).

The operational aspect of a goal-directed action, such as "reaching point N," may therefore vary, depending on such factors as the distance involved or the obstacles on the route to point N, while the goal itself remains constant. This fact indicates the independence of these two levels of analysis in the theory of activity.

In the study of Brazilian adult-child interaction the analysis of operations focused on the specific ways that the subjects carried out the goal-directed action of arranging objects in accordance with a model. In particular, it was concerned with how the members of a dyad carried out actions by dividing up responsibility for the various steps involved. All three levels of analysis in the study may be summarized schematically:

Activity	—	Motive
Action	—	Goal
Operation	—	Conditions

One corollary of the Vygotskian school's social perspective is that the notion of activity applies to collective as well as to individual functioning. The fact that the theory applies to both types of functioning, however, does not mean that it makes no important distinction between them. Indeed, this distinction is of fundamental importance to the forces of change in social history or ontogenesis, since the analysis of individual functioning is grounded in an understanding of the social functioning that gives rise to it.

From a Vygotskian perspective on ontogenesis there are two ways in which activity may be social, and these two ways are typically combined or co-ordinated in the child's experience. On the one hand, activity is social in the sense that it is socioculturally defined. This point derives from Marx's account of productive forces and the ensuing production relations and social structure. On the other hand, the child's experience involves social activity in the sense that he or she participates in "localized collectives," that is, concrete social interactional settings involving one or more other persons. These two ways in which activity is social are combined in a child's experience when he or she participates in joint activity with more mature members of the culture, because these more mature members typically define and regulate the joint activity in accordance with sociocultural patterns. For Vygotsky, participation in activity, which is social in both senses, was the starting point in explaining the development of human consciousness.

Rather than simply asserting that joint functioning somehow leads to individual functioning, Vygotsky argued that the two forms of functioning are tied together in an essential way. Namely, the very processes or relationships that are involved in social interaction are eventually taken over and internalized by the child to form individual cognitive processes. This transition is the cornerstone of what Vygotsky termed the "general genetic law of cultural development": "Any function in the child's cultural development appears twice, or on two planes. First, it appears on the social plane, and then on the psychological plane. First it appears between people as an interpsychological category, and then within the child as an intrapsychological category. This is equally true with regard to voluntary attention, logical memory, the formation of concepts, and the development of volition" (1981:163).

The theory of activity formulated by Vygotsky's followers calls upon us to characterize both interpsychological and intrapsychological functioning in terms of the three levels of analysis. The theory's concern with these levels of analysis makes it a valuable instrument for identifying and examining several other points. For example, it allows for much more specificity in defining the relevant parameters of joint problem-solving and how they lead to improved individual problem-solving. In terms of concrete procedures for empirical research, the theory of activity provides the theoretical apparatus for identifying and varying units at one level of analysis independently of others.

Application of the Vygotskian Approach

In order to clarify some of these issues and to demonstrate the usefulness of the approach we have outlined, we will now turn to a study of adult-child interaction carried out in rural Brazil. In keeping with the social perspective inherent in the approach of the Vygotskian school, the study concentrated primarily on the interpsychological plane of functioning. The task, which was to place toy farmyard objects on a board so that the resulting arrangement matched a model array of identical objects, included a model, a copy, and the pieces needed to complete the copy. This task is of interest from the perspective of the theory of activity for several reasons, the most important being that it is an example of a socioculturally defined routine that is introduced to children in a variety of social interactional settings.

When studying how groups or individuals carry out this task, we can focus on any one or any combination of the units of analysis in the theory of activity. Our ultimate concern here will be the level of analysis concerned with activities. Specifically, in all cases the subjects in our study carried out the goal-directed action of making the copy in accordance with the model, but they differed in how they interpreted the activity setting in which they performed this action. They defined the task setting by importing expectations and assumptions that were part of other, more familiar activity settings, such as formal schooling and household economic activity, as shown by the operational composition of actions. This reflected the fact that the ultimate goal of the theory of activity is to understand the interrelationships among the three levels of analysis — activity, action, and operation.

In order to carry out the goal-directed action of constructing an object in accordance with a model, a problem solver must carry out a series of component actions or strategic steps. The overall action may be broken down into such steps in varying degrees of detail. Our present analysis will be relatively general. It produces the following picture of the component structure of the action:

Step 1. Look at the model to determine the identity and location of the piecè to be inserted next in the copy.
Step 2. Select a piece from the pieces pile.
Step 3. Add the piece selected in Step 2 to the copy object.

In actuality, each of the steps in this strategy is a goal-directed action in its own right. Thus, the primary action is also made up of actions or subactions. However, the overall action has a unique status and cannot be equated with the sum of its component actions. The fact that the representation of Step 3 in the overall action includes a reference to Step 2 reflects its integral nature. The overall action is here called the "action," and the three subactions are referred to as "steps" or "strategic steps."

The action of identifying, selecting, and adding a single piece must be repeated several times in order to carry out the entire task of constructing an object in accordance with a model. Thus, a hierarchical structure of actions is involved in the task setting. On the one hand, what is here called an action actually comprises several subactions or strategic steps. On the other hand, this action is only part of the larger action of constructing the entire copy object in accordance with the model. Again, the primary concern is with the middle level in this hierarchy, the action of identifying, selecting, and adding a single piece to the copy object.

In the level of analysis concerned with operations, the issue is the conditions under which the goal-directed action is carried out. This involves the physical requirements of the task, but of particular interest to us here is how the changes in the distribution of strategic responsibility in interpsychological functioning change the operational component.

Finally, in the level of analysis concerned with activities, the issue is how the participants structure the task setting in terms of socioculturally defined situations. In the case of constructing a copy object in accordance with a model, it might seem unnecessary to consider yet another level of analysis, since the situation has been defined as a problem-solving setting with a specific goal. However, a description of the setting that goes no further than the level of analysis concerned with actions cannot account for striking differences in joint and individual processes in the task setting.

We will postpone our main discussion of the activity level in this task setting until after we have presented our data. One reason for doing so is that it is difficult to deal with this level of analysis on a purely theoretical and abstract plane. A second, and more important reason for postponing our discussion of the activity level of analysis is that subjects' understanding and definition of the task setting in research studies often must be inferred rather than assumed. Especially in cross-cultural and developmental studies, it is often more appropriate and accurate to describe differences in subjects' performance in terms of differences in how they interpret a situation rather than of how they carry out the task that the experimenters thought they had assigned. Researchers such as Cole and Scribner (1974) have shown that the failure to appreciate this point has led to a great deal of confusion. One lesson to be learned from their studies is that experimenters cannot automatically assume that subjects have defined a situation in the way they intended. In the terminology of the Vygotskian school, experimenters cannot be certain that subjects are participating in the activity that they have assigned.

Experimenters must therefore be prepared to assess the subjects' performance at the level of their definition of the situation or at the level of activities as well as at the levels of actions and operations. Verbal instructions and the arrangement of task materials by no means restrict the activity to the one understood by the experimenters. Assessing performance at this level necessarily requires inferences based on subjects' performance. Unless experimenters are willing to rely on introspective reports by the subjects, their task is to infer what situation definition must have guided the subjects' performance.

Methodology

In this chapter we report data from a larger study conducted by Arns (1980). Twelve adult-child dyads participated in the portion of the study reported here. Six of the dyads were composed of a mother with her child whose mean age was 6 years 5 months, ranging from 5 years 11 months to 6 years 8 months. Each of the other six dyads was composed of an elementary school teacher, who was always female, and a student whose mean age was 6 years 4 months, ranging from 5 years 10 months to 6 years 9 months. Equal numbers of girls and boys participated in each group. The subjects were healthy native Brazilians selected from rural areas of the municipality of São José dos Pinhais in the state of Paraná in southern Brazil.

Mothers who participated in the study had no more than four years of formal schooling. Both the mothers and the teachers who participated in the study were born and educated in the municipality where the study was conducted. The teachers resided in the rural community where they were teaching and had completed at a minimum all but the last year of high school. Each of the children who worked with a teacher had been a student in that teacher's classroom for approximately 6 months.

The adult and child in each dyad were asked to construct a copy of a three-dimensional toy barnyard in accordance with an identical model. For purposes of coding and analysis, there were two categories of pieces. Pieces in the first category (a house made of two parts and a fence for the corral made of six parts) fit into only one space in the copy. Hence, it was not necessary for the subjects to consult the model to place the pieces correctly. Correct placement of pieces in the second category (a dog, three horses, three cows, and five pigs) required information from the model. Several extra pieces of this kind were also provided.

The model and copy were constructed on identical boards on which certain features, including a path to the house and six trees, were fixed. Marks on the copy board indicated positions for the placement of missing pieces. The model was placed in front of the adult, the copy was placed in front of the child, and the pieces to be arranged on the copy were placed off to the child's side.

Each session, with both mothers and teachers, took place in an empty classroom and began with an explanation that the purpose of the study was to analyze education in rural communities in order to facilitate possible improvements. Each dyad was then seated at a low table and asked to construct a simple three-dimensional puzzle in accordance with a model.

After the warm-up task was finished, the model of the main task was placed in front of the adult, and the copy, in completed form, was placed in front of the child along with the extra pieces. A research assistant explained how the pieces fit on the copy and told the participants that the child would be asked to make the copy farm, but that if the child did not know how, the adult was to teach him or her how to do it. Audio and video recordings were made of the entire session.

The utterances of the experimenter, the adult, and the child during the task performance were transcribed. Nonverbal behaviors were then added to the transcription, maintaining the sequence of the interaction. Each coded interaction was segmented into a series of "episodes," defined as the interaction of the child and adult required to select and place a single piece. Since the primary purpose of the study was to determine what leads to appropriate or successful strategic behavior, the analysis was limited to episodes that ended in correct piece placement.

The analysis focused on the three observable steps: looking to the model, picking up a required piece from the pieces pile, and placing this piece in the copy. For each of these behaviors there were three stages of analysis, which provided information on the nature of the participation of the adult and child in carrying out the steps. The first stage of the analysis focused on whether the child or adult had physically carried out the step. The second stage narrowed the focus to episodes in which the child had physically carried out the behavior, to determine whether the child had done so independently or with some form of regulation from the adult. The third stage focused on episodes in which the child had carried out a step under some form of regulation by the adult, to distinguish the modes of regulation used according to the extent to which they required the children to understand the strategic significance of their behavior.

At this third stage, direct forms of adult regulation were distinguished from indirect forms. Regulation of the child's look to the model was considered direct when the adult either pointed to the model or identified either the model or a piece in it with an explicit verbal referring expression (e.g. "This other one"). Utterances that did not explicitly refer to the model but required the child to look at it in order to respond appropriately (e.g. "What do we need next?") were considered indirect forms of regulation for this step. In the step of picking up the piece, regulation was considered direct when the adult pointed to a piece or a group of pieces or made an explicit verbal reference to a piece or category of pieces. Regulation was considered indirect for this step when the adult pointed to a piece in the model or produced an utterance referring to a piece in the model (e.g. "Look at what comes next over here"). With placement, regulation was considered direct when the adult either pointed to the proper position in the copy or identified that position with a complete utterance, and it was considered indirect if the adult identified a piece's location in the model through speech or pointing (Wertsch & Schneider, 1980). Where both direct and indirect forms of adult regulation occurred simultaneously (e.g. "What do we need next?" while pointing to a piece in the model), the behavior was coded as direct adult regulation. This was based on the assumption that direct forms of regulation "override" indirect forms.

Results

The analysis revealed substantial differences in the interactions involving mothers and teachers. In general, the mothers tended to perform task behaviors and use direct forms of regulation more frequently than the teachers did. We will now turn to a more detailed discussion of the results of our analysis for each of the three steps.

There were major differences between interactions involving teachers and mothers in terms of the proportion of episodes in which the child actually looked at the model. Children working with their mothers carried out this step in a mean of only 39% of the episodes. In contrast, children working with teachers carried out this step in a mean of 86% of the episodes. This difference is statistically significant (Mann-Whitney $U = 2$, $p < .004$).

At the second stage of analysis there was little difference in the mother and teacher dyads in terms of the proportions of the child's looks to the model that were self- and other-regulated. In both types of dyads, the child's looks to the model followed some effort by the adult to elicit the behavior in slightly over half of the episodes, or a mean of 56% and 59% for mother-child and teacher-child dyads, respectively (Mann-Whitney $U = 17$, n.s.). Further, at the third stage of our analysis the teachers used direct modes of regulation slightly but not significantly more than the mothers did, or a mean of 72% and 55% of the episodes, respectively (Mann-

Whitney $U = 15$, n.s.). Thus both groups of adults tended to rely upon direct means for regulating this behavior.

In summary, sharp differences were found in the percentage of episodes in which children working with mothers and teachers carried out the step of looking to the model. There was little difference in how adults from the two groups regulated those gazes that the children did make.

The first stage of analysis of the strategic step of picking up a piece from the pile revealed that the mothers picked up the required piece in a slightly but not significantly higher proportion of episodes than the teachers did, or a mean of 10% and 1%, respectively (Mann-Whitney $U = 17$, n.s.). Thus in both groups the child picked up the piece in the overwhelming majority of episodes.

As was the case with the step of looking at the model, the second stage of analysis of picking up the piece revealed a strong similarity in the extent to which the execution of this step by the child was regulated by the adult. Mothers provided other-regulation in a mean of 64% of the episodes in which the child picked up the piece, and teachers did so in 66% of these episodes (Mann-Whitney $U = 15$, n.s.).

Differences between the two groups appeared primarily in the third stage of analysis of this step. Here the teachers and mothers supplied other-regulation in different ways. Mothers used some direct form of regulation, either pointing to the pieces or explicitly mentioning them, in a mean of 87% of the episodes in which the child picked up the correct piece. The teachers used direct forms of regulation in only a mean of 24% of these episodes, identifying the pieces indirectly by directing the child's attention to the model. This difference between mother-child and teacher-child dyads is statistically significant (Mann-Whitney $U = 1$, $p < .002$).

The piece placement paralleled the pick-up behaviors. The first stage of analysis revealed that mothers actually placed the pieces in a mean of 14% of the episodes, while the teachers placed them in a mean of only 4% of the episodes (Mann-Whitney $U = 16$, n.s.). As in the picking-up behaviors, children working with both groups of adults physically carried out this placement step in the overwhelming majority of episodes.

The second stage of analysis revealed slightly larger differences between the groups in the proportions of other-regulated behaviors than were found in the steps of looking at the model and piece pick-ups, but the differences were still not significant (Mann-Whitney $U = 12$, n.s.). In a mean of 71% of the episodes, placements made by children working with mothers were other-regulated. This was true in a mean of only 50% of the episodes in interactions involving teachers.

But once again, the third stage of analysis revealed substantial differences in the nature of participation. Of the other-regulated placements occurring in the mother-child interactions, a mean of 87% involved some direct form of other-regulation. That is, the mothers either mentioned or pointed to the position in the copy where the piece was to be placed. In contrast, the teachers used these modes of regulation in a mean of only 46% of the episodes. This difference is statistically significant (Mann-Whitney $U = 8$, $p < .008$). As was the case with the step of picking up pieces, the mothers' behavior here tends to eliminate the need for the child to derive information from the model independently.

In summary, the three-stage analysis of the three strategic steps revealed important similarities and differences in the dynamics of the joint cognitive functioning as structured by teachers and mothers. First, children working with teachers looked to the model in more than twice as many episodes than those working with mothers. In both groups, the children's looks to the model resulted from some form of adult regulation in just over half the cases, and both mothers and teachers tended to use direct means of eliciting these behaviors.

The strategic steps of picking up and placing pieces paralleled one another closely. For both groups, children generally carried out these behaviors. The most significant differences between the mothers and teachers was not in the extent but in the type of adult regulation of the child's pick-up and placement behaviors. Mothers used direct forms of regulation in a mean of 87% of the episodes for both pick-ups and placements, far more often than was the case with teachers.

The overall level of adult responsibility for each of the three strategic steps is shown by the proportion of episodes in which the adults either carried out the step themselves or provided direct forms of regulation to the children. This proportion represents the level of the adults' direct responsibility for the performance of the step. The higher the level of the adults' direct responsibility, the lower the level of participation required of the children. In cases where the adults actually carried out the step, the children could participate only by observation, and in cases where the children carried out the step through direct other-regulation, they did not need to understand the strategic significance of the behavior. For example, when pick-up and placement behaviors were carried out through direct other-regulation, the children did not need to understand the significance of the model.

Comparison of the level of direct adult responsibility for the strategic steps revealed that the mothers were much more heavily involved in the performance of picking up and placing pieces than were the teachers. The mothers were directly responsible for pick-ups in a mean of 58% of the episodes, whereas the figure was only 18% for the teachers; and the mothers were directly responsible for placements in a mean of 69% of the episodes, whereas the figure was only 28% for the teachers. In both cases the difference is statistically significant (for pick-ups, Mann-Whitney $U = 4$, $p < .013$; for placements, Mann-Whitney $U = 4$, $p < .013$).

In the third case, that of eye gaze, the summary measure showed that the mothers were directly responsible for gazes to the model in a mean of 74% of the episodes, whereas the figure was 53% for the teachers. This difference is not statistically significant (Mann-Whitney $U = 12$, n.s.). This result, which contrasts with the finding of a significant difference between groups at the first level of analysis of this strategic step concerned with who physically executed the step, reflects the fact that while children working with teachers looked at the model more frequently than did children working with mothers, they did so primarily through direct other-regulation by the teachers. In other words, children working with teachers were more likely to participate in this step even if they did not seem to understand it well and therefore required close supervision (i.e. direct other-regulation). The fact that they needed most help with this step shows that it is the last of the three steps in this task to be understood and mastered.

Conclusions

The theory of activity as outlined by the Vygotskian school provides constructs that are essential for the interpretation of these findings. In general, to account for the interpsychological functioning and its potential intrapsychological consequences requires analysis at the levels of activities, actions, and operations.

In terms of the level of analysis concerned with actions, both groups of dyads were guided by the same goal of making the copy object in accordance with the model. The two groups of dyads were equally successful at reaching this goal in the sense that they completed nearly identical numbers of successful episodes. In terms of the level of analysis concerned with goal-directed actions, then, they performed similarly. However, the ways in which they reached the goal were different. Even though they all heard the same instructions, used the same materials, and performed the task in the same physical setting, the operational aspect of their performance differed radically. In particular, the two groups of dyads differed in how they divided up responsibility for carrying out the strategic steps in the action. The same steps were carried out in all successful episodes, but systematic differences appeared in the adult's and the child's level of responsibility for them. To paraphrase Leontiev, the two groups differed not in what was carried out (i.e. the level of goals), but in how it was carried out (i.e. the level of operations).

This description is not complete, however, without the analysis of activities. Such an analysis involves inferences about how subjects define or interpret a setting. While the data provide direct evidence about the actions and operations involved in the task, they do not provide direct evidence about the activity. In order to analyze the subjects' activity in this task setting, one must ask why they arranged the operational composition of their performance as they did. That is, analysis at this level is aimed at determining what activity would be most consistent with the operational composition of the subjects' performance. In this sense the analysis is inferential.

The critical variable here is the different levels of exposure that the two groups of adults had to formal schooling, with the mothers having attended school for a maximum of four years, whereas the teachers had all come within at least a year of completing high school. Furthermore, the teachers had continued to participate in formal schooling activity as their profession, whereas the mothers had not. The influence of experience with schooling on adults' interaction with children is consistent with other research (Laosa, 1978, 1979). Laosa (1979) reported that cultural differences in the performance of Mexican and Anglo-American mother-child dyads disappear when mothers have comparatively high levels of formal education.

To argue that the contrast in the performance of the two sets of dyads in the Brazilian study simply reflects a difference in styles for carrying out one and the same activity would overlook an essential point posed by the theory of activity, namely the issue of how activities are related and organized at a societal level. The analysis of activities is concerned with socially defined systems of human activity, such as work and schooling. The specific content and nature of these activities are determined by factors operating at the societal or cultural level. They cannot be understood by focusing on the individual or psychological level alone.

Anthropologists such as Fortes (1938) and Lave (1980; in preparation) have recognized that teaching or instruction as a distinct activity, with a distinct system of motives, either does not exist or is not common in many traditional societies. Fortes remarked of Tale education:

> The Tallensi have no technique of isolating a skill or observance from the total reality and training a child in it according to a syllabus, as, for instance, we train children in dancing, the multiplication table, or the catechism. Tale education . . . works through the situation, which is a bit of the social reality shared by adult and child alike . . . A child repeating the multiplication table is participating in the practical activity appropriate to and defined by the school; but measured by the total social reality it is a fictitious activity, a training activity constructed for that purpose (1938:37).

In these societies, learning and instruction certainly occur, but instead of being a distinct form of activity, the educational process works through the situation of productive work and other forms of activity.

Lave's study of apprenticeship among Vai and Gola tailors in Liberia (1980; in preparation) showed that in apprenticeship, both master and apprentice are aware of the critical importance of the apprentice's learning. This learning is a conscious and important goal of both. Yet it is not this mutual goal but other factors that structure the organization of the learning process. Lave described the "curriculum" of apprenticeship:

> The tailors form a guild and the curriculum, at the highest level, can be seen as a concise summary of the articulation of the guild as a social institution with major dimensions of the social organization of Liberian society. Another major source of organization for learning comes from the work tailors do. Production processes have a logic and order

to them, and these shape the apprentice's learning activities. Economic concerns also impose order on the learning process: it is more costly to make an error when cutting out a garment than when sewing it. Apprentices always learn to sew garments before learning to cut garments out. Add to this the practice that apprentices must purchase for themselves the material to make garments. From this emerges an ordering in which the apprentice works on small garments which can be made of scraps before items which take more fabric or more expensive fabrics (1980:3-4).

This research demonstrated that although learning is an important goal for all involved in the context of apprenticeship, and presumably in both traditional and nontraditional learning settings that are less institutionalized, it has not emerged as an independent activity-motive system. The activity of learning is inextricably linked to productive or economic activity. The motives that define and structure the activity are economic and professional rather than educational.

However, with the development of formal schooling as a social institution and the dominant locus of learning activity in a society, learning and instruction become an independent activity. They are no longer embedded within other systems of activity. Through the development of new forms of activity and new institutions at the societal level they become the dominant motives underlying the organizational dynamics of educational activity proper. Although people often manufacture "products" while engaged in educational activity, this goal does not define the structure of the activity.

In school, students are encouraged to participate in goal-directed actions even if, or indeed particularly if, they are not yet capable of carrying them out efficiently and correctly. Incomplete and incorrect performance of the strategic steps of an action is allowed and even encouraged. Learning that takes place within the context of apprenticeship or household economic activities, where the governing motive is relatively efficient, error-free production of goods and services, has unique characteristics. Where the goal of learning does not directly conflict with the dominant motives of activity, students are allowed to carry out certain steps of a particular action, or relatively simple actions, with which they have developed some level of understanding or competence. Students are introduced into complex forms of productive activity one step at a time. The organization of the process is determined by the motives of making maximum use of the productive capacities of the individual in the production process while minimizing the risk of economic loss.

Thus, for the teachers in the Brazilian study, the goal of teaching or learning functioned as the governing motive of their activity. In accordance with this goal, the children were encouraged to carry out all aspects of the task from the very beginning, with little regard for efficient task completion. In contrast, the rural Brazilian mothers took a much more direct role in carrying out the more difficult strategic steps of the task, such as deriving the necessary information from the model, and delegated to the children only those aspects of the task which they could carry out relatively efficiently and effectively. Many of the mothers' behaviors can be understood only by recognizing their real concern for the children's learning in the task context. But the motive that governed their activity and determined its structure at the operational level was the correct and efficient completion of the task at hand.

It may appear to some that an alternative explanation could account for the pattern of interaction described here. Namely, it might be proposed that the difference between the two groups of dyads is attributable to differences in how the adults interpreted the task instructions. Such an explanation, however, is not really an alternative; it is entirely consistent with the explanation we have proposed. We readily accept the notion that the two groups of adults interpreted our instructions differently. The question remains as to why they did so. The different activity settings provide the most plausible answer. If the mothers viewed the task setting as calling for maximal assistance, whereas the teachers viewed it as calling for maximal independence on the part of the child, this is entirely consistent with the reasoning based on activity settings.

This reasoning and the empirical findings perhaps raise as many questions as they answer. However, they confirm one important point which is closely related to the distinction between social and individualistic perspectives in psychology. Other research with similar findings has consistently attributed the observed differences in performance to differences in factors such as cognitive style and in values relating to factors such as learning and independence. That is, differences in behavior are explained in terms of differences in cognition, affect, and values, which, though perhaps viewed as influenced by the social or cultural systems, are considered to be characteristics of the individual. The theory of activity in Soviet psychology suggests that independent of these characteristics of the individual, the organization of systems of activity at the societal level establishes important parameters that determine the manner in which an individual or group of individuals carries out and masters a particular type of goal-oriented action.

A complete account of the organization of human cognitive activity, manifested in a task carried out on either the individual or the social level, must go beyond narrowly defined psychological phenomena and consider the forces that create the context in which human cognition is defined and required to operate at the level of societal and cultural organization. The theory of activity developed by the Vygotskian school of Soviet psychology provides a useful framework within which to examine this issue. Psychology will continue to encounter seemingly intractable contradictions and disputes as long as it fails to examine the relationship between social and psychological factors at this level.

8. Social Constraints in Laboratory and Classroom Tasks

Denis Newman
Peg Griffin
Michael Cole

From the perspective of a cognitive psychologist, "everyday cognition" might seem to be a contradictory notion. Psychologists have struggled for a hundred years to overcome the limitations that everyday life places on the ability to make precise statements about the mechanisms of mind. In place of "everyday" cognition, with its wide variety of content, different degrees of familiarity, various ways of dividing up labor, and reliance on conversation as a medium of expression — in short, with its lack of control — psychologists have evolved a set of procedures that are termed "the laboratory." Here the investigator constructs a model system within which it becomes possible to make principled, but limited, claims about hypothetical processes, currently referred to as cognitive processes, that can be said to mediate between states of the artificially created environment and behaviors of the subject.

The key to making claims in the laboratory is the psychologist's control over the task and the conditions under which the subjects undertake the task. In terms of experimental methodology, two kinds of control are necessary. One is obtained by carefully contrasting particular conditions in the model system and by having a sufficiently large number of subjects undertake the same task under the same conditions. This is referred to as experimental design. These design controls presume a practical control over the task, such as the goals of the subject's behavior and the conditions imposed on the subject. The experimenter must be sure, for example, that subjects are actually working on the task they are expected to be working on and that the behavior of the subject, not of somebody else, is what is being recorded.

Whether laboratory settings are used for testing cognitive theories or for administering psychological tests, the cognitive processes modeled in them and the cognitive accomplishments tested are thought of as representing more than esoteric games. No doubt performance in these games counts. Cognitive tests are used not only to predict school success but also to make a wide variety of decisions that influence economic fates. But the constraints on activity used to create model systems render them systematically dissimilar to the systems of activity created in the society for other purposes (Bartlett, 1958; Cole, Hood & McDermott, 1978; Lave, 1980). As a consequence, cognitive theories are weak in just those areas where they relate most closely to practice, namely to those "everyday" cognitive tasks that are significant contexts in our lives.

A number of different strategies are available for attacking the broad problem of specifying cognition in nonlaboratory settings. Each speaks to a different facet of the overall problem. One of them is to examine how behavior occurring in one kind of setting, defined in such terms as its social organization and its participants' goals, compares with behavior in another kind of setting in ways that are productive for cognitive theory and also contribute to educational practice. On this basis, a project was designed to collect data in a fourth-grade classroom on children confronting the "same task" in two different settings. The children's performance in a standard, laboratory-derived task was compared with their behavior in a loosely supervised science activity. The way in which the children confronted and were confronted by these tasks showed that the standard "division of labor" between researcher and subject in laboratory settings tends to obscure an important feature of cognition. When experimenters present a well-defined task to subjects in a standarized way, they have little chance to observe the subjects' formation of new goals or their application of a procedure to new situations.

In comparing the two settings, the study did not assume one setting to be more valid than the other for the characterization of cognition. Rather, both kinds of settings make available for analysis different but important aspects of cognitive activity. It is necessary to integrate the analyses of these different settings in order to construct a cognitive science that is relevant to a general range of human environments for learning and thinking.

Making the Same Task Happen in Different Settings

In a study that was a precursor to the current work, Cole and his colleagues (Cole, Hood & McDermott, 1978; Cole & Traupmann, 1981), set out to locate psychological test-like behaviors occurring in classrooms and after-school clubs. The idea was to analyze the nature of known cognitive tasks when they arise in these nonlaboratory settings. Children were administered a battery of cognitive tasks. They were also observed in their classroom and in their club sessions after school. These settings were searched to find the cognitive tasks occurring there.

In the classroom, activities that psychologists recognize as cognitive occurred quite often. Many times each day the children were seen to be dealing with classification, remembering, and problem-solving tasks. However, when the search began for cognitive tasks in the videotapes of the club sessions, it was difficult to identify any of the cognitive tasks that had been posed for children in the testing session or observed in the classroom. There was an enormous amount of activity at a very high level of noise. Somehow cakes were baked, plants grown, rat mazes constructed, and electric circuits lit without anyone doing anything that a cognitive psychologist could recognize as thinking. Despite systematic observations about how cognitive tasks were organized in the club sessions, so much variability had been allowed into the children's activities, in order not to bias the "discovery" of cognitive tasks in the club, that it was difficult to find any basis for comparison of the "everyday" club with the laboratory settings.

The present study then, in a sense, reversed the earlier strategy. Instead of waiting around for something recognizable as a cognitive task to appear, we made deliberate efforts to find ways to make hypothetical "same tasks" happen in several settings inhabited by the same children. Teachers and club leaders helped to construct a set of activities (one-to-one tutorials, small-group lessons, child-guided work groups), in all of which a particular problem structure was embedded. The project went a step further. It put into those various settings what could be called "tracers." The tracer was a bit of knowledge or some procedure that was taught the children in one of the settings, which was potentially useful if they recognized that they were being confronted with what they considered that same task in the new setting. This set of constraints greatly increased the probability of finding good candidates for analysis and of uncovering how the task was transformed, made easier or more difficult, or avoided entirely under the different organizational conditions.

The term "same task" has been placed in quotes because the sense in which two tasks can ever be considered the "same" is a central question. A cognitive task cannot be specified independent of its social context. Cognitive tasks are always social constructions. Transformations of the social organization of the tasks in the study drastically changed the constraints on behavior, thereby rendering the tasks instantly different according to widely shared ideas of what constitutes a task in cognitive psychology. It was hoped that highlighting the way in which efforts failed to make the "same task" occur in different settings would lead to a clearer specification of the class of social constructions represented by such activities as tests and experiments (LCHC, 1978, 1979).

The original idea in trying to make the "same tasks" happen was to create what are called "problem isomorphs" in cognitive psychology. Problem isomorphs are a set of problems that share an abstract structure but differ in concrete content (e.g. Reed, Ernst & Banerji, 1974; Gick & Holyoak, 1980). In the current study, children were asked at one time to make all the possible pairs from four stacks of differently colored cards and at another time to mix all the possible pairings from a set of four chemicals. In cognitive psychological studies, where problem isomorphs are used to study the effects on a subject's performance after experience with a problem "of the same kind," every effort is made to change only the content of the problem, leaving the abstract form of the procedures, initial conditions, legal moves, and goal unchanged. So in this study the content clearly differed but the abstractly defined goal of "finding all the pairs" remained the same.

The problem isomorph formulation might have worked out fine except that one feature of the task environment was changed which is almost never altered in cognitive psychological research. The chemicals activity departed from the one-to-one social organization of the standard laboratory setting in that groups of children worked together. This change in social organization not only increased the social resources available for solving the problem, thereby making it hard to say who did what, but also changed the source of the problem and thus the nature of the task. In the one-to-one situation the tutor motivated the problem as the one to be done; that is, the children were presented with the task of finding all the pairs of problem elements. In the chemicals situation the children had to formulate the problem for themselves as they began to run out of pairs to mix. This shift in the origin of the task clearly changed the nature of the task so that one would hesitate to call the two versions isomorphs.

Because a task in cognitive psychology is a goal plus constraints on reaching that goal presented by the researcher to the subject, the researcher does a lot of work to formulate a clear task. In everyday situations people do not always have the "advantage" of this kind of help; they often have to figure out what the problem is, what the constraints are, and what the available resources are as well as to solve the problem once it is formulated. In everyday situations people are confronted with the "whole" task, not just the solution part.

This broader conception of the whole task makes it possible to analyze the transformation of a task when it is embedded in different social settings. In order to look for the "same task" happening outside of the laboratory, one has to look for how the work of formulating the task which is done by the experimenter in the laboratory is getting done. This analysis will show that the practical methods of maintaining control in the laboratory lead to ignoring the crucial processes of formulating the task and forming the goal which are often the responsibilities of people in everyday settings.

To make the "same task" happen in two different settings required a task that would have as a solution an easily analyzable and recognizable procedure that the children would not already know. This solution was the tracer. An appropriately simple but exotic task was found among a set that Piaget and Inhelder (1975) used in their studies of combinations and permutations. One of these tasks was aimed at the ability to generate all possible pairs from a set of items, using stacks of differently colored chips. There was an accepted "formal operational" procedure for the systematic solution of this combinations problem, which appeared to be both elegant and beyond the capacity of fourth graders as individual inventions. The combinations task was also useful because Inhelder and Piaget (1958) studied another version of it which involved combinations of chemicals. Since the fourth-grade classroom teacher was already planning a unit on "household chemicals," there was an opportunity to embed this well-analyzed cognitive task into the ordinary course of classroom activities. The task was chosen not to test Piaget's theory or the children's "operational level" but rather for its usefulness as a tracer. Although the project occasionally made use of Piagetian analyses, it essentially took the task outside of the theory that generated it (Newman, Riel & Martin, 1983).

In the one-to-one tutorial situation, which served as the "laboratory" version of the task, each child was invited into the library corner of the classroom by a researcher and was presented with stacks of little cards. Each stack of cards was of a different color and bore the picture of a different television or movie star. Starting with four stacks, the child was asked to find all the ways that pairs of stars could be friends. Specifically, the child was asked to make all the pairs of stars and none that were the same. The child then usually went about choosing pairs of cards from the stacks and placing them in a column.

When the child had done as many pairs as possible, the researcher instituted a short tutorial before doing another trial of pair making. The child was asked to check whether all the pairs had been made. If the child did not invent a systematic procedure for checking, the tutor suggested one, asking, "Do you have all the pairs with Mork" (if Mork were the first star on the left). Then she asked about the next star to the right. These hints were designed to give the child the idea of systematically pairing each star with every other star, so as to see whether this systematic procedure carried over to the next trial at making combinations.

When the checking was finished, the stars were put back in their piles, and a fifth star was chosen. Again the child was asked to make all the possible pairs and none more than once. At this point, many of the children began by making all the pairs with the left-most star. This star was combined with each to its right. Then the second star from the left was combined with each to its right, and so on until all the combinations were made. For children who did not arrive at this particular system of producing pairs, the checking procedure was repeated. But this time the tutor gave as explicit instructions as were necessary to get the child step by step through an entire check.

That is, the tutor asked about each star and its pairing with every other star in a systematic left-to-right manner. In the final trial, the child chose a sixth star and attempted to make all the possible pairs with six.

The tutorial accomplished two things. First, it acted as a pretest of the children in a typical laboratory setting on one version of the combinations task. Second, it taught the children a procedure for determining that they had made all the pairs. The procedure of combining each item with every other item could then act as a tracer in a later task with a different social organization. If the children later used the particular procedure they had been taught, and if it were reasonable to assume that the procedure would not be used except for the goal of finding all pairs, then the children's use of the procedure would be evidence that the child participants had identified the "same task."

Piaget's analysis of this procedure, which he referred to as "intersection," is abstract enough to apply to combinations problems presented in other modes. As he conceived of intersection, the child is coordinating several series of correspondences. This can be understood as treating the single array (e.g. four stars) as if there are two dimensions that intersect. Each item on one dimension is paired with the items on the other dimension in the manner of a matrix (Fig. 8.1). With this matrix conception, choosing pairs follows planfully from beginning to end. All the children have to do is work through the matrix. If the children were just checking if all the pairs were done, it was often just as easy to go, say, row by row, even though checks were duplicated. In the production of pairs where duplication was not allowed, the system of dropouts was

	1	**2**	**3**	**4**
1		$1_{and}2$	$1_{and}3$	$1_{and}4$
2	$2_{and}1$		$2_{and}3$	$2_{and}4$
3	$3_{and}1$	$3_{and}2$		$3_{and}4$
4	$4_{and}1$	$4_{and}2$	$4_{and}3$	

Fig. 8.1. Intersection procedure schema.

usually used so that only the top half, say, was produced. In contrast, children without the conceptual matrix typically make pairs without an orderly pattern or make patterns such as 1 & 2, 3 & 4, 2 & 3, 1 & 4. Without the matrix concept, the children cannot be certain they have all the pairs; they "just can't think of" any more patterns. This endpoint lacks the certainty or sense of necessity found in the intersection procedure.

The intersection procedure is potentially general enough to apply to any number or any kind of items should the structure of the activity make it useful. In cognitive psychology, such an abstract and general structure, usually called a "schema," is considered to be a feature of a subject's internal conceptualization (Abelson, 1981; Rumelhart, 1980). Since this study looked for this "schema" outside of the laboratory, it could not be given an exclusively mental status (Griffin, Newman & Cole, 1981). The search for this schema in the peer interaction setting had to allow that it would be found as much to be mediating social interactions as to be mediating an individual's actions. Even when this tracer was used as a frame for comparison between the two settings, the attempt to locate the "same task" was far from straightforward.

The second setting in which an attempt was made to locate the tracer looked very different from the movie star tutorial. In collaboration with the classroom teacher, a unit on household chemicals was developed. A series of lessons and activities led up to this second version of the combinations problem, which was presented as a special work-table activity. Groups of two and three children went to the back of the room where the teacher supervised science activities, one of which involved making combinations of chemicals. Each group of children was given four beakers of colorless solutions that were numbered for easy reference, a rack of test tubes, and a sheet of paper with two columns marked off on which to record "chemicals" and "what happened." The four chemicals had been chosen so that each pair would have a distinctive reaction. The children did two versions of the combinations of chemicals task a few days apart. A second version closely resembled the original Inhelder and Piaget procedure, but the one discussed here was simpler and its goal more closely matched the combinations-of-movie-stars task.

The written worksheet instructed the children to find out as much as they could about the chemicals by making all the combinations of two and recording the results. After getting a child to read aloud the instructions, the teacher reiterated some safety precautions and directed the children to make all the possible pairs without duplicates. The teacher then sat down at the end of the table and busied herself with paperwork so that she could observe the children without directly supervising them. She intervened on occasion when children ran into difficulty or asked for help, but for the most part the pairs of children worked on their own. It was thus more markedly like a peer group activity with fewer laboratory-like constraints on what was to be done or how to do it than is typically the case in cognitive experiments.

Considerable effort was devoted to making the same task happen in the two settings. Most notably, in both cases the researcher or teacher stated the goal of making all of the pairs at the initiation of the problem. This instruction was not always sufficient to make the task happen, a failure that was significant to the study's findings.

There were some difficulties in getting the task to happen in the chemicals setting. The movie star activity posed far fewer practical problems. The movie star cards were just the right size for placing one pair under another in a neat and accessible column, on the mat next to the child. Once a column was constructed, it was easily scanned and checked, as the cards were brightly colored and the pictures were distinctive. The chemicals were much harder to manage. They had to be transferred from beakers to test tubes, and once a pair was in the tube, no visual record of which ones had been put in was automatically available.

If the children were unable to mix and keep track of the chemicals, they could hardly be expected to attend to the task of getting all the combinations. The solution was to set up an earlier lesson in which the children had to place a solution from a beaker into a test tube and record the results on a form which was to be used later in the combinations-of-chemicals task. The recording paper, as well as the previous instruction and practice on using it, provided not only an "external memory" for each child but also a common reference for the groups who were expected to be working together.

There is no way of measuring precisely the relative difficulty of the two situations. But such comparability is not crucial to the analysis. In spite of the long list of differences between the two situations, in an important way they were the same. In both settings the intersection procedure — the tracer — was potentially useful if the children accepted the researchers' notion of the task. However, the nature of the enterprise required taking some chances. In the chemicals activity the children could not be directed to use the tracer or force the task to happen. The lack of teacher-researcher direction was the crucial difference to maintain. If despite that difference, it was still possible to locate the tracer, this would be an anchor point from which to begin an analysis of the "same task" in two different settings.

Comparing the Two Settings

The project started out assuming that these were problem iso-morphs in the ordinary sense. Although this assumption might not ultimately be warranted, the standard approach was pushed as far as it would go to discover how it broke down. The problems that this approach ran into finally forced an alternative analysis.

Once the videotapes were collected, a somewhat naive attempt was made to code the events for occurrences of the tracer. Once coded, they were run through a statistical test to see if performance correlated on the two tasks. For example, if children used the intersection procedure in the movie star task, were they likely to use it in the chemicals task? Or did different children use it in one setting or the other?

The coding of both tasks was designed to spot any instance of a child going through a sequence, like 1 & 2, 1 & 3, 1 & 4, 2 & 3, and so on, in which each item was paired with every other item in a systematic way that could be recognized. The sequence, which could contain duplicates, could be either a complete run-through of the procedure or a fragment of the procedure (e.g. all the 2s: 2 & 1, 2 & 3, 2 & 4). A three-point scale was used, on which "1" meant no fragments of the procedure were found, "2" meant that some fragments of the procedure were found, and "3" meant that the child produced at least one complete run-through of the procedure.

In the movie star task, only 3 children out of 27 started out in the first trial using the intersection procedure. But after the checking tutorial, 17 children used a complete run-through of the procedure, and 4 others used it partially in the second or third trial. In the chemicals task, the coding credited only 4 children with a complete run-through of the procedure, although 8 others did at least one set (e.g. all the 4s). In statistical terms, the conclusion from such a coding approach is a low correlation between performance in the two settings, with 1 child doing a full run-through in the chemicals task but producing only a fragment in the last trial of the movie stars, and 5 children using the procedure in the movie star task but not at all in the chemicals.

These results indicate that in some sense the movie star task was easier, confirming the suspicion that the chemical materials were difficult and unfamiliar. The results were not surprising, given the fact that the intersection procedure was taught just before the second movie star task, a lesson that came months before the chemicals task. But in a more important sense the movie star task was easier. It was far easier to code. For one thing, where to code was known exactly, namely just those testing trials where the children were put on their own to produce the pairs from 4, 5, or 6 stacks of stars. In contrast, in the chemicals activity the intersection sequences were located at various points in the episode in the children's talk about what pairs had, or had not, been done. Also, children were not isolated from sources of help. The intersection sequences which appeared during the chemical task were often collaborative productions which were difficult to code in any but an *ad hoc* way. These differences provided crucial points of comparison. The coder's problems were symptomatic of differences for the participants, including the teacher and researcher, in what the task was and how the work got done.

The chemicals activity presented difficulties from the beginning in locating the tracer, that is, the intersection procedure. There were two kinds of difficulty: knowing where to find the tracer in the course of the children's activity, and knowing to whom to attribute the procedure. It was thought that the children would use the tracer procedure to produce the pairs of chemicals as they had produced the pairs of movie stars in the tutorial. Some of the children would start out with, say, 1 & 2 and proceed to do all the pairs with 1 and so on through the six possible pairs. But this never happened. Instead, the groups of children started with whatever pair was most convenient, or was "thought of first," for lack of a better description. The sequence of pairs either manifested no pattern at all or took on patterns such as doing the middle then the ends. These patterns were not usually produced as part of a single, coherent sequence by the children. For example, one common pattern started with 1 & 2 then 3 & 4 when the two children who were part of the group but working independently each took the two beakers closest to him or herself. When the intersection procedure appeared, it arose in the talk among the children. When the children could not think up another pair that had not yet been done, they would discuss the written record or consult one another's memory.

A group composed of Thomas, Candy, and Elvia provides a good example of this process. At the beginning of the task they settle on a turn-taking order which they maintain throughout. During a turn, one child both mixes the chemicals and records the results. This does not mean, however, that the children work alone; many of the decisions about what to mix and how to describe the result are made after extensive discussion. At each new turn, one child chooses a pair and the other children check it against the record. The sequence of choices follows no apparent order through the six possible pairs, and until the last two pairs the children have no difficulty thinking up a new pair that has not been done. The last two pairs are also arrived at without apparent system but with growing concern about finding more to do.

After Candy's second turn, the six pairs have been done, but Elvia takes an empty test tube from the rack, preparing to mix another pair. With a sigh, Elvia says, "I don't know what color to use now." Thomas suggests 2 & 4, but Elvia finds it on the worksheet. Thomas jokingly suggests 2 & 2, and Candy suggests 2 & 4 again. Thomas thinks of 2 & 1 but finds it has been done. Candy suggests 4 & 2. There is a mild rebuke from Thomas that it is the same as 2 & 4. Elvia comes up with 4 & 3, but Candy finds it has been done. Elvia suggests 4 & 1, and Candy recalls that she did it. At that point Thomas says, "There's no more." Candy thinks of 3 & 1 and Elvia thinks of 3 & 2, but they find both of those on the written record too. Then Elvia suggests 3 & 4. At that point Thomas says, "Wait a minute, 'kay, we got, okay, we got all the 1s." He moves his finger up the record sheet and hesitates when he finds only two of them but then finds the third. Candy says, "All the ones with 2?:2 & 3". She pauses and then says, "They don't have 4 & 1," but Thomas points it out. At that moment the teacher asks, "You have them all?" And Thomas answers, "Yep."

The intersection sequence can be recovered from this interaction. For almost a minute, the three children name off pairs with 4 until Candy moves to 3 & 1, after which Elvia names the other pairs with 3. Then Thomas looks for all the 1s, and Candy suggests looking for the 2s. The order is not "perfect," but as a group they manage to check through all the pairs with each of the chemicals. Usually these checks did not strictly follow the 1 to 4 order but skipped around, partially depending on the order the combinations were recorded on the worksheet. For example, children searched for all the 4s by reading down the worksheet and naming off all the pairs with 4 as they were encountered. This strategy has the advantage of making the search of the record more efficient, although it means the memory load is increased because the children must keep in mind which of the pairs with 4 have been found.

Finding the tracer, the intersection procedure, in the talk among the children as they set about to check their work should not have been a surprise. The tracer was first introduced during the movie star tutorial in the tutor-child checking interaction. The children who used the intersection schema incorporated it as a checking procedure in their production of pairs. They used it in much the same way as they were taught to use it: as a checking procedure.

The second difficulty in the chemicals task was determining who did the procedure. Because the children were not working alone, the procedure could not always be attributed to a single child. In the example of Thomas, Elvia, and Candy the sequence was made up of contributions from all the children, and no child carried out the whole strategy independently. The intersection schema thus regulated the interaction among the children rather than just regulating the individuals' actions.

However, peer collaboration in the chemicals activity did not automatically obscure individual accomplishment. Some children divided the labor in such a way as to make it possible to attribute the schema to an individual. In one case, two boys, Jorge and Mike, who are best friends collaborate closely. Jorge writes down what Mike mixes, and when they exchange turns, Mike records what Jorge mixes. They alternate turns through the six possible combinations, which do not follow any apparent pattern. At that point, Mike takes out a test tube to begin another combination but stops to look over at the record. Mike starts a checking sequence at 1 & 2 and from there continues through the whole sequence, ending with 3 & 4. While he is naming the chemicals, he points to the numbered beakers which remain in a neat array. Jorge, in the meantime, reads the record, finding the combinations Mike is naming. Mike and Jorge divide up the checking roles just as they divided up the roles in producing and recording the chemicals. One deals with the chemicals while the other deals with the written record. Because Mike is the one to name off the sequence of pairs, the schema can be attributed to him. But the schema also regulates the interaction between the two boys. Again, the intersection schema is not just or even primarily an internal knowledge structure. It is also importantly locatable in the interaction among the children. It is, in Vygotsky's terminology, an "interpsychological" cognitive process.

In an important sense the accomplishment of the intersection procedure was always a social accomplishment in the data. The creation in the tutorial of a protected system in which the procedure could be carried out unimpeded was a piece of collaborative social organization. Such organizational support for problem solving is a systematic feature of settings organized for individual assessment. But when individual assessment is the motive for the activity, the organizational efforts tend to go unnoticed because they are background to the data. In the less constrained setting, Mike and Jorge's marvelous bit of organization can be better appreciated.

One thing that the coding neglected to identify in the two settings was the task itself. The tracer was found in most of the movie star sessions and some of the chemical sessions, but what does that say about the existence of the same task in the two settings? The coding of the movie star session assumed that the location of the task was known and that the child's performance on the task was what was being coded. The task was identified with the goal, "Make all the pairs," which was stated by the researcher just before the child began forming pairs of movie stars. The researcher was careful not to give any information until it was clear that the child was not going to make any more on his or her own. The slot between the researcher's instructions and the child's negative answer to the question, "Can you make any more?" provided easy access to the individual child's use of the intersection procedure. It seemed clear that in response to the task of making all the pairs, some children used the procedure or used it partially and some children did not use it at all. The struggle with the chemicals setting, however, led to a questioning of this assumption about the task always being present in the movie star sessions.

When the children started out in the chemicals activity, they clearly were not doing the task. The teacher told them to make all the pairs before they started, but there was no evidence that they were trying to make all the pairs. For one reason, there were other goals that the children were pursuing. For another reason, they were not using the intersection procedure, or apparently any other systematic procedure, for making all the pairs.

The children were doing other tasks than producing all possible pairs. The teacher's instructions at the beginning of the episode stated, but did not emphasize, the goal of getting all the pairs. She emphasized the problem of finding out about the chemicals by seeing how they reacted with other chemicals. The reactions that were produced by different combinations were fascinating to the children, and they were generally interested in the problem of describing the results and writing them down.

Tracy's approach illustrates the common interest in the chemicals themselves. Instead of using the numbers on the beakers, he uses the actual chemical names printed on the beakers. After mixing Chlorox from beaker 2 with copper sulfate from beaker 3, he is excited and describes in detail the blue-green and brown dotted reaction. He appears to want to pursue reactions with "copper." After his partners, who are working together, trade their beaker 4 for his beaker 3, he looks up from the worksheet and objects, "I got copper!" While his partners are attempting to choose their next pair with reference to the worksheet so as to avoid duplication of pairs, Tracy's criterion for choice appears to be interest in a particular chemical.

Children who were not doing the intersection or some other systematic procedure while producing pairs of chemicals were finding the pairs "empirically," according to Piaget. This meant that the children thought up a pair by some means other than the intersection procedure and looked to see whether it had been done. In this case, the children had no way of knowing when they were finished except that they could not think of any more.

Piaget's analysis suggested that a child who was making pairs empirically was doing the same actions, such as mixing pairs or writing the results on the worksheet, but was not doing the same task as a child who knew the endpoint that the researcher had in mind. For the child without intersection, the task was like a request to jump as high as one could. The outcome was an empirical issue and differed for different children. For the child who had the idea of intersection, it provided a definite and general goal to be achieved. In the chemicals activity the teacher's statement of the task goal, "Make all the pairs," was not acted upon. The task, as the teacher and researchers understood it, happened only when the children themselves formulated the goal of finding all the pairs because they wanted to make more pairs.

Tracy's comments about the chemical reactions with copper give a kind of information that was almost never available in the movie star tutorials. The chemicals activity was so loosely constrained that alternative tasks were possible. It was known that the children were not doing the task because they were talking about doing other tasks. In the tutorials, on the contrary, little was allowed other than pair making. Tracy, for example, starts his second trial with five stars by making a row of cards. There is no way of knowing what he might have been trying to do, what his own task was, because he was immediately "corrected" by the researcher and told to make a column of pairs.

The strict enforcement of pair making in the tutorial made it difficult to know whether children were not doing the task of making all of the pairs. Differences in the pattern of pair placements did not stand out as indicating a different goal because they were not accompanied by other behavioral evidence that the children were doing some other task. It was assumed that the children in the movie star activity were all doing the same task but that only some were using intersection to do it.

Piaget's analysis of task performance already implied that some children were not doing his task, which made his analysis somewhat more powerful than other laboratory analyses that cannot distinguish between doing poorly and not doing the task at all. The analytic weakness of the tutorial setting showed up in what Piaget considered to be a transitional level of performance between "empirical" and "intersection," where patterns took place that he called "juxtaposition" sequences, such as doing the ends and then the middle (e.g. 1 & 2, 3 & 4, 1 & 4, 2 & 3, 1 & 3, 2 & 4). He described these sequences as a "search for a system," implying that the child understood the task and was searching for a solution. When such sequences occurred in the tutorial, it was impossible to tell whether or not the child was indeed doing the task. The tutorial design, however, did provide one kind of relevant evidence in that children who made juxtaposition patterns were not significantly faster than "empirical" children in learning the intersection strategy in the tutorial, which suggests that those patterns were not a stage on the way to discovering a solution to the task.

The chemicals activity, however, provided clear evidence that some of these juxtaposition sequences were produced while the children were not doing the task. For example, when Tracy, Leslie, and Rebecca start out, Tracy takes 1 & 2 while Leslie and Rebecca work together on 3 & 4. When they finish their respective mixtures, Tracy offers his 1 for their 3 and mixes 2 & 3, while the girls mix 1 & 4. When the girls finish theirs, Rebecca checks the record and decides to do 1 & 3, so they trade their 4 for Tracy's 3. These trades result in a sequence 1 & 2, 3 & 4, 2 & 3, 1 & 4, 2 & 4, and 1 & 3. This pattern results not from an attempt to create that particular pattern but from trading for chemicals each has not used. In this respect, the unconstrained setting provided better information about task performance than did the laboratory setting. The constraints of the laboratory obscured whether or not some subjects were doing the task.

The original coding scheme must now be drastically reinterpreted. Most of the children in the first and second trials of the movie star task may not have been doing the task at all. Scoring a 1, for no intersection, may not have been a low score; it may simply have been an indication of not doing the task. The coding in the chemicals activity must also be reconsidered. None of the children started out doing the task. For those who finally did, their achievement went beyond the achievement of any child in the tutorial because they discovered the task on their own.

Getting the Task to Happen in Psychology and Education

In both psychology and education there is the need to get people to do tasks which they would be unlikely to confront if left on their own. In both cases an expert must interact with a novice to present the problem and to oversee the methods that are devised for solving it. But the nature of cognitive psychology makes the psychologist's job easier. The psychologist must move the children from not doing the task to doing it when told to do it in the laboratory. The educator must move the children from not doing the task to doing it on their own in everyday life. In everyday situations there is not always an expert getting the task to happen and explaining the procedures. But educators want children to be able not only to solve problems when they are told to do so in a lesson or on a test but also to identify the problems in everyday situations.

Teaching was part of both the movie star tutorial and the chemicals activities. How learning takes place in the course of these interactions is a topic that should play a greater role in psychological research since it may provide an answer to how the task is made to happen in the laboratory situation and also to how the task may be made to happen in everyday situations where there is no teacher.

The movie star activity was designed in part as a testing situation and in part as a tutorial on the procedure to be used later as the tracer. The part of the tutorial devoted to teaching the checking procedure was designed to make use of principles in Vygotsky's (1978) theory of the "zone of proximal development" (Vygotsky, 1978; Brown & French, 1979; Brown & Ferrara, in press; Newman, Griffin & Cole, in preparation). In the procedure used, the tutor started out by giving as much help as the child needed to carry out the systematic check. Where necessary, the tutor asked about every single pair. But as the tutorial progressed, the tutor began giving less and less help until the child was doing the procedure on his or her own. Thus the procedure moved gradually from a location "in" the tutor-child interaction to a location "in" the child.

Following Vygotsky's theoretical formulation, the study assumed that tasks would be found first in the interaction between expert and novice and later in the novice's independent activity, because the novice not only lacked the skills necessary for carrying out a task on his or her own but, more important, did not initially understand the goal. The expert must ensure that the task itself occurred in the interaction between the expert and novice. Teaching in the study not only provided most of the children with the intersection procedure but also gave them the goal of finding all the pairs. That is, it introduced them to the task in such a way that the goal and the procedure were simultaneously internalized in the course of the interaction.

In the movie star tutorial, the children first produced a column of as many pairs as they could, and then the tutor began teaching the checking strategy. The conversation at this point was important. The tutor asked, "How do you know you have all the pairs?" The child usually answered vaguely or, like Tracy, with a hint of frustration, "I can't think of any more." The tutor then asked, "Could you check to see if you have all the pairs?" The child usually said little, and the tutor said, "Well, I have a way to check. Do you have all the pairs with Mork (or the first star on the left)?" From there she proceeded through the checking procedure, allowing the child to take over more and more as they went along.

The tutor's question, "How do you know you have all the pairs?" presupposed that the child was trying to get all the pairs. This may have been a false presupposition, but it was strategically useful (Gearhart & Newman, 1980). The question treated the child's column of pairs as if it had been produced in an attempt to get all the pairs. The teacher then invoked the intersection procedure as a means to fix up the child's "failed attempt to produce all the pairs." In other words, she appropriated the child's pair-making, turning it into an example of how to achieve the stated goal. When their own "empirical" production of pairs was retrospectively interpreted in terms of the intersection schema, children probably began to learn the researcher's meaning of "all the pairs."

This retrospective appropriation process was also seen at the end of the chemicals activity. The teacher always checked when the children thought they had finished and attempted to elicit a rationale for their thinking. Like the tutorial, the teacher was working with a concrete set of already produced pairs which were not necessarily produced by the children using the intersection procedure. In the chemicals task far more than in the movie star activity, the researcher's task completely disappeared from the scene in many cases. The teacher's questions at the end brought the task back to the interaction. Her discussion demonstrated to the children how the work they did could be understood as doing the teacher's task.

In an important sense the tutor and teacher were treating the child's production as if it were a poorly executed attempt to achieve an agreed-upon goal. In education, such assumptions may be a useful way of importing the goal into the teacher-child interaction and, from there, into the child's independent activity. The original coding scheme also treated many of the children's productions as poor strategies for getting all the pairs. In psychology, such overinterpretation can be dangerously misleading. Children are scored as doing poorly when they are not doing the task in the first place.

It is one thing to get tasks to happen when the teacher or researcher and the child are in direct interaction. It is another thing to get tasks to happen in the everyday world over which the teacher or researcher has little or no control. One important difference between everyday and laboratory-style tasks showed up in the chemicals activity.

Take the case of Rebecca, Leslie, and Tracy, who are working together. When it seems that no more combinations of chemicals are to be made, Rebecca looks to the record sheet and begins naming off the combinations following the intersection schema. She does not use the canonical order, however. The first pair on the sheet is 4 & 2. She starts with 4 & 2 and scans the record for the other combinations with 4 and then for the combinations with 3. Within each group (i.e. the 4s and 3s) she names the combinations in the order they appear on the sheet. When she gets to the end, she says, "We're done," and the teacher comes over and asks, "How do you know?" Rebecca repeats her intersection strategy, but this time she speaks more clearly and does the sequence in a stricter numerical order: 4 & 1, 4 & 2, 4 & 3; 3 & 1, 3 & 2, and so on.

The difference between Rebecca's first and second intersection procedure corresponds to a crucial difference in the source of the task. As Lave (1980) pointed out, everyday tasks usually arise from and are constrained by the actor's own higher-level goals. When Rebecca checks the worksheet the first time, it is to establish for herself that all the combinations are done. The order in which she names the pairs follows fairly closely the order on the worksheet she is checking. When she checks the sheet the second time, it is to display for the teacher how she has arrived at her conclusion, and she keeps closer to the canonical order. She answers the question, "How do you know?" rather than trying to find out if more chemicals are to be done.

A "whole task" thus becomes specifically a task considered in the context of the activity or higher-level goals that motivate it. Whenever there is a task, there is always a whole task. But in some settings, like the laboratory, the classroom, or wherever there is a hierarchical division of labor, the higher-level goals may not be under the actors' individual control. In other cases, the actors must formulate the instrumental relation between the goal of the task and the higher-level goal they are primarily trying to achieve. This was what happened in the chemicals activity. The children wanted to mix more pairs of chemicals, so they tried to figure out if they had done them all. Finding all the pairs was not a task which was presented to them by somebody else; it followed from the concrete situation in which they were engaged. In standard laboratory practice, where it is necessary to have as complete control as possible over the goals that the subjects are trying to accomplish, subjects are never called upon to formulate their own goals and so are confronted with only part of the problem — the solution part.

This is not to say that whole tasks are not part of the social interaction in the laboratory. The subject may be very much aware that the researcher has goals which are the reasons for getting the subject to do the task, even though the subject has no part in formulating the task. When Rebecca changes the order of the procedure, she appears to be displaying the procedure for the purpose of the lesson that the teacher is conducting. In short, there is always a whole task, but standard laboratory cognitive tasks are organized into a division of labor such that the subject is confronted only with the solution part.

Education is an attempt to make children able to do the whole task when an appropriate occasion arises. To provide such opportunities as were found in the chemicals activity, where children were allowed to discover a task in the course of doing some higher-level problem, is probably an important kind of experience for children to have if they are going to learn how to apply what they know to new situations. They will not learn to do this if they are always presented with a ready-made task. A teacher's retrospective discussions are also a crucial part of this experience. For the children who did not formulate the task themselves, such discussions were an opportunity to see that a task had been a potential part of the activity.

Conclusions

The effort to make the same task happen in two settings led to identification of two very different ways in which people are confronted with tasks. In one case the task was made to happen by the researcher, who not only stated the goal but also provided training in carrying out the solution. In the other case the teacher stated the goal, but the goal was not acted upon until the children themselves found a function for it in the course of their own activities. This difference calls for analysis in terms of the whole task. That is, any time a task happens, one must ask how it has come to happen. How it was made to happen is not an incidental aspect of the task.

The traditional business of cognitive psychological research has been to identify knowledge and processes in the head of the subject. It is only natural, then, that the subject should be isolated and the part of the experiment during which the experimenter and subject interact, namely the initial instructions or training, should be ignored. But just as the laboratory setting does not have privileged status as a place to study what people can do, "in the head" does not have privileged status as a place to locate schemata. They can also be located in the interaction between the experimenter and subject, or in the interaction among a group of subjects collaborating on a task, or in the interaction between a teacher and a child who is learning to do something new.

A framework that has schemata moving from the interaction to the individual makes the interaction and how it changes over time the central topic of analysis rather than an incidental aspect. Learning a task is accomplished in interactions. The ability to find the same task in everyday settings may also arise in interactions during which the expert turns the child's concrete actions into actions that have a new significance within the interaction. Methods must be developed for bringing those teaching interactions into sharper focus, so as to begin to discover how tasks can move from the classroom to the everyday world.

9. Children's Difficulties with School Mathematics

Herbert P. Ginsburg
Barbara S. Allardice

This chapter reports on our efforts to understand children's difficulties with elementary mathematics. We begin by describing the relevant problems and children, namely the cognitive difficulties of normal children in the social context of school. Next we consider two substantive bodies of research. The first deals with informal knowledge of mathematics. The basic issue is whether children who are likely to fail in school lack the informal mathematical concepts and procedures which seem useful for assimilating formal, written mathematics. The second body of research deals directly with failure in school mathematics. We present both case studies and controlled investigations of cognitive factors involved in children's difficulties with arithmetic. Finally, we suggest new directions for research and education.

The Problem

The issue is why children who are otherwise intelligent exhibit poor performance in school mathematics. The population of interest is the broad spectrum of children, generally at elementary school level, who persistently exhibit low academic achievement in mathematics and usually perform poorly in other subjects as well. These children are not seriously retarded nor severely emotionally disturbed. They display obvious academic failure, defined in terms of low grades, teachers' judgments, standard achievement test scores, and self-reports. Often they are children about whom teachers feel a sense of helplessness, since nothing seems to improve their performance in arithmetic; and some of the children have so much difficulty that they are referred to a special clinic for diagnosis and remedial work. Often, the children are poor and black. In the United States, school failure is associated with class and race.

Here is an example of the kind of child with whom we are concerned. Butch, a member of a working class family, is in the third grade of an upstate New York elementary school. His teacher identified him as having severe problems in learning ordinary school arithmetic. Both his grades and his achievement test scores are low, in arithmetic as well as other school subjects. Butch is a candidate for repeating third grade. He is not retarded, nor is he psychotic or otherwise severely emotionally disturbed. Outside of the classroom, in the playground, he is lively and boisterous. His everyday behavior seems to reveal at least average intelligence. Yet in the classroom he is quiet, appears depressed, and obviously neither performs school arithmetic well nor understands it. When asked what he is doing in school, Butch says he is working with fractions:

Interviewer: Fractions? Can you show me what you are doing with fractions?
(Butch writes $8\overline{)16}$.)
Interviewer: Okay. So what does that say?
Butch: 8, 16.
Interviewer: 8, 16. Okay. What do you do with it?
Butch: You add it up and put the number up there.
Interviewer: Okay. What is the number?
$$\overset{23}{8\overline{)16}}$$
(Butch writes $8\overline{)16}$.)

Obviously, Butch is doing something unusual. He confuses division with fractions, and he cannot calculate simple division. He seems to have a lack of understanding of school arithmetic and engages in highly irregular procedures. The basic aim of our research was to understand why children like Butch act as they do when they are working with school arithmetic.

Informal Knowledge

Our attempt to understand children's mathematics difficulties began by investigating the "spontaneous concepts," or "informal knowledge," of children who are most likely to do badly in school arithmetic, that is, lower-class and black children. Cognitive theorists, most notably Piaget and Vygotsky, have pointed out that in their natural surroundings preschool children spontaneously develop informal concepts and strategies, many of which are related to the academic knowledge taught in school. Thus, the preschool child develops elementary notions of mathematics, physics, causality, and the like. In Piaget's view, the child then assimilates academic material into these already existing spontaneous concepts. The child's informal knowledge thus serves as a kind of cognitive underpinning or scaffolding for school learning.

There seem to be two different systems of informal mathematical knowledge operating concurrently in individual children (Ginsburg, 1982). System 1 knowledge appears before children enter school, or outside the context of formal education. Early in life, children develop "intuitive" mathematical concepts and techniques for solving quantitative problems, especially those that do not demand a numerical response. Consider the perception of more, originally described by Binet (1969). Given two randomly arranged collections of blocks, a child of three or four years of age can easily determine which of the two collections has "more" than the other, at least when relatively small numbers of elements are involved. The child's speed of judgment, requiring only a second or two, indicates that counting is not necessary to solve the task. The child achieves the solution by employing such aspects of stimulus information as the area covered and density of the elements. Since System 1 knowledge develops outside the formal school setting, it is termed "informal." Cultural influences, such as parental training, books, and television, do not appear to be major determinants of the development of System 1 skills, such as the Piagetian operations or the concept of more. Indeed, most parents are surprised to find that children possess such skills. It is conceivable that System 1 knowledge is tied to a biological component and thus is "natural."

System 1 skills appear in infants and preschoolers. Starkey and Cooper (1980) showed that elementary forms of quantity discrimination may even be present in early infancy. Piaget described the precursors of seriation in infancy and the development of functions in the preoperational period. There can be no doubt that untaught and non-numerical mathematical concepts and skills develop in the preschool years.

System 2 knowledge appears during the preschool years, when the child learns counting, a culturally derived tool, and uses it in the service of problem solving. Hebbeler (1977) has shown that preschoolers can use counting, sometimes on the fingers, to solve elementary problems of addition, particularly when objects are involved. System 2 knowledge is informal, insofar as it develops outside the context of schooling, but also cultural, since it depends on social transmission, direct and indirect, as by adults, television, or books.

System 2 skills develop in the preschool years. Gelman and Gallistel (1978) showed that children base their counting on certain implicit principles, for example, that the order in which they count a set of objects makes no difference. Fuson and Hall (1983) showed that the young child invents rules for generating novel number words. Again, there can be little doubt that in the preschool years System 2 skills are well developed and relatively powerful.

Given this theory and research concerning children's informal concepts of mathematics, we can ask whether children who are likely to experience difficulty in school, especially lower-class and black children, possess the informal knowledge, defined in terms of System 1 and System 2 skills, which could serve as a basis for learning school arithmetic. Can school failure be explained by weak informal knowledge of mathematics, that is, by spontaneous concepts that are not sufficiently powerful to assimilate what is taught in school? There are conflicting views on this issue. One class of theories proposes that certain groups of children, especially the poor and the black, suffer from cognitive deficits which prevent adequate understanding of academic subject matter. The environmentalist view, for example, posits that poor children develop in a "deprived environment" which stunts their intellectual growth. According to Hunt, "cultural deprivation may be seen as a failure to provide an opportunity for infants and young children to have the experiences required for adequate development of those semiautonomous central control processes demanded for acquiring skill in the use of linguistic and mathematical symbols" (1964:236).

The nativist theory also postulates a cognitive deficit but offers a different explanation of its origins. Jensen (1969) proposed that lower-class children and blacks in particular suffer from an inability to engage in "conceptual learning," which involves cognitive activity mediating between stimulus and response, and that this deficit is the result of genetic inheritance. Moreover, the deficit prevents poor children from learning the conceptual material taught in school.

An alternative approach proposes that poor children possess fundamentally sound cognitive skills and exhibit few cognitive differences, so that their school failure must be explained on grounds other than cognitive deficit (Cole & Bruner, 1971; Ginsburg, 1972). According to this cognitive difference view, the evidence suggesting a deficit is faulty, typically deriving from standard tests which may be culturally biased. Adequate testing procedures would reveal cognitive strengths or perhaps even differences, but not deficits. For example, Labov (1972) found that blacks who perform poorly on standard, school-administered tests of language nevertheless exhibit basic syntactic competence in their natural environments. While Black English contains some features which are superficially different from Standard English, the underlying syntactic structure is the same. Similarly, in cognition generally, blacks may possess basic skills and their intellectual activity may differ from that of whites only in superficial ways. To explain why these children nevertheless do so badly in school, Ogbu (1978) suggested that many blacks perceive themselves as members of a caste who can realistically anticipate little in the way of economic opportunity. Hence, poor blacks and other lower-class individuals have little incentive to work hard at academic studies. The problem is primarily economic and motivational, not cognitive.

While these views have aroused considerable controversy, particularly concerning the possible origins of the hypothesized cognitive deficit, little research has been conducted on the prior issue of whether the deficit in fact exists. We have been able to locate only one such study concerning mathematical thinking. Kirk, Hunt, and Volkmar (1975) used tasks involving counting and enumeration to compare the numerical thinking abilities of Head Start children, black and white, with those of middle-class children. In general, the differences among the Head Start and middle-class groups were of a large magnitude, but there were no racial differences within the Head Start group. Although supporting the deficit position, this study was not conclusive since it dealt with only a limited array of mathematical skills and the procedures may not have been maximally effective in eliciting children's competence. The investigators themselves reported that their tasks "taxed the children . . . the test evoked efforts to leave the field and escape the examiner" (p. 137).

In view of the paucity of available evidence, we undertook several studies designed to examine the generality and robustness of System 1 and System 2 skills. Our purpose was to find out whether these informal concepts and skills are characteristic chiefly of American middle-class children, developing in what some consider to be a privileged and enriched environment. We did not think that this would be the case. Rather, we expected System 1 and System 2 skills to resemble language and the various Piagetian operations, at least up to the stage of formal operations. That is, the hypothesis was that System 1 and System 2 skills are extremely widespread and robust, being exhibited by the vast majority of young children, regardless of social class, race, or culture. If so, then virtually all children would possess a set of cognitive skills that could serve as the basis for later mathematical learning. Social class differences, if any exist, would be of only a minor nature. Evidence to this effect would contradict cognitive deficit theories.

To investigate this possibility, studies were carried out both in the Ivory Coast and in the United States. The cross-cultural studies generally involved a comparison of children and adults from three ethnic groups: Baoulé, Dioula, and American. The Baoulé are an animist, agricultural group, placing no particular emphasis on mathematics. The research took place in areas where some Baoulé children attend schools, while others do not. The Dioula, a Moslem group scattered throughout West Africa, have traditionally engaged in mercantile activities. While often illiterate, they need to employ calculational processes in the course of commerce. Like the Baoulé, some of the Dioula attend school and others do not. These two African groups provide a useful contrast in terms of hospitality to mathematical ideas and procedures. The groups were therefore used to investigate the effects of culture and schooling on the development of System 1 and System 2 skills.

Posner investigated the development of a variety of mathematical concepts, including the perception of more, as measured by the Binet task, in Baoulé and Dioula children ranging from 4 or 5 years of age to 9 or 10 years of age. One striking finding was that young children in both cultures "possess the basic notion of inequality; by the age of 9-10, regardless of schooling or ethnic background, they display a high level of accuracy. Moreover their methods for deter-

mining the greater set are similar to those of American children . . . suggesting . . . a universal capacity" (1982:207).
While African children may acquire this concept at a later age than
Americans, the former do acquire it, without the benefit of schooling or American middle-class culture. As for elementary addition,
both schooled and unschooled Dioula were extremely skilled in
this area, and schooled Baoulé were also adept. Only unschooled
Baoulé, members of the agricultural society, did relatively badly,
perhaps because their culture places little emphasis on counting. In
any event, unschooled Dioula children were competent at elementary addition, using counting and other effective strategies, and
even the unschooled Baoulé achieved some success in addition and
employed similar strategies.

Ginsburg, Posner, and Russell (1981a) investigated more complex forms of addition in schooled and unschooled Dioula children
and adults and in American children and adults. In general, unschooled Dioula children eventually exhibited a high degree of
competence in the solution of verbally presented addition problems. The young Dioula began with rather elementary counting
procedures, but older Dioula switched to the extensive utilization
of regrouping methods (e.g. $23 + 42 = 20 + 40 + 3 + 2$), which are
more efficient, especially in the case of larger numbers. Furthermore, the unschooled, particularly in adulthood, made significant
use of remembered number facts, which presumably they had
acquired through everyday experience in calculation. At first, the
Dioula did not employ the various strategies with great accuracy,
but with age they became increasingly proficient in their use,
learning to discriminate among different types of problems and to
apply different strategies where appropriate. The strategies employed by the Dioula, counting, regrouping, and number facts, are
essentially the same as those observed in American children.
Schooling and American culture are not necessary for the development of mental addition strategies.

Petitto and Ginsburg (1982) studied the use and understanding of
the four basic arithmetic operations — addition, subtraction, multiplication, and division — in unschooled Dioula adults and American college students. Dioula adults were competent in all forms of
mental arithmetic. Their accuracy was the product of efficient
cognitive strategies, often employing regrouping and various
counting procedures. Implicit in some of the strategies were mathe-

matical principles like associativity and commutativity. Further-more, subjects often used such principles to short-cut the process of calculation. For example, after calculating a problem like 46 + 38, subjects used commutativity to avoid calculating the answer to the problem 38 + 46. Thus, unschooled Dioula adults were skilled in mental calculation and even possessed an implicit understanding of certain basic mathematical principles.

These cross-cultural studies suggested that unschooled Africans, from both agricultural and commercial cultures quite different from those in the United States, who generally grow up in extreme poverty and environments that would be considered "deprived" by Americans, nevertheless exhibit basic System 1 and System 2 skills. Schooling and American middle-class culture are not necessary for the development of these skills, although they may accelerate their appearance.

To find out if this is also the case of poor children in American culture, Ginsburg and Russell (1981) investigated social class and racial differences in the early mathematical thinking of American children. They reasoned that basic cognitive skills should be no less prevalent in lower-class Americans than in unschooled Africans or middle-class Americans. The investigation, conducted in the Washington, D.C., and Baltimore areas, involved children at the prekindergarten and kindergarten levels, black and white, lower and middle class, from intact and single-parent homes. Each child, seen individually, was given seventeen mathematical tasks, many derived from the Ginsburg, Posner, and Russell work in Africa and from the work of investigators like Gelman. Table 9.1 summarizes some important ANOVA results.

In the vast majority of cases no social class differences were found or, at most, statistically insignificant trends favoring mid-dle-class over lower-class children. Children of both social classes demonstrated similar competence on the various tasks and similar strategies for solving them. If these competencies and strategies were not evident at the preschool level, they emerged by kindergar-ten age in all groups. For example, by kindergarten, the lower- and middle-class children performed well on several tasks designed to measure their understanding of addition operations, such as simple addition, inverse, and complex addition. Similarly, middle- and lower-class children made effective use of counting strategies to solve addition calculation problems involving objects present. In

Table 9.1. Summary of Ginsburg and Russell results

| | Significant main effects | | | | | Significant interaction | |
	Social class	Race	Age	Family	Sex	Vanishing interaction[a] involving age, race, or social class	Other
1. Perception of more	—	—	X	—	—	—	—
2. Seriation	—	X	X	—	—	—	X
3. Conservation	X	—	X	—	—	—	—
4. Addition operations	—	—	X	—	—	—	X
5. Equivalence	X	—	X	—	—	—	X
6. Counting words	—	—	X	—	—	X	X
7. Enumeration	—	—	X	—	—	—	X
8. Cardinality	X	—	X	—	—	X	X
9. Order invariance	—	—	X	X	—	—	X
10. Abstraction principle	X	—	—	—	—	—	—
11. Which number is greater?	—	—	X	—	—	X	X
12. Unit rule	—	X	X	—	X	—	X
13. Repair sets	—	—	X	—	—	—	—
14. Addition calculation	—	—	X	—	—	—	X
15. Representation of number	—	—	X	X	—	—	X
16. Reading numbers	—	—	X	X	—	—	X
17. Writing numbers	—	—	X	—	—	—	X

a. A vanishing interaction is a social class or racial difference at the preschool level which essentially disappears by kindergarten.

general, the only large differences involved age: developmental changes from preschool to kindergarten far outweigh social class differences in this area. Furthermore, the research showed fewer racial than social class differences, which themselves were few. Even if one foolishly granted the existence of "race" as a pure variable, it would have only trivial associations with early cognitive functions. Jensen's (1969) notion that lower-class and black children exhibit weaknesses in "abstract" thinking is thus wrong, at least with respect to early mathematical cognition. Also, a "deprived environment" does not necessarily produce children deficient in basic intellectual skills. Of course, we do not argue that such an environment, specifically lower-class poverty, is beneficial for those growing up in it, nor that it exerts no effects on psychological functioning. Rather, the study demonstrated that basic mathematical thought develops in a robust manner among lower- and middle-class children, black and white. School failure cannot be explained by initial deficit in basic cognitive skills, specifically System 1 and 2 mathematical skills. Instead, poor children display important cognitive strengths, developed spontaneously before the onset of formal schooling. These strengths should provide a sufficient foundation for later understanding of school mathematics. As Piaget maintained, "It is difficult to conceive how students who are well endowed when it comes to the elaboration and utilization of the spontaneous [patterns] of intelligence can find themselves handicapped in the comprehension of a branch of teaching [mathematics] that bears exclusively upon what is to be derived from such [thought]" (1970:4).

Academic Knowledge

On entrance to school, young children are faced with the necessity of assimilating and accommodating to written culture. They are taught symbolic, codified arithmetic and other forms of elementary mathematics. They encounter written symbolism, algorithms, and explicitly stated mathematical principles. These cultural inventions and discoveries are more powerful than counting and, used properly, can provide children with considerable efficiency in problem solving. Children therefore must develop a new set of intellectual skills, System 3 skills, for dealing with written culture. Since System 3 knowledge typically develops in school or through contact with written materials, it is formal. Since it is transmitted by social agents, it is also cultural.

Children often experience difficulty in developing System 3 skills and knowledge of written arithmetic. What could go wrong? Why should this occur when on entrance to school most children possess adequate informal knowledge, namely System 1 and System 2 concepts and skills? The reasons for the difficulty are unclear; virtually no research on these issues has been conducted. An investigation was therefore initiated to obtain preliminary information concerning such questions as whether children with mathematics difficulties display unusual patterns of error or distinct types of procedural and conceptual knowledge.

The research was based on a clinical cognitive case study approach. It was "clinical" in two senses. First, it directly investigated a clinical population, namely children experiencing learning difficulties so severe as to require treatment at a clinic or special attention in the classroom. Second, it employed the clinical interview method, which is based on a sound rationale and for certain purposes is in principle superior to standard tests and experimental procedures (Ginsburg, 1981). In particular, the method is useful in establishing competence, conducting exploratory research, and measuring the complexities of cognitive process. The research was "cognitive" in that it attempted to identify cognitive processes underlying the observed learning difficulties. And it involved "case study" in the sense that it dealt with the long-term investigation of individuals, some of whom might receive remedial treatment.

The clinical cognitive case study approach was used to accomplish several aims. First was the aim of exploration and discovery. Since so little is known about cognitive problems, it was necessary to engage in extensive exploration of the relevant phenomena. The case study permits this in a way that controlled laboratory investigation does not. A second aim was the systematic study of cognitive complexity in the individual. In the case study, the investigator attempts to get a comprehensive view of the complex system of the child's academic knowledge of mathematics. The focus is not just on a particular mental addition strategy or on a single error strategy, but on these and other cognitive processes as they operate within the larger context of the child's mathematical knowledge and efforts to learn and the examiner's attempts to teach. The resulting portraits may or may not be typical of children with learning problems, but they represent different ways in which cognitive systems can function to generate school failure. Normative research is required to determine what is typical and what is not.

The case studies were conducted in a local elementary school serving both middle- and lower-class children. The teacher of a combined third- and fourth-grade class was asked to select those students who were having the most difficulties with mathematics. We wanted to know nothing about the children other than that they were having difficulty. Nevertheless, the teacher could not keep from observing that all the children suffered from "perceptual problems." At the time of testing we knew little about the kind of instruction the children had received, except that they were using a New Math text and were participating in a programed learning system. Each child was interviewed once a week for a period of four to six weeks. Most interviews were recorded on videotape in a room adjoining the classroom. At the outset of the interviews, videotaping was demonstrated to all the children so that they would be familiar with it. After the first few minutes, the children seemed to ignore the video camera, which was in full view throughout all sessions. At the outset, intensive interviews were conducted with four children. Later, interviews were conducted with 15 more children.

One important finding of these case studies was that children with mathematics difficulties (MD), despite their real weaknesses and low level of performance, nevertheless possess extremely important and basic intellectual assets — or cognitive processes and states, described in "qualitative" terms — which are manifested in several ways. One of these cognitive assets is the ability to use informal procedures. While some MD children are unable to deal with virtually any type of written problem, such as column addition, they are able to solve essentially the same problem when concrete objects or spoken numbers, without written representation, are involved.

For example, at the outset Stacy does quite poorly. Her behavior seems chaotic and she seems retarded (Ginsburg, 1982). She is unable to deal with the most elementary written arithmetic problems. But soon the clinical interview begins to reveal Stacy's strengths. Perhaps this process is facilitated by the interviewer's encouragement of Stacy's counting on the fingers, which her teacher discouraged. In any event, Stacy shows that she can perform addition by combining and counting, or by counting on, when real objects are involved. She can also deal with absent objects when she is given concrete supports. This pattern repeated itself in many other children who, though severely deficient in written arithmetic, were able to employ informal procedures, typically involving some form of counting.

Another cognitive asset of MD children is the use of invented procedures. While these children often cannot accurately employ the standard algorithms, they may be able to solve written problems by means of procedures that they have at least partially devised. These invented procedures are usually a blend of the standard algorithm and informal methods, such as finger counting. In one case, Patty does column addition partly in the standard manner, by adding numbers in columns, and partly by counting on her fingers (Ginsburg, 1982). Both informal procedures, which are typically System 2 counting methods, and invented procedures, which are typically System 3 strategies involving the assimilation of written methods into existing cognitive structure, are hardly unique to MD children. Both are observed extensively in normal children.

The last cognitive asset of MD children is standard arithmetic knowledge. Often MD children possess many ordinary arithmetic skills, like simple standard algorithms (e.g. "carrying" with two-digit numbers) or number facts. MD children are not totally ignorant of mathematics.

In addition to these cognitive assets, MD children have a number of cognitive weaknesses. Again like normal children, they often produce consistent errors as the result of a systematic rule. Examples are:

Reading or writing numbers as they sound: writing "403" for "forty-three"

$$\text{Misalignment: } \begin{array}{r} 23 \\ +2 \\ \hline 43 \end{array}$$

$$\text{Carrying errors: } \begin{array}{r} 56 \\ +56 \\ \hline 1012 \end{array}$$

$$
\begin{array}{r}
34 \\
\text{Diagonal addition:} +5 \\
\hline
89
\end{array}
$$

$$
\begin{array}{r}
3 \\
\text{Zero as an eliminator:} +0 \\
\hline
0
\end{array}
$$

These are among the "bugs" or error strategies found in ordinary school children (Brown & Burton, 1978). MD children do not seem to display unusual species of bugs.

Another cognitive weakness is wrong number facts. MD children are sometimes incorrect because they have the number facts wrong, as in $2 + 2 = 5$. Wrong number facts may be extremely widespread in the work of MD children.

Still another cognitive weakness is counting errors. Occasionally the MD child miscounts, which has deleterious effects on informal or invented strategies.

Still another cognitive weakness is arbitrariness. Sometimes MD children believe that mathematical procedures are completely arbitrary, bearing no relation to reality. They are willing to accept absurd results (Patty's belief that $100 + 1 = 200$) or contradictions between incorrect written calculations and correct informal calculations, because, "That's the way you do it on paper." Thus, finger counting gets one answer, written work another, and both are acceptable.

Still another cognitive weakness is wild guess. Occasionally MD children make wild guesses, apparently without any calculation or thought, formal or informal. Perhaps anxiety and panic are major causes.

Still another cognitive weakness is misunderstanding of principle. MD children may misunderstand basic principles on an explicit, verbal level. A common misunderstanding involves place value. Thus the child fails to understand that the "1" in "13" stands for "ten." Such misunderstandings are again quite typical of normal children, despite their success on standard tests of achievement.

There is also a kind of gap or "cognitive schizophrenia" between MD children's informal and invented strategies, on the one hand, and their written calculational skills and formal understanding, on the other. That is, such children perform very poorly on written calculation and understanding of principles as taught in school, while at the same time they possess relatively sophisticated informal procedures like mental addition or invented strategies.

All these findings from the case studies — the gaps, the informal skills, and the bugs — may apply generally. Ginsburg, Posner, and Russell (1981b) used the same case study method to show that four African children experiencing learning problems display the same pattern of strengths and weaknesses and gaps as are typical of American children. Indeed, aside from a few cultural idiosyncrasies, like talk about francs, it is virtually impossible to distinguish the African children from the American. The phenomena uncovered are indeed widespread.

Further investigations were conducted to settle three other questions left unanswered by the case studies. First, the case studies suggested that school-age children with mathematics difficulties possess some degree of informal knowledge, yet they did not establish with precision the extent of this informal knowledge. Additional data were needed to show how MD children compare with normal children in various informal skills like mental addition.

Second, the case studies suggested that MD children do not exhibit unusual modes of thinking, either generally or specifically in mathematics, even though their written work sometimes gives the appearance of strangeness, at least on the surface. Thus, Butch writes $8/\overset{23}{16}$. Yet the apparently bizarre overt behavior is usually generated by sensible underlying strategies. Butch's result was obtained by a minor execution error in the process of adding 8 and 16. In general, the bugs and other forms of misunderstanding displayed by MD children seem typical of normal children. Nothing MD children do seems so unusual that it might not be done by normal children as well. Systematic data were required, however, to settle the question whether MD children suffer from various cognitive disorders, such as illogical thinking or poor memory capacity, which then result in disordered forms of mathematical cognition.

Third, the case studies suggested that MD children resemble, but do not perform as well as, normal children. It may be that math difficulty children bear a strong similarity to younger normals. Weinstein proposed a strong form of this "developmental lag" hypothesis in arguing that poor performance in mathematics may be the result of "slower development of the cognitive structures underlying the acquisition of arithmetic processes and concepts. [The] pattern of development of arithmetic competencies is said to be that of the normal child, except for the delay in their maturation" (1978:25). In this view, MD children are very much like their younger peers, in that they suffer from a developmental lag in underlying cognitive structure. Again, further data were required to shed light on this possibility. In brief, the case studies and Weinstein's work suggested as areas for systematic research comparing MD and normal children: the extent of informal knowledge, the existence of cognitive disorders, and the possibility of a developmental lag.

Russell and Ginsburg (in press) shed light on some of these issues when they investigated various aspects of mathematical thinking among fourth-grade children performing poorly in school arithmetic (grade equivalent $= 2.8$) but scoring in the normal range on IQ ($\overline{X} = 100.07$). These children were compared with fourth-grade peers, matched for IQ and performing at grade level on arithmetic, and with a randomly selected group of third graders, for whom IQ and achievement test scores were not available. There were 27 children in each of the three groups. This design permitted the comparison of MD children with normals at the same age and younger age levels.

Each child was interviewed individually in three separate sessions. The first two sessions lasted approximately 20 – 30 minutes, the last about 10 minutes. Lengthy testing was required, since each child was given several tasks in each of five areas: number skills and concepts, informal calculation, number facts, written arithmetic, and story problem solving.

Some of the data bear on the extent of informal knowledge, specifically informal addition. Each child was asked to solve eight addition problems without using paper and pencil. Two sums were under 20, two were between 20 and 50, two were between 50 and 100, and two were over 100. The third grade (TG) and MD groups were moderately accurate, with roughly equal mean accuracy scores of 5.37 and 5.18, respectively, of a possible 8. The fourth-grade control (C) group, with a mean of 6.37, was more accurate than the MD group ($p < .01$). As one might expect, children had more difficulty with the larger problems. The TG and MD groups were similar, and in absolute terms the C group was not much different from the others.

The proportional use of the various strategies for solving these addition problems (e.g. mental algorithm, counting on, regrouping) was similar among all three groups, as well as being similar to the strategies displayed by Africans. Moreover, among all three groups there was an adaptive deployment of strategies for different-sized sums. Counting on was used for about half or more of the small sums and declined in use until it was never employed for sums over 100. The mental algorithm (picturing in one's head the usual written algorithm) was used for a minority of the sums under 50 and increased in use to nearly half or more of the sums over 50. Finally, while the MD group selected adaptive strategies on most problems, these children executed the strategies with less accuracy than the C group but with similar accuracy to the TG group.

Other data bear on the issue of cognitive disorders. Subjects were examined on the use of principles, an insight task. Each child was presented with addition and subtraction problems in which commutativity of addition or the reciprocity of addition and subtraction could be used as a short cut to finding the answer, which were similar to problems originally developed by Petitto and Ginsburg (1982). Two problems involved commutativity and two involved reciprocity. Most of the children in all three groups, or 81% of the TG, 85% of the MD, and 89% of the C, used commutativity to solve at least one problem. Reciprocity was much harder, and the spread among the groups was greater; yet even here, 52% of the MD group used reciprocity at least once, while the corresponding figures for the TG and C groups were 38% and 70%, respectively. Thus, a majority of the MD group had knowledge of simple mathematical principles — commutativity and reciprocity — and were able to use it to short-cut the process of problem solving. This knowledge and this behavior are examples of insightful problem-solving (Wertheimer, 1954). The use of principles is highly "intelligent" and demonstrates that at least in this case a majority of MD children were not observed to exhibit bizarre modes of thought. In brief, with respect to mental addition and the use of principles, MD children behaved in sensible ways, showed no sign of cognitive disorders or bizarre thinking, and used strategies quite similar to those employed by normal children, but did so somewhat less efficiently.

While displaying some relatively impressive skills, MD children exhibited weaknesses in other areas. One weakness involved written calculation. MD children made more errors than C subjects and about the same number as TG. The strategies underlying the errors, such as faulty carrying algorithms, were quite similar for the MD and TG groups. Another difficulty involved elementary addition facts. Each child was asked to give quick answers to ten addition fact problems with sums under 20. The MD group, with the mean number correct of 4.74, knew somewhat fewer facts than the TG group, with a mean of 5.63, and substantially fewer than the C group, with a mean of 7.52 (all statistical comparisons were significant). Over 50% of the MD group knew only four or fewer facts, whereas 44% of the TG group and 15% of the C group knew such facts. Clearly, the MD children exhibited a serious problem with respect to memory of elementary number facts. Whether this signifies some kind of memory disorder requires further investigation.

The data bear only indirectly on the question of whether MD children suffer from a developmental lag, whereby poor performance in school mathematics is the direct result of a slow-down or retardation in underlying cognitive processes, since the study did not include measures of Piagetian operations or other basic cognitive processes. Nevertheless, MD children's performance levels on many tasks, such as number of correct responses on mental addition, were generally more similar to those of younger children than same-age peers. This developmental lag in performance should come as no surprise since by definition MD children score below the norm on standard tests. MD children also exhibited a developmental lag in the strategies underlying written calculation: MD and TG children made similar numbers of mistakes and used similar strategies to produce the mistakes. Thus, the typical MD child not only got wrong answers on written computation problems, as might be expected, but also arrived at these wrong answers through common bugs exhibited by younger children.

MD children did not necessarily exhibit a similar lag with respect to informal mathematical concepts and strategies. On at least some tasks, such as mental addition, MD children used the same strategies as normal peers but did so with less accuracy. On other tasks, such as use of principles, MD children used the same strategies (short-cuts via principles) as same-age peers but did so less frequently. There was little evidence of a lag in informal concepts. Even though their performance was retarded, MD children's mathematical cognition, particularly their informal concepts and strategies, appeared to be essentially normal. On the basis of these data and clinical experience, the strong form of the developmental lag hypothesis — namely, that retardation in basic cognitive processes, like the concrete operations, causes poor mathematics performance — is not a valid explanation for the vast majority of MD children. Further research bearing directly on the developmental lag hypothesis is necessary.

The fact that MD children lag behind in performance but not necessarily in mathematical cognition, particularly in informal skills and concepts, does not mean that there is nothing distinctive about MD children. The study showed that in at least one area, number facts, MD children seem to experience unusual difficulties. Although the reason for this is as yet unknown, some kind of memory disorder is conceivably responsible for the low level of performance. Also, clinical observation of MD children shows that they are distinctive — different from both same-age and younger normals — in at least one very important way. MD children are failing, usually know they are failing, and feel very badly about it. And the failure is not transitory; indeed, it feeds on itself and over time produces a cumulative deficit.

Conclusions

The research fails to support the view that school failure in mathematics and other areas stems from a cognitive deficit, originating in either the deprived environment or the genes. Informal knowledge of mathematics is widespread, appearing in non-Western, illiterate cultures as well as in lower-class and black preschoolers in American society. On entrance to school, those children most likely to exhibit academic failure nevertheless possess the basic concepts and techniques of informal mathematics. Later, in the context of elementary school, MD children display certain basic informal strengths, like mental addition strategies, which are similar to normal children's strategies, deployed adaptively, and executed somewhat inaccurately. Also, MD children do not seem to think in bizarre or unusual ways, for gross cognitive disorders have not been detected in these children. MD children display a developmental lag with respect to performance and the strategies for written calculation, but not necessarily with respect to informal mathematical concepts and strategies. On the whole, MD children appear to be cognitively normal and not to suffer from a lag in basic cognitive processes. MD children are distinctive in some ways, such as their poor knowledge of number facts. Perhaps more important, they differ from younger and same-age normals in their experienced and cumulative failure.

These findings suggest several new directions for both the theory of mathematical thinking and educational practice. Contemporary cognitive research has focused mainly on what might be called the "technical" aspects of mathematical cognition, such as informal concepts of more or invented strategies for written addition. Yet these technical processes cannot be considered in isolation; they are embedded within a larger psychological context. For example, Papert (1980) stressed the affective component of learning mathematics, arguing that falling in love with mathematics, or one's relationship to the subject matter, is at least as important as knowledge of the subject matter itself. This "new" emphasis on the affective context is a return to ancient themes in psychology. One of Freud's greatest works, *The Interpretation of Dreams*, was an examination of the interplay between "personality" factors — repression, id impulses — and the cognitive processes of the dream work.

Our own case studies attempted to examine mathematics difficulties within the context of emotion, cognition, and personality. Consider Arnold, a 9-year-old boy in the third grade, who was referred to the Rochester Institute of Technology clinic because of his extremely poor work in school mathematics and reading. The first exchange illustrates the role of affect:

Arnold: I usually hate math because it hurts my fingers like —
Interviewer: How does it hurt your fingers?
Arnold: I don't know. It . . . it makes my fingers feel frail. It feels like I can't write.
Interviewer: Show me how you hold the pencil. What makes it hurt?
Arnold: Like this, after, when I first start, it doesn't hurt, but when I start to learn, then it hurts. I feel like I'm going to snap the pencil in half.
Interviewer: Gets really tight?
Arnold: Yeah.

Arnold's statements to the effect that doing mathematics "makes my fingers feel frail" and "I feel like I'm going to snap the pencil in half" suggest strong affect concerning mathematics, as well as defenses for dealing with the affect. Arnold probably feels a great deal of anxiety and anger. Perhaps the anxiety finds bodily expression, and the anger is displaced to the pencil. Whatever the specific psychodynamic interpretation of these episodes, an emotional system of high power and salience is clearly operating in the case of at least some children with cognitive difficulties. For these children, the affective system and the defenses for dealing with it are paramount, and they no doubt color all activities in school mathematics. Indeed, the affect is as much a part of the mathematical activity as are the reasoning and other cognitive processes. Mathematical thinking is not simply a matter of information processing. Although anxiety and hostility are known to be disabling and to exert other major effects on intellectual work, much more needs to be known concerning the interplay between cognition and affect. Obtaining such knowledge demands a general psychological approach rather than a narrowly cognitive one.

Another exchange with Arnold illustrates the importance of cognitive style. Later he solves a problem correctly, writing the number 100 in expanded notation as $100 + 00 + 0$:

Interviewer: Okay. That's good. How did you know what to do with this stuff? What did you say to yourself?

Arnold: Well, she usually, like she does it on the board like that so you can get it.

Interviewer: Now, what did you know, how did you know to put down these numbers here?

Arnold: Hundreds.

Interviewer: Umhm.

Arnold: Well, like she says on the board, like what 139 and 149, the first number is 100, the second is 30, the last is 9.

Interviewer: So that's how you would do it then?

Arnold: The way she does it on the board.

Interviewer: So you just kind of follow along with what she does.

Arnold: Yeah.

This episode suggests that Arnold's thinking is heavily influenced by authority figures. He minimizes his own contribution and stresses that of the teacher. Although many children take this approach and the schools encourage it, Arnold carries it to an extreme. He often does things not because he understands them or wants to do them but because the teacher tells him to. While inferences concerning "reliance on adult authority" are risky, they make a good deal of sense. The difficulty of obtaining conclusive evidence in this area does not indicate that the phenomenon is unimportant. The phenomenon is one of cognitive style, which is a characteristic of cognitive function or is perhaps the "personality of cognition." In Arnold's case, cognitive style may be conceptualized as an overall plan to the effect that, "I do things as the teacher says; my thought is not my own." To provide a link between personality and cognition requires reexamining notions like cognitive style. The clinical interview method may prove to be an effective technique for exploring cognitive style within domains of academic knowledge like mathematics.

The next exchange illustrates the role of metacognition in Arnold's work:

Interviewer: Now you said you'd show me the things you were doing in school in math.
Arnold: Well, usually, like, um, well, I'm not sure of the things we do.

Arnold may have formed an accurate assessment of his own abilities, for he is generally "not sure of the things we do." Or perhaps he also has a low level of self-confidence.

In a later exchange, Arnold provides a clear and presumably accurate account of his problem-solving procedures. After solving $42 + 31$, he is questioned about his strategy:

Interviewer: Good. Now you got the 3 pretty fast and you had to wait a minute to get the 7. How'd you get the 3 really fast?
Arnold: Well, $1 + 2$ is 3. It's easy.
Interviewer: How about $4 + 3$? How'd you get that answer?
Arnold: Well, I counted.

Arnold then explains his method, which essentially involves counting on from the larger number. In this case Arnold not only distinguishes between his direct memory procedure for $1 + 2$ and his counting on procedure for $4 + 3$ but also knows which is easier.

That Arnold is so articulate about his problem solving and can make realistic judgments of difficulty is surprising. The finding raises questions concerning the processes of metacognition, which according to Brown (1978) play an important role in cognitive development. In general, more needs to be known about how the processes of metacognition function within the overall problem-solving activities of both normal and MD children. Is it useful, for example, to be able to introspect on one's calculational procedures? How and why does self-knowledge develop within the larger context of mathematical cognition? Do MD children display a distinctive pattern of performance in this area?

Another exchange illustrates the learning potential of MD children. In the course of the interview the examiner introduces problems involving simple series, such as, "What comes after 2, 4, 6?" With some effort, Arnold is able to use a counting procedure to solve problems involving increments of two. Most likely the counting method is his own invention, although it may have been taught in school. In any event, Arnold is unable to use the method consistently and accurately for increments of 3, as in 2, 5, 8. The interviewer then instructs Arnold how to extend his counting method to the new situation, and Arnold rapidly learns the generalization.

The topic of learning potential is too often slighted in cognitive developmental psychology, where most research focuses on questions of cognitive process or structure, such as, what do the children know about addition when they enter school, or how do they understand place value? In general, more questions should be asked about learning potential. For example, what can a child at a given point in development actually learn? Or to what extent is poor performance the result of poor environmental conditions or inadequate motivation, as opposed to a genuine learning disability? From a practical, educational point of view, learning potential is the main issue. The basic question for any educational system is not what children now know or how they currently solve problems but whether and how easily they can learn. Yet no literature directly investigates the issue of whether and how children with mathematics difficulties can learn! Brown and French (1979), Feuerstein (1980), and Papert (1980) have recently stressed the necessity for research into issues like these, and we concur. Notions like the zone of proximal development (Vygotsky, 1978), scaffolding theory (Greenfield, this volume), and the social context of learning (Rogoff & Gardner, this volume) may prove useful. Theorizing, in short, must go beyond the technical aspects of mathematical thinking to consider such matters as affect, style, metacognition, and learning potential.

Finally, our work has several implications for the ways in which psychologists can contribute to educational practice. First, diagnostic procedures must be drastically revised. Standard tests like the Key Math may not be well suited, both methodologically and theoretically, to reveal the complexity of children's mathematical thinking. Standard administration is often too rigid to capture the complexity of mathematical cognition. The notions of computational skill or quantitative ability which underlie many standard tests appear outmoded, vague, and of little practical use. Instead of employing standard tests, diagnosis should employ flexible methods, like the clinical interview, which for the purpose of describing cognitive process are generally superior to the standard test. Further, the diagnosis needs to be based on modern theories of children's mathematical cognition. Diagnosis should focus on cognitive processes like informal skills, error strategies, and invented procedures. Above all, diagnosis needs to be sensitive to children's intellectual strengths and cognitive complexity. The work of developmental psychologists can make an important contribution to the creation of more effective diagnostic procedures.

A second implication has to do with improvement of the educational system. Our research suggests that the vast majority of MD children do not suffer from deep-rooted cognitive deficits or fundamental disorders of mathematical thinking. On the contrary, MD children possess informal mathematical concepts and skills and, in general, appear to be cognitively normal. This is not to deny that a small percentage of MD children may suffer from genuine and severe cognitive deficiencies, neurological disorders, and even "learning disabilities." If this view of MD children is correct, a major contribution to mathematics difficulties is made by schooling itself, defined in the broad sense to include teaching, tests, textbooks, school atmosphere, and social values. The majority of children experience difficulties primarily because of inadequacies in teaching, curriculum, textbooks, and the educational system generally. While the result is cognitive, namely poor knowledge of mathematics, the basic causes may be educational. One does not need research to demonstrate that textbooks are often confusing and mathematically inaccurate; children with varied needs and knowledge are taught in the same, rigid way; schools frequently discourage independent thinking and idiosyncratic styles; and many teachers are themselves uncomfortable with school mathematics and would much prefer to be teaching something else. The failure of American mathematics education is obvious. Is there any doubt that it is a major cause of learning difficulties?

Given this analysis, several approaches to helping children with mathematics difficulties seem not to be fruitful. One involves the use of psychological diagnosis to blame and abandon the victim. The child is given intelligence tests, Benders, and other diagnostic instruments. The psychologist, having inferred that the child suffers from cognitive defect X, reaches the explicit conclusion that he cannot learn mathematics at the normal level and makes the implicit conclusion that the school is not to blame for the child's situation. This approach mainly stigmatizes the child and does little to help him. A related approach is to follow the diagnosis of defect X with cognitive treatment designed to remove it. Thus, if the child is diagnosed as suffering from retardation of the concrete operations, she may then be given remedial training in them. This approach may be useful for some children insofar as the diagnosis of cognitive defect is correct and insofar as the defect is directly related to mathematics learning problems. But since most MD children do not suffer from any basic cognitive deficit, removing one is quite beside the point. These children are not cognitively defective; they are poorly educated.

MD children need something else altogether. They need good education—to be taught mathematics properly from the outset. And if they get into difficulty, they need suitable remedial instruction. The longer the children experience difficulty, the harder it will be to provide effective remedial treatment. But the solution—however difficult it may be—should be mainly educational, not psychological.

The primary burden of creating effective educational environments lies on educators. But one way in which psychologists may assist is to emphasize the study of learning potential in stimulating environments rather than focusing on cognitive deficits in the current, defective environment. As Papert (1980) points out, studying how the current system is deficient or how children in it function poorly may be basically irrelevant to improving children's lot, and, in fact, may imply a commitment to preserving the status quo. Instead, psychologists may help by providing knowledge of how MD children could learn under a different system. Psychologists can examine what is now usually undeveloped, hidden, or suppressed—children's learning potential—and what may emerge in radically new environments, such as those suggested by Papert or Feuerstein (1980). Math difficulty children's intellect is fundamentally sound. By studying what they can do in a favorable situation, psychologists can make a real contribution to education.

10. Children's Reasoning and Peer Relations

David Lubin
David Forbes

The development of peer relations is a universally recognized aspect of socialization in humans and animals alike. Social scientists have recently made serious efforts to understand this developmental process by investigating how children comprehend and act in their social world (Hoffman, 1977; Forbes, 1978; Hartup, 1978). The study of social cognition, a field essentially unknown in the 1960s, has taken a central position in developmental psychology. Investigations of children's social behavior, an enterprise neglected since the child study movement of the 1930s, have reemerged as an important and fertile area. Recognizing that meaningful relations must exist between the development of organized behavior and the development of cognitive regulation, investigators have also begun to assess both social behavior and social reasoning, in the hope of describing how these two areas of development are intertwined.

Shantz (1975) distinguished two approaches to this line of synthetic inquiry. In one, independently formulated measures of social cognition and social behavior are administered to children, and the correlational relationships between these measures are examined. In the other approach, targeted children who are experiencing difficulties in their peer relations are trained in selected social cognitive skills, and the effects of training are assessed in terms of observable behavioral changes. Others have demonstrated reliable correlations between reasoning and behavior by abandoning the relatively global reasoning and behavior constructs, such as egocentrism and altruism, used in past work and focusing instead on carefully delineated variables, such as the relation of understanding distributive justice concepts to actual distribution of rewards, or the relation of conceptualizing relations between social behaviors and internal psychological states to strategies of persuasion (Clark & Delia, 1976; Damon, 1977; Delia, Kline & Burleson, 1979; Haslett, 1980; Forbes & Lubin, in press). Training efforts have shown increased success, particularly when social learning models guide the modification of children's social behavior (Cooke & Apolloni, 1976; Bornstein et al., 1977; Oden & Asher, 1977).

A research project was undertaken to explore this problem of synthesizing diverse cognitive and behavioral findings within a general theory about the role of cognitive regulation in the construction of organized behavior. It was designed around concepts of theoretical psychology that lend themselves to the generation of a conceptually integrated program for the study of relations between reasoning and behavior, for which the most general covering term is "planfulness" (Werner, 1948; Piaget, 1950; Miller, Galanter & Pribram, 1960; Bruner, 1974; Schank & Abelson, 1977). The study examined planfulness in the social reasoning and action of five- and seven-year-old children, who were brought together in laboratory play groups for the purpose of "getting acquainted."

Because the study was based on the view that social behavior is a goal-oriented activity, the phenomena selected for study were thought to reflect an individual's pursuit of identifiable social goals. Some of these phenomena involved "third-party entry" episodes, as in the case of a child approaching and attempting to join two or more other children who are already at play. These episodes were thought to be easily assimilated to the notion of a goal-directed sequence of social interaction, and thus the behavior in these episodes was examined as a strategic element of planful interaction. Third-party entry episodes were also chosen for study because they are a frequently occurring and important aspect of peer relations (Corsaro, 1979; Putallaz & Gottman, 1981; Forbes, Katz & Paul, 1982).

Another focus of behavioral investigation was the larger process of peer-group formation. The fact that the children in the study were initially unfamiliar with each other provided the opportunity to examine temporal patterns of isolation and affiliation which reflect children's integration into their play group. This variable too could indicate children's responses to a social problem, that of becoming acquainted. The study showed how patterns of affiliation during the acquaintanceship process may reflect developmental changes in children's conceptions of the nature of friendship, especially the role that psychological intimacy plays in relations with friends (Forbes & Katz, in preparation).

Social reasoning was also examined in the study, as the mechanism of cybernetic regulation, and specific social-cognitive skills were delineated for assessment on the basis of their distinctive contribution to a general process of planning. These social reasoning skills derived from the basic distinction between "test" processes, aimed at evaluation of the environment, and "operate" processes, directed at formulation of action plans (Miller et al., 1960). The procedures called "interpretive" in the study, which were analogues of Miller et al.'s test processes, consisted of skills needed for evaluating the social environment, including decisions about the need to employ certain plans during social interaction and evaluations of feedback from the social environment about the impact of social actions. The procedures called "operative" in the study, which were analogues of operate processes, consisted of skills needed for carrying out social action, including accumulated knowledge of past outcomes for particular action strategies and general principles for deciding between alternative strategies for particular persons and contexts.

Two specific skills were considered. One was "script knowledge," an operative procedure, defined as children's ability to construct strategies for solving hypothetical social problems and to explain why they think their chosen strategies might work. The other skill was "psychological inference," an interpretive procedure, defined as children's ability to infer internal states of specific individuals, based upon witnessing social interactions in which those individuals are engaged. The social reasoning assessments, which utilized videotapes of actual social interactions, provided the opportunity to make the interview stimuli approximate as closely as possible the phenomena to which a child's attention was directed during actual social interaction.

In previous reports we have identified a variety of features of children's behavioral organization and related them within a developmental perspective to levels of script knowledge and of psychological inference (Forbes & Lubin, 1981a, 1981b; Forbes, Katz & Paul, in press). There were age-related increases in children's ability to provide scripts for common social events and to make inferences about the thoughts and feelings of others involved in social interactions. Relationships were also found between the psychological inference skill and one other important form of children's social interaction, interpersonal persuasion. Two other phenomena that are less clearly tied to emerging cognitive capacities nonetheless emerged as important influences on children's planful social action. One was age-related changes in the motives that guide children's planning in the third-party entry situation, based on the behaviors with which children typically initiate an entry attempt (Forbes, Katz & Paul, 1982). The other phenomenon was the existence of peer cultures among children of different age groups, within which optimal social behavior appears to derive from regulation via age-normal levels of social reasoning ability rather than via the highest levels in an absolute sense.

Methodology

Subjects in the study were twenty-four children drawn from kindergarten and second-grade classrooms in the Cambridge, Massachusetts, public school system. Four play groups were composed of six children each, three males and three females. Two of the play groups consisted of five-year-old children (ranging from 4 years 9 months to 5 years 3 months) and two groups consisted of seven-year-olds (ranging from 6 years 9 months to 7 years 3 months). Children were of mixed racial and socioeconomic groups, with parent occupations ranging from blue collar to professional. Each play group was composed of children who had had no contact with one another prior to the investigation. Parents of children in the study were asked not to allow outside contact between their child and other play-group members until the study was completed.

The children met for free-play sessions one hour per day four times per week for three weeks, totaling twelve hours of play time for each group. The groups met in a large playroom with age-appropriate toys and games selected by a teacher consultant who supervised each session. Generally, this teacher remained in a small kitchenette adjoining the actual play area and did not intervene in the play activity except to provide new materials and occasionally to prevent physical injury or property damage. All behavior during the play-group sessions was recorded on a custom-designed surveillance system which allowed for individual access on playback to the record of each child's verbalizations, while providing three camera views of all play-group action. The resulting data were of the best possible quality for subsequent coding of the subjects' social interaction and for the use of edited videotapes as stimuli in social reasoning interviews.

The behavioral data of the study were of two types: third-party entry sequences and behavioral sociometric data reflecting the integration of the child into the group (Forbes, Lubin & Anderegg, 1980). A third-party entry sequence was defined as any occasion in which a child physically approached a group of two or more children, with or without verbally addressing them, and appeared to seek entry into the group activity. Third-party entry sequences terminated when a child exchanged more than one round of interaction with the group that was related to the group's activity, or when the child left the area of the group. Using this definition, trained coders located 824 sequences in the videotape records. Of these sequences, 205 were discarded from the analysis because they involved approaches to the snack table, where access was guaranteed by group rules, or they involved sequences in which the child's bid for entry was mediated by the teacher. There remained for analysis 619 episodes of third-party entry.

Each third-party entry sequence was coded in several ways (Forbes, Lubin & Anderegg, 1980). First, the initial attempt and all subsequent attempts of the entrant child to join the group were recorded. For each entry attempt made by a child, the response of the group was also recorded as being positive, negative, neutral, or unclear to the coder. And the final outcome of the entry attempt was coded, in terms of the possible relationships that could eventuate between the entrant child and the group.

The coding of children's integration patterns during the play groups was documented by using a "scan sampling" technique (Altmann, 1974). Children's social involvement was recorded every minute on the minute throughout all twelve hours of play-group activity. Codes included whether or not the child was at play with others, who those others were, and what the status of the child was in the outgoing activity.

Social reasoning assessments were based on interviews. Prior to the beginning of the play-group sessions, the children were each administered an interview that tapped their script knowledge. This interview elicited the children's suggestions of behavior which they might do in four typical peer situations: making overtures to unfamiliar peers, distributing play materials, constructing themes for play, and negotiating entry into an ongoing group of children at play. After completion of the twelve play-group sessions, the children were each administered another interview aimed at evaluating their psychological inference. This interview utilized a standardized videotape stimulus depicting unfamiliar children interacting in the four peer situations that had been examined in the script-knowledge interview. This tape was a carefully edited seven-minute synopsis of approximately twenty minutes of interaction, designed to provide optimal facial views and audio records of the stimulus social interaction.

The tape was first played uninterrupted for the interview subjects, to create familiarity with the stimulus and lessen the memory demands of the interview task. The tape was then reshown to the subjects with pauses at predetermined points, when a still-frame portrait of the action appeared on the screen for later reference by the children during the interview inquiry. At that interview the children were asked to make inferences about the thoughts, feelings, and intentions of the children, in the course of the social interaction depicted on the television screen. The interview focused on eliciting explanations for the children's inferences in terms of the relationships that they could posit between the actions they had observed and the psychological states they had inferred.

The scoring of both types of social reasoning interview focused on how children understood the relations between a social action or action sequence on the part of one child and a psychological reaction on the part of a second, target child. The form of their understanding was inferred from verbal explanations that they had to make in each of the two interview tasks. Children's explanations of why they thought a particular behavior strategy would produce a desired effect were scored from the script knowledge interview, and children's explanations of why a particular pattern in observed social interaction might give rise to a certain type of thought or feeling state on the part of the interactants were scored from the psychological inference interview.

There were three levels for scoring of social reasoning assessments. The first level was mechanistic sterotypy. At this level the child appeared to posit a mechanistic one-to-one relation between environmental events and individuals' psychological reactions. The child thought that all persons perceive a social behavior in the same fashion, think the same thoughts about the person who did the behavior, and have the same feeling states as a result of experiencing the behavior. Thus the child had a "naive realistic" conception of behavioral phenomena, thinking that the behavior had only one significance independent of the observer. The child also had a "mechanistic" conception of how behavior gives rise to psychological reactions in those who witness it, thinking that variance in individuals' psychological states derives from external determination in "real" events. The mechanistic sterotypy of level one may in fact have been a product of egocentrism. That is, children may have felt that all persons view and react to events as they do.

The second level was reactive subjectivism. At this level the simple mechanistic relation between environmental events and individual psychological reactions had been transformed via the recognition that reactions to events may differ from person to person. Subjects at level two acknowledged that different persons may have a variety of feelings in reaction to social behavior and may think various things about the individual who exhibited the behavior. Subjects still, however, possessed a naive realism concerning the status of the environmental event. That is, they still regarded their interpretation of the meaning of a social behavior as the "real" one. In other words, children at level two acknowledged individual variance in affective or evaluative reactions to a social behavior but still assumed invariance regarding interpretative reactions, namely constructions of the event.

The third level was constructive subjectivism. At this level the subjectivism of level two has been transformed, based on the child's newly acquired conviction that not only affective or evaluative reaction but also interpretation of social behaviors can vary from person to person. In some sense, the level three child was acquiring the rudiments of a "constructivist epistemology," which placed the perception of events, as well as reactions to events, within the domain of subjectivity. At level three the person-environment relation was truly a subjective one, with the environment providing the aliment giving rise to the individuals' reactions, but with the individuals' subjectivity playing a role in defining "reality" from their perspective. Thus at level three not only the impact but also the meaning of a social behavior was a subjective and interpersonally variant phenomena.

The total range of measures used for the study are summarized as follows:

1. Behavioral Measures
   A. Behavioral Sociometric: Scan sample of affiliation patterns on minute-by-minute basis yielding a weekly participation score for each subject.
   B. Third-party Entry Coding: Event sampling of entry sequences yielding record of entry strategy and response to entry strategy and outcome of episode for each event.
2. Reasoning Measures
   A. Psychological Inference Assessment: Video-based interview taps structure of explanation of children's inferences about thoughts and feelings of others depicted in interaction.
   B. Script Knowledge Assessment: Hypothetical interview taps explanations of efficacy of children's strategies for interacting with others in problematic social situations.

Age-related Change in Entry Behavior

The children's bids for group entry took different forms at the two ages of five and seven. In particular, the study showed a distinction between "direct" and "indirect" strategies for gaining entry into a group. A direct entry bid was one in which the children's behavior made explicit their desire to join the group. An indirect bid, in contrast, avoided direct announcement of a group entry goal by pursuing more casual interaction with group members. In the entry bid coding scheme, direct bids included "asks to join," "suggests role for self in group activity," "offers incentives for group acceptance," "suggests new activity for self and group," and "directly enters play." Indirect entry bids included "gives information about self," "seeks information about other," "asks instrumental question," "makes instrumental comment," and "approaches and observes."

In a study of children's third-party entry strategies in preschool and early childhood years, Corsaro (1979) documented an age-related change in the use of direct versus indirect entry bids, with the latter replacing the former as age increases. The use of indirect bids by children might be explained as an adaptation to the low probability of success in group entry. That is, such strategies are chosen because they are low-risk strategies in a relatively high-risk situation.

Sullivan (1953) characterized the juvenile period of social development, from about seven to nine or ten years, as a time when peer status becomes especially important to children. Prior to seven, the children's orientation is more toward simply participating in peer play rather than toward gaining the psychological acceptance of their peers. If these motivational values of peer acceptance are correct, then the choice of low-risk strategies can be seen as a reflection of age differences which are primarily motivational in nature. That is, the increased salience of peer acceptance or rejection in older children may lead them to perceive greater psychological risk in the entry situation and hence to use indirect bids that minimize risk.

The study clearly supported the notion that older children show increased reliance on indirect entry bids. The ratio of direct to indirect bids used by the two age groups was such that 80% of the five-year-old children fell above the mean for the total sample, while 75% of the seven-year-old children fell below this grand mean. Evaluation of this pattern using a chi-squared procedure yields a significant relationship between age and entry bid type $(x^2 = 8.22 \ p < .01)$.

Other data related to older children's use of indirect bias involved responses made by the children to negative feedback from the group being approached. In children's responses to initially negative feedback to an entry bid, five-year-old children tended to respond to negative feedback by simply proceeding "as if" it did not occur; that is, they made little or no attempt to address the issue of resistance. For example, the most frequent strategy employed in response to negative feedback in the five-year-old group was to ignore the response and repeat previous requests or move to another bid in which the desire to affiliate with the group remained clear. The ignore and move-in strategy accounted for 65% of all negative feedback sequences among five-year-olds and 47% of all sequences in the seven-year-old group. Failure to meet statistical assumptions made significance testing of this difference unadvisable.

The other strategies were status-maintaining moves, in the sense of either choosing to leave or saving face. That is, following the receipt of negative feedback, the children either criticized others in the group or asserted superior qualities of self. In both of these cases the children attempted to maintain their status by either devaluing the group and its rejection or making their departure from the group appear voluntary. In the five-year-old group these strategies accounted for only 17% of all sequences. Seven-year-olds employed such strategies more frequently, to the extent that choosing to leave and face-saving accounted for 37% of all sequences, or more than double the frequency in the five-year-old group. Again, failure to meet statistical assumptions made significance testing of this difference unadvisable.

These data indicate that the five-year-old children and the seven-year-old children were indeed motivated differently in the third-party entry situation. The seven-year-olds relied far more heavily on indirect strategies for entering groups. There were no differences in success rates between the five- and seven-year-olds; for both groups, entry attempts were successful about 30–35% of the time. Thus, the two groups were differentially affected by the risky quality of third-party entry situations. That is, the seven-year-old children recognized that they might not succeed in gaining entry and used their superior power of regulating behavior not to pursue the goal of gaining entry through a strategic choice of moves, but to create uncertainty about whether or not entry was desired via indirect overtures. In so doing, they attempted to enter or exit the scene sideways, creating uncertainty about whether or not entry was desired. They were therefore able to preserve status in the face of possible rebuff, while still pursuing the goal of group entry.

The children's responses to negative feedback regarding their entry bids also supported the notion of differential motivation in the third-party entry situation. While the five-year-old subjects tended to ignore this feedback and proceeded as if it was not received, the seven-year-old subjects were far more likely to respond to the negative feedback by saving face or choosing to leave — behaviors that preserved social status in what had become an increasingly "risky" encounter. This form of responding in the seven-year-old sample may be viewed as working hand in hand with the use of indirect entry bids, motivated by an overarching desire to preserve status in peer affiliation situations.

On an intuitive level, most people are familiar with the indirect bid. In the adult social world, a young man who approaches a young woman in the park with the question, "Do you have the time?" is recognized as potentially employing the indirect approach. In so doing, he evokes some behavior from the young woman, and this behavior contains information which allows both actors to decide if this will be a simple request and response or the beginning of a conversation. The curt response "12:30" will signal to the young man that the young woman is not interested in providing anything more than the time and that, if he is to keep his pride intact, he would do best to define her response as satisfying his request in full.

This feature of social relations is called the "creation and management of ambiguity." From the planfulness perspective, the use of indirect bids in entry attempts has the goal of simply eliciting more behavior from those approached. The behavioral rule becomes: if you don't have enough information to decide, then proceed in a manner which cloaks the goal under consideration. In creating a smokescreen, people allow the individual approached to provide them with an opportunity to make inferences about how they have defined their goals in the situation and, most important, how they feel about those goals. Thus, the event can be defined only at its conclusion, and the events that transpire will allow the participants to create the definition. Ambiguity is used by the actors to ease the anxiety-provoking aspects associated with acceptance and rejection: status can be maintained without sacrificing opportunities to explore the social environment.

The behavior patterns observed in the study might have been described as the result of cognitive rather than motivational changes. Older children are generally more able to infer others' thoughts about self (Shantz, 1975), and this increased awareness of what others are thinking (in the study, that other children did not want the subjects to join them) might result in an increased sensitivity to the risky nature of the third-party entry. But while such an explanation might have adequately described the thoughts of the children, to account for the relations between their ability to evaluate the situation and their tendency to select a particular type of response required a motivational analysis (Sullivan, 1953). The differences between the five- and seven-year-olds thus resulted from an increased awareness of the thoughts and feelings of others and a heightened sensitivity to maintaining status in the peer group.

Impact of Social Context on Behavior Regulation

Behavior regulation is an interactive process in which individuals work together to create one definition of their moment-to-moment relationship. Interaction involves the exchange of information which is embedded in a variety of social cues and messages. This information is encoded by senders and decoded for interpretation by receivers. When information is encoded by senders they typically take into account the decoding ability of the receivers and modify the change so that it can be understood. Typically this kind of modification takes place when there is a discrepancy between the communicative competence of the participants and when there is a desire to have the message understood. Most often the modification is made by the more competent to assist the less sophisticated in comprehending the message sent (Shatz & Gelman, 1973).

However, not all components of messages in social interaction are intentionally sent. There is a phenomenon of "leakage" in social interaction, whereby an individual unwittingly sends messages in an everyday interaction that are likely, if received by the target, to be at odds with the verbal communication (Eckman & Friesen, 1969; Rosenthal, 1979). Typically, leakage is composed of negative reactions to another that the actor does not intend to communicate, which belie the intended veneer of another's polite and friendly exchange. Such events are common in everyday life. When a friend recently asked us if we liked the new woman in his life, we answered, "Oh, sure, you look like you're just right for each other." We were obviously "leaking," since the friend then asked what it was about her that we disliked. From an interactive perspective, the problem of leakage becomes real only if the unintended message is received and comprehended by the target. This situation is most likely to occur when one individual is a less competent communicator and therefore more leaky and the other individual is more sensitive to subtle messages and therefore more likely to receive the unintended message.

On this interactive aspect of the leakage phenomenon, Rosenthal (1979) suggested that individuals scoring high on their ability to read subtle nonverbal cues experience problems in social relations. In a sense these individuals "over-read" the information, either detecting and processing unintentionally leaked information that is negative in character or reading such information into social exchanges where it may not exist. The problem of over-reading in third-party entry appeared in the study when a child, upon approaching a group and receiving "neutral" or "unclear" feedback from that group, abruptly abandoned the entry attempt or otherwise failed to join the group, despite the absence of negative feed-back. Such a pattern was expected to be more likely in children who scored high on the measure of psychological inference relative to their age group, since these children were better able to process subtle social cues, or leaked information, than were their less sophisticated age mates to control the leakage of such cues.

The ability to infer the thoughts and feelings of others was also expected to encompass the capacity to detect leakage in social situations like the third-party entry. Therefore, children scoring relatively high for their age group were compared with children scoring at or below the norm for their age group on the psychological inference assessment. The success of entry episodes for these two groups of children was examined in cases where the child received no explicit negative feedback but rather a response that the coder could not classify as either negative or positive.

There was indeed a significant relationship between being relatively high on psychological inference and being below the mean rate of group entry following unclear/neutral feedback. Of the eight children scoring high relative to their age group on psychological inference, six fell below their age-group mean for entry in the unclear/neutral feedback situation. Of the sixteen children scoring relatively average or low on the psychological inference measure, thirteen were above the age-group mean for entry in the unclear/neutral feedback situation. This 2×2 matrix results in a Fisher Exact Probability equal to .02.

The problem of over-reading, which appeared to be responsible for aborting entry attempts, was expected to lead to high levels of isolation in these children. Moreover, a problem of "under-reading" was expected to lead children relatively low in psychological inference ability to be too unresponsive to the social signals of their peers and to experience more isolation as a result. Thus, children classified as either high or low on the psychological inference measure relative to their age group — that is, as over-readers and under-readers — were expected to experience higher levels of isolation in the play groups than those whose ability to read cues matched their peer group. Furthermore, this effect was expected to be most pronounced in the early phase of acquaintance, at which time children rely more on moment-to-moment inferences for understanding of others, since little or no prior experience exists.

To examine this question, analysis was made of the behavioral sociometric data that indexed the amount of time a child spent alone in each third of the play-group data, thus generating a weekly participation rate for each child. The level of isolation, or percentage of time alone, during the first week of play-group sessions was calculated for each of the subjects classified as relatively high, average, or low on the psychological inference measure (Table 10.1). As the data indicate, there was indeed a curvilinear trend. In all twenty-four subjects, there were only two violations of the expected results. One high-scoring five-year-old and one high-scoring seven-year-old were less isolated than the most isolated child scoring average on the psychological inference measure in their respective age groups.

In all cases, subjects who were most isolated within their play groups had psychological inference skills that were either relatively higher or lower than those of their group. In six of eight cases, children who were least isolated were matched with their peer group in psychological inference skills. The Fisher Exact Probability for this distribution is .005, which represents strong support for the curvilinear hypothesis.

Table 10.1. Relative psychological inference scores and degree of isolation (% time alone) during Week I.

High		Medium		Low	
Subj.	%	Subj.	%	Subj.	%
		Seven-year-old			
43	38	44	19	41	25
46	35	45	23	42	28
64	24	61	14	63	38
66	8	62	24		
		65	9		
	$\bar{x} = 26$		$\bar{x} = 18$		$\bar{x} = 30$
		Five-year-old			
33	46	34	14	31	37
54	26	36	15	32	57
55	20	52	23	35	24
51	24	56	20	53	48
	$\bar{x} = 29$		$\bar{x} = 18$		$\bar{x} = 42$

The curvilinear pattern in the psychological inference data contrasts with the data concerning levels of script knowledge and children's degree of isolation. Psychological inference is typically employed in the reactive process of interpretation. Greater sensitivity to another's social communications may indeed bring an individual into contact with the unintended message and thereby create problems for the individual. By contrast, script knowledge is proactive in nature (Schank & Abelson, 1977). It is relevant to the formulation of action plans and therefore not tied directly to messages received from others. The problem of leakage has no parallel that is directly related to the process of scripting. Therefore, higher levels of script knowledge were expected to allow for greater flexibility in interactions with peers and thus to be important in helping children establish contact with their peers. The benefit of high levels of script knowledge was expected to be most apparent in the first week of play-group sessions when children must rely primarily on generalized scripts in their relations with unfamiliar others.

The degree of isolation was calculated for each subject classified as relatively high, medium, or low on the script knowledge measure (Table 10.2). The group as a whole provided some support for a linear relationship between children's script knowledge and their

Table 10.2. Children's age-relative script knowledge scores and degree of isolation (% time alone) during Week I.

High		Medium		Low	
Subj.	%	Subj.	%	Subj.	%
36	15	41	25	31	37
44	19	42	28	32	57
51	24	46	35	33	46
62	24	54	26	34	14
65	9	55	20	35	24
66	8	56	20	43	38
	$\bar{x} = 16.5$	63	38	45	23
		64	24	52	23
			$\bar{x} = 27$	53	48
				61	14
					$\bar{x} = 32.4$

level of integration into the group, although the picture is complicated. All of the children scoring high on the measure of script knowledge had levels of isolation that were lower than the average for the medium-script children. Six of the eight children scoring medium on script knowledge spent less time alone than the average for the low script-knowledge group. Four of the six least-isolated children scored low on the script-knowledge measure. However, there was great variation in levels of isolation among the children who scored low on script knowledge, with some children in the group showing very low levels of isolation in spite of their lack of script knowledge. Consequently, script knowledge was not a significant correlate of isolation in the peer group, although to the degree that it was involved, this involvement took the form of a linear relationship rather than a curvilinear relationship, as in the case of psychological inference. When the children's isolation scores were ranked, six of the nine rank violations of linearity between script knowledge and isolation occurred in the five-year-olds, suggesting that perhaps the relationship between script knowledge and isolation is least strong at this age.

Thus, while psychological inference appears to function in a complex manner in terms of its relation to behavioral outcomes, such may not be the case for script knowledge. Over-reading of cues seems to be a danger of highly developed interpretive ability, and its outcome is not dissimilar from that of under-reading, with the latter's more usually accepted pejorative tone. Taken in combination with the probabilities of eventual acceptance in a third-party entry when feedback is neutral or unclear, the problem of over-reading is likely to be displayed by the high-inference subjects.

Since there is an age effect in the measure of psychological inference, the fact that a five-year-old had a lower absolute ability to make psychological inferences than seven-year-olds might still classify the five-year-old child as high for that age group. The results indicate that over-reading is still a problem for a five-year-old child, despite a lower absolute score in comparison with the seven-year-olds. Perhaps the levels of leakage are also greater at the younger age; that is, the peer group of five-year-olds may show greater levels of unintended negative feedback. If so, the lower absolute levels of psychological inference would still lead to maladaptation in the five-year-old group.

Conclusions

This study showed that some relations between children's social reasoning and behavior lie outside the domain of development in the formal sense of that term. These findings contrast with most descriptions of children's socialization, which place a heavy emphasis on age-related changes that can be described as a sequential unfolding of increasingly complex forms of thought or action, each of which is logically related to its successor in a hierarchical fashion. This structural developmental perspective is an important one for child socialization, and the bulk of research should probably be done within this framework. However, other phenomena in children's social psychology also deserve attention.

Two very different avenues of research may serve as supplements to the structural developmental approach. Our findings on children's third-party entry behavior indicate a need to study changing child motivation over age vis-à-vis social encounters and to relate some patterns of behavior change observed in maturing children to changes in motivation. Understanding the changing motivational background in which children apply their social skills is as important as understanding structural developments in the skills themselves.

Our findings on relations between children's psychological inference ability and their levels of isolation in a group of unfamiliar peers illustrate that the advent of structural maturation *per se* does not always imply increased adaptation for the child. These data suggest the importance of defining adaptedness in relation to a social context and recognizing that increased sophistication of thought or action in purely structural terms may not always imply increased adaptedness in every social setting, especially in settings which are themselves characterized by immaturity in structural terms. In a situation like that in which the five-year-olds in the study found themselves, for example, the possession of skill at reading the nonverbal cues of others and making inferences about their internal psychological states can prove to be a handicap. Sophistication in the social reasoning ability of young children can lead them to make attributions on the basis of behavior in another person that is not under the other's intentional control and perhaps to receive messages that the other does not intend them to receive. Ignorance may indeed be bliss in circumstances like this, where optimal social adaptation may require that children not possess reasoning skills which exceed the capacity of their peers for intentional control of social behavior. The data thus indicate a need to study the adaptative value of less sophisticated modes of thought or action *per se*, as these may represent coordinated systems of competence within a peer culture that is immature, rather than limiting studies to a structural perspective which often views lower levels of organizations as only way-stations on the route to higher ones.

11. Cognitive Development in Time and Space

Sheldon H. White
Alexander W. Siegel

The study of cognitive development has traditionally been confined to two kinds of places, the arranged environments of experimental rooms and classrooms. Children's performances in these places reveal changes with age in learning, memory, conceptualization, language, reasoning, and problem solving. Usually, such changes with age are interpreted by presumptive mechanisms of cognitive growth and quasi-embryological structural development.

Yet other obvious and important facts about the everyday lives of children deserve attention. Children travel from place to place in their everyday environment. Cognitive changes in growing children depend upon both the functional needs imposed upon them during this process of travel and the requirements of cooperation with people near and far that children experience as they come out into adult society. We discuss in this chapter the cognitive development of children moving among natural contexts of human interaction distributed across space and time. To approach cognitive development in this way requires modification of certain assumptions about what cognitive development is and what its proper study should entail.

· The central issues of research on children's cognitive development over the last decade have centered upon the fact or the promise of structural models of logical and linguistic competence. The structural development of competence, it has been argued, must be adaptive. But such arguments have never been very specific about adaptation for *what*. The research movements of the last ten years have been woefully short of efforts to explore those contexts toward which adaptation is directed. Life is not predominantly a matter of getting along in school classrooms or experimental rooms. A new functionalism is needed, which includes a broad analysis of the contexts of children's behavior.

· The contexts in which children live are, with minor exceptions, social contexts. Children in experimental rooms and classrooms are not engaged in solitary achievement. They are working with other humans. To abstract the cognitive part of a social encounter imperils the texture and meaning of the cognitive phenomena. To understand cognitive development across time and space requires seeing it as deeply embedded in a social world of occasions, formalities, etiquettes, and dramaturgy.

· Linked with traditional notions of a generic cognitive and language development in children are parallel notions of a generic socialization. Socialization is treated as a universal process through which all children in a society acquire a common stock of knowledge, attitudes, beliefs, and customs. But this is a superficial view of what happens as a cadre of age-mates find places in a working society. Socialization makes children not alike as it makes them alike. Children of a modern society occupy only a fractional part of the contexts of the town or city which nominally they inhabit as a whole. Part of the socialization of children is negotiation to find a viable and unique set of social contexts to be used and lived in by the individuals.

· Nowadays, socialization encompasses a second kind of travel involving symbols. Children learn to engage in cooperative activity with people who are far away in space and time. Reading, writing, and the electronic media connect the mind and memory of the growing child with the minds and memories of individuals thousands of miles and hundreds of years away. What is often spoken of as a trend in cognitive development toward more "abstraction," "decontextualization," or "distancing" of children's thought must be regarded as an expression of the child's enlarging capacity for long-range communication and cooperation with others.

· Finally, a new functionalism should entail an enlarged view of self-knowledge in children. If children move from one place to another, they not only experience other people in those places but also experience themselves in other settings. They have an opportunity to see other facets of their capacities and incapacities. Multiple adaptation on the part of the small child may be accompanied by the marginal development of a "multiple personality," and it is surely accompanied by a knowledge-about-self that directs the child toward some sites of action as promising and away from others which, in the child's experience, have proven threatening.

The several new assumptions we have been discussing suggest a functional approach that is akin to various current attempts to create an ecologically valid, more naturalistic kind of developmental psychology (Cole et al., 1971; Bronfenbrenner, 1979; Cole, Hood & McDermott, 1978). However, American children do not have one privileged, natural, and valid scene of action. Each child has many. Is an experimental room less natural to a child than piano lessons, or a session in Sunday School? Children live in many situations. A statement about a child may not travel across any pair of them. A naturalistic developmental psychology can be achieved only through the creation and use of a theory of situations. This is, of course, exactly what Bronfenbrenner (1979) has begun to sketch out in his ecological psychology.

Bronfenbrenner maps out the nested social settings in which children lead their everyday lives. He implies that scientific methods, as currently known and taught, can be brought away from laboratory settings toward work in natural environments (Bronfenbrenner, 1977, 1979). All it takes is the willingness to contend with larger and somewhat messier research designs. But controlled experiments require controlled environments. Twenty years of policy studies have demonstrated that society at large does not open all situations to researchers. Ultimately, the problem may not really be to find ways to take psychological research everywhere in the natural environment, but to locate selected places and issues that call for research on child development.

The natural environment of child development is large and complex. If children's cognitive development is located in time and space, it may be necessary to locate research on cognitive development similarly in time and space. After all, researchers with children have not existed everywhere, in all times and all places in human society. They are creatures of modernity, existing only in the twentieth century and only at special niches within the social frameworks of highly developed, complex, modern countries. Research may take place in those niches because of the special circumstances of children in those countries.

White (1978) argued that research in developmental psychology is uniquely tied to the emergence of "distal bureaucrats" in modern society. Children in modern societies are facilitated in their socialization by people holding specialized occupational roles, such as teachers, ministers, and youth group leaders, who share the responsibilities of socialization with families. This distributed socialization system, complexly organized in bureaucratic and political forms, requires certain kinds of symbolic information about children in order to be envisioned, controlled, and managed. Elsewhere, we have traced the emergence of child study as the first union of professional children's services and professional researchers (Siegel & White, 1982). Research on child development emerged as a response to new necessities of modern societies. When societies develop, as when children develop, new functional needs are distributed across time and space.

Nearby Contexts

A prominent theme in children's cognitive development is a movement of thought away from the concrete and toward the abstract, or away from the material and toward the formal, or away from ideas rooted in the here and now and toward ideas addressing events that are distant in time and space.

In a psychobiological stage theory of children's cognitive development written in the late nineteenth century, the Russian physiologist Ivan Sechenov argued that children's thought moves from the sensory to the extrasensory:

> This mysterious work of the transformation of the sensory products into apparently less and less sensory symbols, together with the innate capacity of speech, enables man to combine the products of the experience of another person with those of his own (i.e., to learn what is taught to him), and is the most characteristic feature of all his mental development . . . the child was thinking in terms of concrete sensations and suddenly the objects of his thoughts, instead of copies of reality, become reflections of this reality; at first, these reflections are very close to reality, but gradually they deviate so far from their source that all noticeable connections between the sign or symbol and its sensory origin disappears (1878:455).

A century later we find Werner and Kaplan (1963) anticipating the current trend toward a semiotics of cognitive development in their pioneering study of symbol formation. They state repeatedly that distancing is at the heart of a child's development of symbol usage:

For the designation of the process of differentiation in the domains of object formation and symbolization, we shall employ the concept of *distancing or polarization* . . . in the course of development there is a progressive distancing or polarization between person and object of reference, between person and symbolic vehicle, between symbolic vehicle and object, and between the persons in the communication situation, that is, addressor and addressee . . . A distancing between vehicle and referent with respect to space and time reflects the increasing use of the linguistic medium as a means for transcending the immediately given, and hence as a means of extending the human universe into the realms of the non-present, that is, into the spatially remote and into the temporally past and future (1963:42, 113).

Sigel and Cocking described distancing as a principled educational strategy, intended to encourage children to engage in acts of distancing:

The development of representational thinking is fostered by those life experiences which create temporal, spatial, and psychological distancing between the self and object. *Distancing* [is] proposed as the construct defining those classes of behavior or events which function to separate the individual from the immediate behavioral environment. For example, asking a child to reconstruct a previous experience poses a challenge to the child to bring an awareness of previous experiences. Thus, the child separates or *distances* himself at that moment from the present in order to reconstruct the past. The child is responding to the *distancing behavior*, to the request to represent previous experience through separating the self mentally from the here and now (1977:116).

Although many others have recognized the principle of distancing in children's cognitive development, curiously few have considered in detail a real-world distancing phenomenon that goes on parallel with the cognitive phenomena. Children travel in larger and larger circles as they get older. They range across larger physical distances, and they go to school where everything draws them toward communion with people and events that lie at far distances in time and space. The theme of distancing found in cognitive development must depend upon the fact that growing children are called upon to travel and to think about things at a distance.

The Enlarging Adaptive Environment of the Small Child

Fortunately, we have some views of children in a community that allow us to estimate the ways in which children travel as they grow up. Barker and Wright (1954) have studied children among the scenes and situations of a midwestern American town. Self-consciously trying to create an ecological psychology, Barker and Wright gave careful attention to issues of definition and method. They sought to lay a foundation for what we have above called "a theory of situations." What does their work suggest?

1. *Children who begin life in a small town enter a milieu composed in part of family behavior settings and in part of community behavior settings.* Barker and Wright establish a type of unitary, psychological situation. A *behavior setting* is an organized, repeated behavior pattern engaging several human beings but existing independently of any particular group of people that happen to be active in it at any given time. The behavior setting is a stage that many can act upon, similar to what Burke (1941) called a scene.

Having a defined unit of social interaction makes it possible to decompose the social life of a community into its presumptive constituents. A town may be viewed as a system of behavior settings. Barker and Wright and their associates mapped the psychological ecology of Midwest, a town of 721 inhabitants, as it existed from July 1, 1951, to June 30, 1952. They identified 2030 reasonably independent ("K-21") behavior settings. Of these, 1445 were located within the homes of the town and were called family behavior settings, such as *Home Meals, Home Bathroom, Home Festive Occasions. Community behavior settings* were located in relatively public areas of the town. There were 585 such settings, such as *Everging Variety Store* (with an *occupancy time* of 10,325 *person hours* during the year), *Burris University Choir at Methodist Church* (occupancy time 180 person hours), *School Boys' Basement Rest Room* (occupancy time 2819 person hours), *Cancer Control Committee Meeting* (occupancy time 3 person hours), *Trafficways* (occupancy time 78,000 person hours).

2. *Children spend their earliest years predominantly at home.* In the survey year, the citizens of Midwest spent 5,130,000 hours in family settings, 1,030,658 hours in community settings, and 330,620 hours in foreign settings, namely settings outside the borders of the town in which activities relevant to the functioning of the town occur. Infants (0–2 years) spent an average of 95% of their time (22.8 hours/day) in family settings, preschoolers (2–6) an average of 92% (22 hours/day), younger school children (6–9) an average of 76% (18.3 hours/day), older school children (9–12) an average of 73% (17.6 hours/day), and adolescents an average of

65% (15.7 hours/day). Hart (1979) similarly found that the *free range* of five-year-olds, as contrasted with their *range with permission* and *range with other (older) children,* was limited to the visually accessible environs of their home in a small New England town.

Barker and Wright, and Hart, offer data indicative of a regular feature of human societies. Small children live in limited and protected niches, usually within eyesight and reach of solicitous adults. The children gain small freedoms, movement, and release from control and protection as they grow older and more knowing and responsible. Significant movement out of family contexts seems to coincide with the time of life at which children begin to be initiated into adult roles and responsibilities (Rogoff et al., 1975; Rogoff et al., 1980).

3. *There are several kinds of change in children's occupancy of their environment as they enter school age. They move out into the community. They experience a more differentiated set of psychological environments. They begin to establish secondary "home bases."* Hart (1979) observed that the *free range* of children increased after age five. The statistical indices of the Midwest children's use of family settings indicated a drop at the beginning of school age and another at adolescence. The number of hours these children spent in community behavior settings increased from 1.2 hours/day/child in infancy to 2.0 in the preschool years, 5.7 in the younger school years, 6.4 in the older school years, and 8.3 in adolescence. Preschoolers spent an average of 747.3 hours/year in the community, younger school children 2087.8 hours/year, and adolescents 3341 hours/year.

Midwest children not only spent more time in community behavior settings as they got older but also used a greater variety of settings. Infants had a *territorial index* (the proportion of all 585 community behavior settings inhabited by members of a subgroup) of .59, preschoolers .65, younger and older school children .67, adolescents .78, and adults .99. The figure of .59 looks surprisingly high for infants, and other indices reveal that they participated very little in the settings they entered. Children went to more places as they got older, and they were more active and central in them. A slight "regression" of this outward travel occurred in old age in Midwest, where the territorial index for citizens over 65 years of age was .81.

Both children and adults preponderantly use a nuclear set of family settings, ranging over more and more community behavior settings as the individual gets older. A majority of time is spent at home by everyone. As growing children "move out," they establish secondary nuclei of activity and, conceivably, secondary "home bases."

Generally, spatially mobile and territorial creatures occupy new territory in a stepwise fashion. They find a secure place, use it as an anchor point, explore out from it, and retreat back toward it depending on their needs. This pattern is embodied in the toddler's ranging out from mother as an emotional base (Rheingold & Eckerman, 1970). Rats explore a new environment by using a known part as an anchor point or base of operations. They then appear to construe the rest of the environment as a network of topological relationships extending outward from that anchor point. If a familiar object is put into the environment, the animals use that as a secondary anchor, and their network apparently changes to reflect something like two home bases (Yamamoto, Wapner & Stevens, 1980).

Midwest children entered community behavior settings as they grew, but this was not entirely synonymous with entry into adult society. Some of the new places children entered were transitional behavior settings. Midwest had some places wholly or partially dedicated to use by various age groups of children. The Midwest study included a canvass of the community behavior settings most frequently used by different age groups. Outside their homes, infants spent an average of 169.7 hours/year in baby care and 48.5 hours in trafficways. They spent minimal time in such places as Clifford's drugstore, the Pearl Cafe (16.4 hours), and Methodist and Presbyterian Sunday-school classes (12.1 hours). Preschoolers spent an average of 160 hours in trafficways, 61.3 hours in Clifford's drugstore and Culver's shoe repair, 58.3 hours in child care, 39.6 hours in Methodist and Presbyterian kindergarten Sunday-school classes, and 46.3 hours in Midwest Theatre.

4. *As children get older, they enter more and more centrally into community activities.* Barker and Wright defined *penetrance* as an index of an individual's involvement in a behavior setting and the degree to which the individual takes responsibility for the standing pattern of activity of that setting. Six degrees of penetrance were scored: *onlooker, audience or invited guest, member or customer,*

active functionary, joint leader, single leader. The three highest degrees of penetration entitled the individual to be called a *performer* in a behavior setting. Although very young children entered a good number of community behavior settings in Midwest, they were not for the most part performers. Infants were performers in 13% of all the behavior settings they entered, preschoolers in 23%, younger school children in 41%, older school children in 48%, and adolescents in 73%. Midwest adults were onlookers or audience in less than 1% of the settings they entered.

These figures may depict an unusually high community standing for children. Much of the work in Midwest was subsequently done a second time in Yoredale, a larger British town (Barker & Barker, 1963; Schoggen, Barker & Barker, 1963). The data there indicated significantly less penetrance of children in community behavior settings, perhaps because a larger pool of adults provided people sufficient for the performances needed to keep Yoredale going. This is another difference between small towns and large cities: not only do children enter more adult places in small towns, they play more prominent roles.

5. *There are trends suggesting a principle of progressive entrance. Perhaps children are invited to participate with adults first in motor activity, second in emoting, and last in thinking.* Behavior settings in which children of different ages participated were rated on seven prominent qualities of activity embodied in them: *affective behavior, gross motor activity, listening, looking, manipulating, talking,* and *thinking.* Infants came into settings where there was talking, affective behavior, and gross motor activity. Preschoolers came into settings where there was gross motor activity, affective behavior, and thinking. Younger school children came into settings where there was gross motor activity, thinking, and affective behavior. Older school children and adolescents came into settings where there was gross motor activity, thinking, and manipulation.

Some Cognitive Consequences of Travel

The fact that children progressively enter the working society into which they are born, going into a larger and larger proportion of the community around them, establishing secondary home bases with their age cadre, and penetrating the places and activities of adults to become more and more central performers, is in a sense obvious. It is known to any adult who moves around in a community and is familiar with where children are more or less likely to be. Yet the Midwest work has been largely ignored, because of a preoccupation with the learning of free-floating, placeless cues and symbols.

Most psychological experiments are designed to deal with decontextualized signs and symbols, signaling the same thing anywhere they are. What complicates such experiments is the fact that young children, as well as animals, use place, space, and position as cues guiding their behavior. They do so easily, often in preference to dealing with free-floating cues. In fact, it is quite awkward to deal with place and space in a stimulus-response psychology. Although Piagetian genetic epistemology explicitly addresses the child's construction of time and space, research has for the most part explored children's reactions to a tabletop world of physical phenomena (White, 1980).

Building Cognitive Maps

When children move around in the world, they learn large quantities of spatial arrangements easily. Spatial learning comes so easily to people that they "spatialize" nonspatial things to make them easier to learn (Siegel & White, 1975). As children travel, they map a geographic terrain. They use a large, quick, recognition-in-context memory to retain images of objects encountered sufficient for those objects to seem familiar the second time they are seen (Livingston, 1967; Kirasic, Siegel & Allen, 1980). At the same time, children somehow annotate their retained images so that directions and distances between objects can be estimated. Using first-order route maps, which allow them to retrace a path used before, and higher-order survey maps, which allow them to generate productive, never-before-used routes, growing children store more and more things and places of their world into their mental stock of known loci (Siegel, Allen & Kirasic, 1979).

The growth of spatial representation in children directly reflects the range and variety of travel that has been permitted to them. Preschoolers and kindergarteners can produce sophisticated survey maps of the environs of their home, but at that age more distal settings are not well represented (Hart, 1979).

A map is a kind of metaphor. In the relationships among its

graphic elements, it initiates spatial relationships among things in the physical world. A child who draws a map or makes a model transforms the world into an imitative symbolic code. The sequence of acts by which a child creates a map imitates sequential features of the child's larger encounters with the environment. Just as children's walking and running range out from home base, so does children's map construction. When children make maps, they start with home. They put in places that can be seen or easily reached from the home. Then they put in less visually and physically accessible places.

Until 8½ years of age, children produce dual-level cognitive maps, which are survey maps of the environs of the home, built out with route maps representing fragmentary knowledge picked up in occasional trips out into the world beyond (Hart, 1979). Without data about the movement and travel of children, such dual-level maps might well be interpreted as instances of structural "decalage." With data showing that children before the school years spend much time near the home and only occasional time in the larger environment, such maps make another kind of sense. Children escalate their maps as they gather more and more data about a spatial arrangement, moving from stringy route maps to configured survey maps. Their maps become more complete, more metric, and more accurate (Acredolo, 1977; Allen et al., 1979; Herman, 1980).

Mapping Things of Importance

Maps are not targets of learning in and of themselves. Children take note of the places that are meaningful in their everyday lives, bringing forth notations of those places as landmarks on the maps they make. When adults teach children landmarks and routes, they do so as part of teaching about where the important things lie. Hart (1979) told of Davy, a 6-year-old who could draw a pretty good map of his town. Davy's father had shown him around the town, pointing out places of interest as a part of preparing Davy for citizenship, hunting, and wayfinding. Adults and children are purposive. Whitehead once remarked, "The object of symbolism is the enhancement of the importance of what is symbolized." The knowledge that people take in during their travels and the maps that they draw selectively enhance those things that seem important to them in the light of their purposes. A casual visitor to a city and a prospective home-buyer will construct maps that probably differ in nature and detail (Siegel, 1981).

Piaget, Inhelder and Szeminska recognized the interrelationships of travel and cognitive development:

> At four years of age, a little boy is brought to school by his mother; he is aware only of the school, of his own home, of "the house with the surprises" (i.e., the traveling circus on the Plaine de Plain palais); he makes up a plan of the area with the few reference-points which he is required to show, and he indicates the journeys he makes on the plan. At seven, a child knows several roads; those which take him to school where he now goes by himself and those which he walks along with his family when they go on their customary walks; he can therefore describe several fragmentary routes, and he can draw a plan showing a number of discrete areas. At nine or ten, a child is free as a man and can roam at will all over the town; he therefore answers all the questions satisfactorily (1960:23–24).

Knowledge and movement feed one another in the life of the growing child. Children "overlay" social learning on their cognitive maps. They learn who the other people are in the community. They become aware of the range and extremes of social, physical, and behavioral differences that people in the community expose to them. They develop normative expectations about social life. Much more is entailed in their social learning than the simple social attribution mechanisms recognized as central issues in social cognition. Training in style and manner is part and parcel of skill training in everyday settings, as it is in school. For example, when a 4-year-old Midwest child "regularly spent Friday morning with his father, brother, and two other mechanics in the machine shop of the Midwest Hardware and Implement Co., he was being educated in the ways of adulthood and in the skills of a mechanic" (Barker & Wright, 1954:115).

Scribner and Cole (1973) point out that children in modern societies characteristically take training in places like schools, away from the real adult world. Children of traditional societies learn by apprenticing to adults in real work situations. This is an important difference in approach to occupational or "career" training in the two kinds of societies. Children in modern societies still get much training by adults in both the obligatory and optional competences shared by modern adults.

Children traveling around in the community make maps. They locate behavior settings on their maps, learning what goes on where. They develop expectations about people. They learn how to act properly and skillfully in a number of community behavior settings. Important aspects of their situational learning are attitudinal and motivational. Community settings differ in the emotional atmospheres that they maintain or hold out to a child who enters. Roy Eddy, a Midwest 6-year old, entered 17 community settings in one day and received an interesting variety of greetings: "In some settings Roy was ignored, restricted, and coerced; but in others he was warmly welcomed, helped, and given great freedom. He had ample opportunity for satisfying his need for social approval and self-esteem" (Barker & Wright, 1954:96).

Not only do children encounter different emotional atmospheres in different settings, but they experience changes in tempo (Wapner, 1980a). Children must learn how to manage their behavior sufficiently to operate in a setting. Age differences occurred in Midwest children's "attitude span" in everyday behavior settings quite akin to what is commonly observed in schools: "The younger children tended to shift from one action to another, to do things sequentially, one at a time, and to abandon episodes before completing them more frequently than the older children; the latter tended to engage more often in episodes of longer duration, to carry on more than one action at a given time, and to complete a higher proportion of their episodes" (Barker & Wright, 1954:301).

As children pick up the tempos, the emotional atmospherics, and the self-management demands of diverse behavior settings, an emotional overlay appears on their cognitive maps:

In a predominantly black area of northern Philadelphia, Ley (1972) mapped a large sample of the local people's fears on an environmental stress surface. There was an invisible, mental topography of psychic stress in this neighborhood, where the peaks are places to be avoided, while the lower areas and valleys are areas of greater safety. The peaks generally coincide with the headquarters of gangs close to the center of their turfs, areas of abandoned building, and places where drugs are peddled. For an adult or child living in the area, information about this invisible topography literally lets them survive in a physically dangerous environment that is solely the creation of man (Gould & White, 1974:30).

Different Development in Different Ecologies

The different settings that children experience and subsequently map during the process of travel are by no means randomly chosen. Whiting found that the power of parents and other socializing agents to shape social behavior lies largely in their role in the assignment of children to settings. The most critical characteristics of a setting for developing patterns of social behavior are the actors who occupy the set, particularly the age and sex of these actors. Sex differences in behavior may be created through differences in assigned behavior settings. In many traditional societies, girls are placed in villages where they are with the old and young, who call forth respectful and nurturant kinds of behavior. Boys are placed with like-age children, who call forth competitive behavior. Among the things that children learn in and about settings are their differential etiquettes: "Each setting is characterized by an activity in progress, a physically defined space, a characteristic group of people, and norms of behavior—the blueprint for propriety in these settings. Thus a child moving from the classroom to the playground interacts with adults and peers in a different manner" (1980:104).

The cultural and sex differences often found in spatial ability may arise from different travel experiences that the members of a society are afforded. Ladd (1970) found that the quality and detail of maps drawn of their neighborhoods by American urban adolescents were positively related to the extent of the children's normal activity range. Berry (1966) found that the spatial abilities of the Baffin Island Eskimos, who led a far-ranging hunting and trapping life, were superior to those of the Temne of Sierra Leone, a settled, village-dwelling culture. Munroe and Munroe (1971) studied the relationships between activity range and spatial ability in young Logoli children of western Kenya, while Nerlove, Munroe, and Munroe (1971) studied young Gusii children of southwestern Kenya. In both societies, boys spent a relatively greater amount of free time further from home and performed significantly better than their age-matched female counterparts on tests of spatial ability. When girls spent a greater amount of free time far from the home, they performed better on the tests than age-matched boys.

Among the Walbiri of Australia, Munn found sex differences in the embodiment of space in iconographic representation. In Walbiri society, women stay close to home and men travel. The women typically make *yawalyu*, a class of designs whose functions center on procreative aims, curing, and the growth of children. The designs are formal arrangements of meaningful graphic elements, but they are not typically map-like. The *guruwari* are a class of designs used almost exclusively by men, whose function is to commune with ancestral spirits and manage nature and the universe. The *guluwari* are part route maps, part arrays of mythic emblems: "This site-path or site-list structuring of experience firmly binds story and dream to particular, spatial loci — actual places which can be directly encountered outside the story (or dream) context. Names are the detachable, linguistic aspects of places that serve to mediate them to individual experience when the visible reality of the place is not directly within the actor's presentational field. An ancestor may thus be 'followed' through the listing of his site names" (1973:133–134). As a function of their wide movement and freedom, Walbiri males tie together symbols of events and symbols of space.

Motive for Development

Free movement and issues of freedom are important aspects of a child's development. Midwest children usually added new, "older" behavior settings to their territorial range one at a time. The children's first entrance into a new setting was often brief, limited, and controlled by others. The children then consolidated behavior in this new setting before beginning in a next setting the process of entry and mastery: "Growing up in Midwest brought continually expanding opportunities and increased status. The 6-year-old had privileges and opportunities not available to the 4-year-old, and the 8-year-old had more freedom, more status, more power than the 6-year-old" (Barker & Wright, 1954:102).

Cross-cultural reports of children's entries into adult roles and responsibilities in the school years suggest that freedom, mobility, status, power, and responsibility rise together as children gradually enter the behavior settings of the adult world (Rogoff et al., 1975). Part of what brings the child forward is surely what White (1959) called a need for competence. Barker and Wright (1954) also alluded to the freedom, status, and power that accrue to the growing child. Piaget et al. (1960) described the child of nine or ten as being as "free as a man." Conceivably, what drives a child to enter adult behavior settings and to penetrate to central, performing roles is partly the child's need for freedom and dignity.

Building Selves to Fit a Set of Social Worlds

It is the somewhat pleasant, but scary, destiny of small children to be faced constantly with the task of going to where they have never been before, of meeting and dealing with people they have never seen before, of doing things they have never done before. In a new environment, they have to arrive at emotional and social settlements before they begin to enter into the problems and processes of intellectual problem-solving. They have to ask, "Is it safe here?" "Can somebody like me be here?" "Can I trust the people here?" "Can I trust myself to manage what I have to?"

These adaptational imperatives are by no means obvious in everyday life, because adults and older children for the most part travel across familiar, negotiated, and routine territory. But adults ask these questions in strange situations no less than children. Emotional and social problems are associated with major transitions in the everyday environment (Wapner, 1980b; Wapner, Kaplan & Ciottone, 1981).

In everyday life, cognitive development takes place as children gradually make their way toward a system of adult existence in the community. The adults live in the community using a sufficient number of its behavioral settings. Adults never use all the scenes of a middle-sized town, nor could they if they wanted to. A fraction must be used, properly assorted. There must be places to find shelter, food, companionship, work, care, love, and recreation. The combinatorial possibilities offered by even a small town such as Midwest are large in number.

Children must acquire knowledge to form such an adult system of existence. They have to become able to perform in a good number of local behavioral settings. They have to have maps and decision rules so that they can choose the settings they want. Since children's local community life is linked in thousands of little ways with the human community that lies beyond, they have to learn something about the beyond. All children will go to school and pick up some reading, writing, and arithmetic, together with some history, geography, and literature — codes for long-distance communication, together with crude mappings to tell where communicants may be found, what they care about, and what they are like. Much of higher education simply refines this process. But schools do not, and cannot, create the cognitive development necessary to be a viable adult.

Children in the community extend their knowledge of the distant by specializing, so that children who move toward farming learn more about crop loans, commodities markets, manufacturers of farm machinery, and federal agricultural policy; children who move toward work in clothing stores learn about credit systems and how garments and textiles are made and shipped. In its everyday context, cognitive development is not uniform across children. Every boy and girl constructs a unique solution to community life in the course of becoming an adult.

Some of the apparent uniformities in children's cognitive development are socially created. Societies use standardized institutions and conventions as vehicles of socialization, such as schools, books, clubs, and the norms and legal codes applying to children of different ages. Studies directed toward the average child tend to retrieve what all children experience, but this may be misleading. A school, like a train, is a social convenience that allows a number of people to move from different points of origin to unique destinations. One does not ordinarily think of people on a train as going through a standardized travel experience. It is a mistake to think of children in school as going through a standardized sequence of cognitive development.

Studying Children's Cognition Across Situations

To understand cognitive development in everyday life, it is necessary to examine children who are moving across different behavior settings. One approach would be to study the relation of culture and cognition. A second approach might be to look at transforming experiments, where a child is shifted to a radically new cognitive context and expected to adapt to it. A third approach might be to look for larger or smaller examples of context-dependent pluralism in cognitive performance (Cole & Traupmann, 1981; Cole & Means, 1981).

More detailed clinical and case-study material is needed dealing with cognitive transition and change. One of the more spectacular cases of ecological transition on record is that of Victor, the "Wild

Boy of Aveyron," who moved into nineteenth century French civil society. Lane described the elaborate program of education that had been created by the physician Itard for Victor, which had five principal aims:

1st Aim. To interest the wild boy in social life by rendering it more pleasant for him than the one he was then leading, and above all more like the life he had just left.

2nd Aim. To awaken his nervous sensibility by the most energetic stimulation, and occasionally by intense emotion.

3rd Aim. To extend the range of his ideas by giving him new needs and by increasing his social contacts.

4th Aim. To lead him to the use of speech by subjecting him to the necessity of imitation.

5th Aim. To make him exercise the simplest mental operations, first concerning objects of his physical needs and later the objects of instruction (1976:99).

The purely cognitive aspect of Victor's program began at the fourth or fifth aim. The program, unhappily, did not work. Victor could not learn speech, perhaps because he was not a "wild boy" after all but simply a retarded child who had been left in the woods to die. The educational program created for Victor is of more than antiquarian interest, however, because it was the basis for Itard's creation of an oralist method of training the deaf, Seguin's methods for training retardates, and Montessori's development of a pre-school training regimen.

Clinical study of cognition should cross time and space with a child, showing a child's cognition and personality as reflected or refracted through a number of situations of action. It might well examine the multiple development of a child across behavior settings and perhaps reveal something like a multiple personality of everyday life. On the basis of everyday observation, James argued that normal people develop multiple selves: *"A man's Social Self is* the recognition which he gets from his mates . . . We may practically say that he has as many different social selves as there are distinct *groups* of persons about whose opinion he cares. He generally shows a different side of himself to each of these different groups. Many a youth who is demure enough before his parents and teachers, swears and swaggers like a pirate among his 'tough' young friends. We do not show ourselves to our children as to our club-companions, to our customers as to the laborers we employ, to our own masters and employers as to our intimate friends. From this there results what practically is a division of the man into several selves" (1890:293 – 294).

James spoke confidently about man's multiple selves, because he felt he was laying out the obvious. Yet even today psychologists do not fully "know" what James knew. Perhaps people do not have traits, but the data are not clear, so when psychologists began to envision the laboratory as a controlled context of inquiry, one problem was that of "seeing" the obvious in the multiple behavior settings of everyday life. American psychologists have not "seen" the multiple behavior settings of everyday life in which children dwell, except for the heroic ecological work of the Midwest study.

The clinical psychologist has done the discipline a service by keeping the vicissitudes of everyday life awkwardly in view, mediated and mitigated by the phenomena of psychopathology. Psychologists have often been fascinated by reports about psychopathology, hypnosis, psychotherapy, and odd states of consciousness, thinking that the basic structures of the mind and soul are perhaps outlined by these psychic phenomena. (James, 1901 – 1902; Ellenberger, 1970). Multiple personalities are a special curiosity (Thigpen & Cleckley, 1954).

Prince (1900, 1906), for example, made a special study of the several personalities of Christine Beauchamp ("Sally," "The Woman"), from which he concluded that the exotic abnormality of the multiple personality might be an enhancement of the normal:

Man is a many sided creature . . . No one is wholly good or wholly bad; or wholly hard or wholly sentimental; or wholly self-centered or wholly altruistic; or wholly self-assertive and self-reliant or wholly shy and self-depreciative; and I may even say wholly intelligent or wholly stupid . . . The individual reacts at one moment with one set of traits and at another with another, perhaps of an opposite character. Indeed he may possess . . . traits that are antagonistic to one another, such as sentiments of hatred and love, or interest and disinterest, for the *same* objects; or he may manifest both charitableness and uncharitableness; intelligence and stupidity, etc. Obviously such opposing traits cannot be manifested at one and the same moment. But let the conditions of the organism be altered, such as occurs in fatigue, or in illness, or intoxication, or states of dissociation, and the other of these opposing traits comes into functional activity (1925:269, 290).

A clinical, idiographic view offered Prince the outline of a dramatic and unusual configuration of human personality. Casting an eye about him at everyday human behavior, he saw that something like this configuration is general and part of the normal. Like James, he appealed in the end to obviousness in everyday psychological experience.

Formal observations directed at people acting in several contexts can pick up relatively circumscribed but exact indications of behavior changes across behavior settings. Labov (1970) showed that adults speak to one another differently in different social contexts. There are times and places where they take pains to speak properly and correctly, and other occasions when they do not care so much. Labov argued that people give more or less attention to monitoring their speech depending upon the formality of the situation.

As children grow up, they have to pick up somewhere an ability to recognize the formality of the situation and to respond appropriately to it. They recognize some situational demands on language about as early as they have extended language. Shatz and Gelman (1973, 1977) showed that the mean length of utterance when 4-year-olds speak to 2-year-olds is significantly shorter than when they speak to adults and peers. Young children can apparently modify complexity and a miscellany of other features of speech (Snow & Ferguson, 1977). Children must be able to estimate the communicative demands of various contexts of speech (Shatz & Gelman, 1977).

Gleason (1973) showed that restricted observations across contexts can be informative and that complex behavior can be modified to suit the pragmatics and style of various behavior settings. Parents constitute not one but a developmental series of sociolinguistic environments for their children, and children reciprocate on their side of the "socializing game" by forming not one but a series of parent-specific linguistic forms. The phenomenon of parents shifting their form of address to children of different ages is a case in point: "One mother, for instance, spoke in a normal voice to her husband, a high voice to her 4-year-old, a slightly raised voice to her 8-year-old, and when she talked to her baby she fairly squeaked" (1973:161).

As mothers shift their gaze toward older or younger children, they change their voice register. They speak in a higher voice to small children. They change the complexity, speaking in shorter sentences to younger children. They change the frequency of terms of endearment. Little children get a lot of "honey," "sugar," "sweetie," and "love." Older children get "Ted," "Mary Ann," "Jimmy," or, if there is trouble, "Theodore!" and "Mary Ann Brown!" Raising the voice, drastically shortening the sentences, and sprinkling in endearments is typical of the baby talk used with small children from birth to about four years of age. Apparently the young children reciprocate by forming a baby talk that they use selectively with their parents and other adults they know well. The high nasal tone of voice, or whining, used frequently by small children is selective for their parents and is not commonly used with their peers or miscellaneous adults. This may also be the case for the mindless repetitions of nagging.

Parents move to a "language of socialization" to address their children of four to eight years of age. This is a heavily instructional language full of real and implied imperatives. Both the form and the content of the language are shaped toward training in civility and etiquette. At this age, parents are heavily engaged in setting forth standards, rules, courtesies, social forms, and mores. The language of parents is very controlling, telling children what to do, what to think, and how to feel. The language is generously predictive of the real or possible dangers of situations. This is about the same time when the Midwest children marched out to new situations (Barker & Wright, 1954). It is also just about the point in cognitive development when children might be expected to understand and remember a modest amount of futurology.

In the 4- to 8-year-old range children begin to develop a context-sensitive set of languages. They respond as best they can to the directive language of their parents. At the same time, they show an emerging ability to adjust their speech sensitively to context. Five- and 6-year olds, having only recently emerged from baby talk of their own, show a clear emergence of an ability to reproduce baby talk when babies seem to call for it. But this, according to Gleason, is only one of an array of languages that children begin to use: "Four year olds may whine at their mothers, engage in intricate verbal play with their peers, and reserve their narrative discursive tales for the grown-up friends. By the time they are 8, children have added to the foregoing some of the politeness routines of formal adult speech, baby-talk style, and the ability to talk to younger children in the language of socialization" (1973:167).

In summary, a developing child adapting to multiple behavior settings may form plural selves and styles. How much fractionation and division there is in children's self-development is not known, but the clinical material is suggestive. Erikson (1968) proposed that an "identity crisis" is normal in adolescence. Studies are needed to examine the identity crisis not as a psychoanalytic foible but as a reasonably responsive outcome of real experiences of differentiation in an enlarging psychological environment.

Cooperation at a Distance

Cognitive development as psychologists usually speak about it — meaning to know more, have more concepts and ideas, and have more skills — is potentiated not only by physical travel in childhood, but also by a kind of traveling in thought created through a highly regulated use of the imagination.

Vygotsky (1934) argued that children learn to use two kinds of concepts as they develop, spontaneous concepts built out of their own experience and scientific concepts given to them from others. Children talk about things they have seen with their own eyes: Dad, Harris' drug store, Tommy the dog, Myrtle Street. As they get older, they know more and more things that other people have told them about: Santa Claus, Charles DeGaulle, President Reagan, Shangri-La, Toledo. Adults might separate this list into the real and the imaginary, holding, for example, that Santa Claus has never been real while Charles DeGaulle has existed. But most adults have never laid eyes on Charles DeGaulle. Their separation of Santa Claus as fictional from Charles DeGaulle as real would be part of a consistent system that they have for treating the many imaginaries they deal with each day as cold, hard pieces of reality.

Adults treat many imaginaries as things in the real world, well located in time and space with respect to the here and now, interactive with the tangible and connected to it in lawful and predictable ways. We authors have been doing exactly that in this chapter. We have never laid eyes on Barker and Wright. Yet we addressed them as real people writing about the circumstances of a real place, Midwest. Although the exact location of Midwest was left a little vague, we know that it is in Kansas. We know generally where Barker and Wright were taking our thought in space, and we know precisely where they were taking us in time, to the year July 1951 – June 1952. At these bearings in time and space, certain things were true of the imaginary town, its activities, its adults, and its children. Thus we now have a teeming imaginary world, so well and lawfully grounded in the technologies and regulated procedures that link us to Barker and Wright that we treat it as an extension of the real world about us.

Barker and Wright are linked with us by our common purpose, psychological science, and within the framework of that purpose, they offer us certain facts and arguments about the way things were with children in Midwest. The reality of the facts we accept or reject following various methodological principles; the arguments we consider. Barker, Wright, you, and we are engaged in a cooperative body of activity. We regulate our individual activities so that we are able to use one another's perceptions and memories to "observe" and reflect upon events that are distant in time and place. Scientists cooperate at a distance in gathering knowledge, using complex physical and institutional devices to create a synergy of many people's thought and action. As children grow up, they enter into the use of physical, symbolic, and institutional technologies which provide that they will know about people and events at a distance, productively mingling such knowledge with their knowledge of the everyday world.

Children do not have to become aware of things and people at a distance. Some people today are born, live, and die within a tribal area of a few square miles. They know mostly what they have seen. Things beyond are vague and legendary to them, conveyed by word of mouth from travelers or outlined in oral histories. A few hundred years ago most Europeans knew little of the world beyond their village or manor. Literacy creates the possibility that widely distributed people can deal with one another knowledgeably. A wealth of social and psychological changes flow from that possibility (Goody, 1968; Clanchy, 1979; Scribner & Cole, 1981). As Spengler observed, "Writing is the grand symbol of the Far" (Goody & Watt, 1968). Literacy tells people about things that are far away in time and space.

Literacy brings about a complex body of physical, social, and psychological rearrangements in human society. When children are born and reared in a society that has been so rearranged, they face developmental tasks that implicitly offer the possibilities and require the abilities entailed in communication with the far. The children pick up special motives, such as a love of books, the need to do well in school, or a ham radio hobby. They elaborate a characteristic intelligence, somewhat like literate mentality (Goody, 1968). Adults tend to regard the developmental tasks that confront their children as reasonable, normal, and natural, as in a sense they are. Adults may even regard the child's struggle with the tasks of literate civilization as a species of growth or mental evolution, but this is at best only a partial truth about the matter.

Some of the gateways to the distant the child finds in a modern society are the following:

• Children encounter print and paper all around them. They are spared the necessity to read it all until they go to school, but they grow up in a world in which people send and receive mail, read newspapers, and buy magazines and books. The children see this. Now and then, they trace the paper paraphernalia around them back to mailboxes, postmen, post offices, paperboys, bookstores, and printing shops. Part of their cognitive development is learning about the art and sciences that help to manage and predict usage, such as how to use the post office, how the mail moves, or how paper is made and priced.

• Children encounter radio and television, taking in some messages through them from their earliest years. You do not have to have special training to use these gateways to the far.

• Children find that any community behavior setting they deal with may be the outcropping of a system or may be coupled with the distant. Any human activity nowadays is apt to be serviced occasionally by some form or other of long-range transportation or communication. Children visit bus stations, railroad stations, and airports.

• Children go to school. The basic skills offered to children in school are the codes of distant communication. From kindergarten through graduate school, the young develop more facility at sending and receiving messages from afar and at embodying productive calculations within those messages.

These are some of the larger artifacts of a communicative society to which the developing child must adjust in order to pick up the cognitive development of communication (Innis, 1951; Olson, 1970; Olson & Bruner, 1974). Whorf listed the smaller and subtler artifacts and attitudes that children are apt to find lying about them in a society adapted to distal communication:

1. Records, diaries, bookkeeping, accounting, mathematics stimu-
lated by accounting.

2. Interest in exact sequences, dating, calendars, chronology,
clocks, time wages, time graphs, time as used in physics.

3. Annals, histories, the historical attitude, interest in the past,
archeology, attitudes of introjection towards past periods, *e.g.*, classi-
cism, romanticism (Goody & Watt, 1968:64).

This is only a casual list of the artifacts and attitudes of a modern
society. The environment children face as they grow up is man-
made in many of its most important aspects, designed so that
long-distance communication, computation, record keeping, and
inquiry are normal and natural to it (Goody, 1968, 1977; Eisenstein, 1980). Children have to meet the thoughtfulness and design-
edness of their physical and social world (Vygotsky, 1978).

Much of the data on cognitive development do not and cannot
reflect absolute progressions in reasoning or intelligence. No one
can pull apart the private vs. the public sectors of cognitive development. It is likely, however, that some of the cognitive changes seen
in children have as their primary value the coupling of the child's
mind and activity with that of others. Teaching a child to read or
write would be irrelevant in a society without others who could
read or write. The development of mathematical and scientific
reasoning as those terms are usually understood might be of little
consequence outside of a society committed to technology.

Symbols and the Social Mind

The development of symbols is a force at one and the same time in
the psychology and sociology of the growing child. Symbol systems
mediate the growth of the individual child's thought toward what
Piaget (1954) called "the construction of reality in the child" and
what Berger and Luckmann (1967) called "the social construction
of reality." There are private and public functions of symbol development. Simple functional explanations of what symbolic thinking
does for a child are probably not possible, simply because symbols
may act simultaneously to change the mind of the child and the
relationship of that mind to the "group mind" of the society
surrounding the child.

Growing children use symbols to create "travel" in imagination,
that is, to extend their ideas outward to the imaginatively known

people, places, things, and events of the larger human world within which their local, physically accessible community is nested. Mental development is identified with symbol formation (Piaget, 1952; Werner, 1957; Werner & Kaplan, 1963). The nature of thought is tied to what symbols are and how they are used.

Peirce (1931) saw logic as a form of semiotics and human thought as a form of symbol usage. Problems of thought therefore required both psychological and philosophical analysis. How does the mind, he asked, form general ideas of things? How are people persuaded that invariant things are "out there?" At one moment people glimpse a tree. A few moments later, in a slightly different light, with different shadows, and at a slightly different visual angle, they glimpse the same tree again. How do they sort through their impressions to infer that they are seeing a constant tree in the midst of a few little changes? They make an ever-so-slight leap to accomplish the objectification of the tree.

Or people see one tree and then another, and they say that they have seen "two trees," that is, two of the general type "tree." The "tree" they have instanced is not any one tree that they can find anywhere on earth. Where did this unreal "tree" come from? They made a leap into a constructed world of symbols, because they could mentally "digest" their experience only by projecting it in symbols that portray experience in general terms. Helmholtz remarked:

> The process of our comprehension with respect to natural phenomena is that we try to find *generic notions and laws of nature.* Laws of nature are merely generic notions for the changes in nature . . . When we cannot trace natural phenomena to a law, and therefore cannot make the law objectively responsible as being the cause of the phenomena, the very possibility of comprehending such phenomena ceases. However, we must try to comprehend them. There is no other way of bringing them under the control of our intellect. And so in investigating them we must proceed on the supposition that they are comprehensible. Accordingly, the law of sufficient reason is really nothing more then the *urge* of our intellect to bring all our perceptions under its own control (Cassirer, 1944:34).

Peirce's position would today be called an analysis-by-synthesis approach to perception. Part of people's perception, at least, is sensitive to the symbol systems that they have available. They construe out of the flux of experience, or see that to which their building-block symbols give coherent form. This in turn lets society in as a participant in an individual's perception. Society shapes the perception and thought of the individual by its symbol systems. Indeed, Baldwin argued that the meaning and discursive knowledge of the individual is always intrinsically social: "Society, genetically considered, is not a composition of several individuals; on the contrary, the individuals are differentiations of a common social protoplasm. The conclusion is drawn that the individual is a 'social outcome not a social unit.' We are members of one another. The oppositions, conflicts, antinomies of personal and social life are late developments which are sharpened with the rise of reflective and ethical thinking "(1930:5).

Societies that use long-range communication and cooperation set forth the physical and intellectual tools for such activities as part of the curriculum for the child who seeks to be a competent adult. Some of what is called cognitive development and is tested for as "intelligence" is such specialized cultural apparatus. Particularly central is the development of symbolic activity.

From Adaptive to Symbolic Action

Children begin to make complicated symbolic constructions in the second year of life after organized adaptive action has been perfected. They engage in activities whose function is representational and symbolic. Piaget (1952) discussed three symbol-making activities of children: symbolic play, language, and drawing and painting. These might be considered the child's first media or languages of art (Olson & Bruner, 1974; Goodman, 1976). A central feature in the use of these symbol systems is the translation of external relations into internal relations. Selected events of an outing in the park are represented in an arrangement of words. A few blocks and a few imitative gestures reconstitute the activities of a bricklayer seen on a walk. A cat and her new kittens become one large and six small daubs on paper plus some "romancing" discourse before the easel. In each case, significant arrangement of things in the world, external relations, are translated into arrangements of symbolic activity and of signs created by that activity. The child does not follow formal rules in making these translations. Nevertheless, the translation process must be regular and systematic, because other children and adults can usually "read" the symbolic constructions.

Clark (1973) analyzed the movement of features of the surrounding environment from perceptual space (P-space) into linguistic space (L-space). In the representational use of language there is an orderly translation of aspects of the physical environment into the linguistic terms. What is selected for representation depends on the saliency and complexity of the physical features. Symbol systems, like spoken language, print, drawing, and numbers, capture parts of the world in their special terms. Aspects of the everchanging world so captured are held in the symbols, "remembered," and made available for many to see and know.

Extending Thought Through Symbols

As children perfect their symbolic activities, more complex kinds of collaboration with others becomes possible. Typically, parents are delighted by an infant's early use of symbols because this establishes contact and communion with a child's thought in a new way. Parents and children experience intellectual communion, richer communication, and richer possibilities of cooperation. How much of this there can be depends upon how long and strong are the bridges of symbolic activity between parents and child.

Two-word utterances at age two tell something about what a child is thinking and feeling. The fully grammatical but short sentences of 5-year-olds tell even more. As more elaborate transmissions between children and others, or children and themselves, become possible, more and more of the world all around is drawn into the system of internal relations of symbolic discourse and thus becomes "known." The microcosm is made richer. More can be said, done, and negotiated using it. Controlling functions of parental language, existing in the "bridge" of language between children and their parents, can be adopted by children as cognitive control principles. Luria saw social control mechanisms being transmuted into psychological cognitive controls in exactly this way in the 3–3 ½-year-old: "However, the most essential and fundamental fact, characteristic of this stage of the child's development, is that similar results can be obtained if we replace the external sanctioning afferentiation by the child's own speech . . . we replace the regulatory action of the external signal by the child's own verbal command" (1961:76).

A child's elaborating symbol system has a bearing on language development. The grammatical devices that emerge in the first five years of life create a more and more complete world view embodied in and expressed in a child's language. This more complete world view potentiates the child's ability to communicate with others about distal events. The holophrastic utterances of the toddler have meaning in the tiny intimate world of caretaker-infant face-to-face interaction. "Doggie?" uttered in a room from which the dog has just left and where a mother is standing who has seen and knows it, means, "Where has the doggie gone?" "Fa'down" said when the infant is being fed and has just dropped a spoon, clearly signals, "I have just dropped my spoon. Would you mind picking it up for me, please?" It is manifestly evident that this kind of language will not work outside of a context of face-to-face communication about things immediately present and ongoing.

Gradually the child organizes all the grammatical devices necessary to build who, what, where, when, and why notations into every sentence (Bloom, Lightbown & Hood, 1975; Hood & Bloom, 1979). Children become able to talk with themselves and others about things that are far away. They develop what White and Pillemer (1979) called a "socially accessible memory system." One important feature of a long-term memory system, private or collective, is the need for powerful indexing and cross-referencing devices. If a memory system is to be practically useful, individual memories must be "filed" in such a way that they remain connected to ideas of things, people, and places on which they have a bearing.

People cannot just throw books into the library. They need something like a Dewey Decimal System that tells them where to put a book in the library and then, later, how to find it. The Dewey Decimal System depends on ideas. People have to think about a book in just the right way, generate just the right set of comments on the book, in order to handle the book within the format of the system. Exactly the same holds true for human memories to be shared in a socially accessible memory system. If the memories are to be retrieved when and where they are needed, there must be internal reference systems that direct thought to appropriate ideas when conditions call for them.

Children develop relatively precise ways of communicating with others about things distant, such as the ability to deal with clock time, days of the week, and months of the year. Basic terms for time and distance are present at about age eight. A major problem in speaking about things far away arises from the extra demands imposed by distal communication. Not only must people use the symbol system to make their statement, but they must also build into the system an auxiliary set of communications to generate or summon the context and things to which the statement applies. If two people are standing in front of Niagara Falls, it is an adequate communication for one to say, "Beautiful, isn't it?" But if they meet in New York and want to say something similar, the communication at the very least must be, "I've just been to see Niagara Falls, and they are beautiful."

Dimensionalization, Calculation, and Prediction
Through Symbols

The emerging symbol systems of a preschool child allow thought, communication, and cooperation to project to a world beyond the here and now. But the child's reference to things beyond has locational accuracy rather than metric accuracy. It is conventional to separate human cognitive maps into two kinds. In route maps, the relationships of things in space to one another become known only as those things are recognized to be landmarks on known paths. In survey maps, in contrast, objects are understood as placed on a grid or set of coordinates, so that any objects on the grid can be located with respect to any other (Siegel & White, 1975; Downs & Stea, 1977). The symbolic devices of young children have limited coordinating power. A child may know local orderings of events in space and time but may lack devices for placing the local orderings into a larger ordering. The child may lack calculational devices that for adults would more completely exploit the possibilities offered by the ordering.

Preschoolers may know that *Road-runner* comes before *Bugs Bunny* on Saturday morning, and *Little House on the Prairie* comes before *Brannigan* on Wednesday night, but since these hypothetical children do not know the days of the week, they have no way to interconnect these two local orderings. To unite the local temporal orderings, they need symbolic devices that allow them to project all local orderings on a master temporal grid, and they need calculational devices that allow them to compute locations, relations, and distances on the grid. This is the work of what Piaget called "operational thought."

In book after book, Piaget has explored the school child's elaborating understanding of the symbolic grids people use to locate things and calculate relationships among them. This is the heart of the genetic epistemology program. On the one hand, Piaget has explored what he takes to be the genetic formation of the Kantian categories in monographs dealing with the growth of children's ideas about number, time, movement and speed, geometry, and chance (Piaget, 1953a, 1970a, 1970b; Piaget & Inhelder, 1956, 1976; Piaget, Inhelder & Szeminska, 1960). On the other hand, Piaget has sought to model the child's growing ability to calculate as, presumably, a genetic series of logics is built during the course of cognitive development (Piaget, 1942, 1949, 1953b; Piaget & Inhelder, 1958, 1964).

His goal was to articulate the successive logics that govern a child's thought. Children presumably want more powerful logical structures because such structures equilibrate the child's experience more adequately. One cannot overlook the everyday functional utility of logical reasoning. Children are more than theorists looking for consistency in everyday life. They need to become able to use the calculational possibilities entailed in sentences like, "I'll meet you at 10:00 A.M. on the corner of Fifth and 42nd on Tuesday, December 30"; "I'll be carrying 5% interest on the money"; or "I may be late. My plane gets in at 8:32, and I'll have to come in crosstown through the 9 o'clock rush."

Operational thought improves the precision with which the child can estimate the consequences of present actions. Bearison (1969) argued that fourth graders have a quantitative set, a habitual framework of thought that permits the child to envision exact solutions to a diversity of problems. A child must learn where to calculate as well as how to calculate. Flavell described the quantitative attitude of the school child: "There is a general characteristic of middle-childhood cognition [7–11] . . . More than is true of the preschooler, the elementary-school child has what might be called a *quantitative attitude* toward many cognitive tasks and problems. He seems to understand better than the younger child that certain problems have precise, specific, potentially quantifiable solutions, and that these solutions may be attained by logical reasoning in conjunction with well-defined measurement operations" (1977:85).

The Creation of New Kinds of Formal Operations

Generally, children spend the school years acquiring socially conventional mappings of the world. Some children go on in late adolescence to engage in artistic planning or scholarly, scientific, and design activities that allow a society to come into possession of new languages of order. The natural tendency of many adolescents is to go beyond the actual toward the possible and the fanciful. They think in terms of systems. Having absorbed the the rituals and symbols of their native religion, some children begin skeptical inquiry into religions-in-general. Others dabble in politics. Some read science fiction. Some become hot rodders or computer buffs. The highly organized imaginaries of conventional social symbol systems are now addressed by a mature intelligence that explores the possible invention of new systems of imaginaries. Riegel (1973) and Basseches (1978) argued that after "formal operations" there is a normative movement of children's thoughts toward "dialectical operations." Again, these structuralist arguments are worth considering from a functional perspective. Planning, design, research, and development are all normative activities in modern societies. People make their living doing these things. Many occupational roles embody responsibilities for the creation of new codes and new routines for cooperative human behavior.

The Sacred and the Profane

As children grow up, they travel outward into the symbolic world constituted by their society even as they physically travel to the full range of here-and-now behavior settings offered by their community. In the end, children's knowledge of symbol usage allows them to stock an imaginary world with distant others, to deal with imaginaries in a highly regulated and rational way, to know about the structures, events, and processes of the human society lying beyond the community, and to communicate and cooperate with people at a distance. There are intimate relationships between communication-with-the-beyond and power in many societies.

Eliade's studies of tribal religion have led him to argue that, generally, everyday life in tribal societies is perfused with the sacred and the influence of the beyond. The myths of many human societies posit special times and places at which legendary beings engaged in acts that have special significance for those presently on earth. Through magic, ritual acts, and symbol, people commune with that world beyond. The world is given meaning by its connection with the beyond. The beyond enters constantly into everyday life, and there is a touch of the sacred about most human activities (Eliade, 1959; Beane & Doty, 1975). Religion has not been bottled up on Sundays and in churches. The world of everyday affairs is explained by its connection with the distant: "The man of the societies in which myth is a living thing lives in a world that, though 'in cipher' and mysterious, is 'open.' The World 'speaks' to man, and to understand its language he needs only to know the myths and decipher the symbols. Through the myths and symbols of the Moon man grasps the mysterious solidarity among temporality, birth, death and resurrection, sexuality, fertility, rain, vegetation, and so on. The World is no longer an opaque mass of objects arbitrarily thrown together, it is a living Cosmos, articulated and meaningful. In the last analysis, *The World reveals itself as language*" (Beane & Doty, 1975:8).

Western societies use scholarly and scientific histories to explain where man came from and why human societies look the way they do. White (1978) argued that such histories may constitute a corrigible mythic system for Western societies with social functions resembling those of the tribal myths.

In the environment of the developing child there are many things whose nature and meaning is given by their extensions into distant human society. Homes, schools, and stores all hold the paraphernalia of communication. A toddler plays beside television sets, radios, newspapers, typewriters, magazines, books, telephones, and maps. Children are expected to deal with these and to understand the beyond to which they lead.

Some children are carefully trained in civility, courtesy, and etiquette. In medieval Europe, the rise of a middle class was associated with spreading education and with special training in civility. A style is customarily found among people who are adept at the codes and habits of education and literacy. Part of that style is undoubtedly functional. Part of it is perhaps dramaturgic, offering signals to those around that the individual is certified, qualified, and competent to participate in the esoterica of symbolic debate.

It has been customary in academic writing to picture the stylistic differences among more and less educated people as class markings. The class markings associated with socioeconomic status are taken to be serious in what they betoken but frivolous in their substance. Calhoun (1973) argued that in the nineteenth century, United States small towns regularly chose one among their number to go to college and get educated. Political debate was conducted in a florid literary language generously garnished with Greek and Latin quotations. If one could not manufacture the discourse, one could not be effective politically. In this view of a classical education, its predominant function was to create class markings and to segregate some individuals from others as a power elite. A similar argument is made about the social meaning of the nonclassical college curriculum today. There is probably something to the argument. Human beings use all kinds of small personal qualities and stylistic differences to create status hierarchies. But one kind of functional validity in both the classics curriculum of the past and the liberal arts curriculum of the present might be to bring to a high-polish artistry in sending and receiving messages in words and numbers.

In a world of extended behavior settings, special human qualities other than the strictly intellectual may be necessary for successful functioning. Lorenz (1966) argued that humans who can kill by pushbutton may have outstripped their biological mechanisms controlling aggression. The ethics of face-to-face human encounters may be regulated, canalized human social competencies (Fishbein, 1976). But some extensions of human ethical and moral sentiments may be necessary if children are to accept someone unseen as human like themselves and as fully qualified for an ethics of reciprocity and justice. In other words, some of the "moral development" that Piaget and Kohlberg identified as intimately associated with cognitive development may be an extension of modernization. A child growing up in a face-to-face society may not need an elaborated cognitive apparatus of morality.

As early as 1894, Schallenberger offered a developmental study of 3000 children in which she found a transition from a morality of consequences to a morality of intentions: "Almost as striking as children's reasons for punishment are their attitudes regarding the motive that lies back of the action. The intellectual and moral condition of man can be fairly estimated by his ability and willingness to judge of the motives which actuate those about him . . . The young child thinks of the results of an action. If the result is bad, punishment should follow; if not, the offender should be allowed to go free . . . The older child, on the contrary, thinks of the motive that led to the action. If this be good, punishment should be light or not at all" (1894:94). If there is to be a morality of the symbolized other, then the significant behavior of others must be codified in a communicable symbol system. It must specify which are the morally salient aspects of others' behavior, their motives or their intentions. Communication about people demands some kind of a motivology. Psychology was born in part because people wanted a language of motives.

Children in modern society, in short, must be able to talk about the goals and purposes of people. They participate in extended behavior settings. The physical world must be fully represented in an elaborated discourse; so too, must the psychological world. Since cooperation and communication are two-way streets, children must become able to discuss themselves no less than others. As children do so, their motives become "conscious," that is, couched in discourse addressable by a rational memory system, susceptible to mental processing, open to self-management, and open to the morality-of-the-other, that is, guilt.

The Self As Glimpsed Through Symbols

In order to transform external relations into internal relations — to build symbolic models of experience — people need to put tokens of their selves and their actions into the model. Arbib set forth this strictly logical requirement, which must be as fully respected in the design of robot machines as in the human brain: "In other words, the 'brain' (controller + identification procedure) interacts with the 'environment' (which includes the body as well as external objects) on the basis of an internal model (the latest set of adaptation parameters), and *its interactions must be designed to update its internal model as well as to change its relationship with the external world in some desired way*" (1972:82). An intelligent system that plans must have self-knowledge, and it must update or upgrade self-knowledge no less than knowledge of the outside world.

The child adapting to a set of behavior settings must build self-knowledge for a set of worlds. Self-consciousness, the elaboration of conceptual representations, procedures, and algorithms sufficient to rationalize self's behavior, is an intellectual feat of a relatively high order. The human mind departs from that of animals in its property of self-consciousness (Romanes, 1889; Gould, 1980). The question is how self-consciousness emerges in children.

Luria suggested that cognitive development entails changes in thought and feelings about the self, because peasants transplanted to collective farms after the Russian revolution showed a number of changes suggestive of "cognitive development" and an increase in verbalization about the self. These changes had emotional overtones that were strikingly reminiscent of the Freudian theme of civilization and its discontents. Luria asked Nurmat, age eighteen, a barely literate peasant from a remote village, "What shortcomings are you aware of in yourself, and what would you like to change in yourself?" Nurmat replied, "Everything's all right with me. I, myself, don't have any shortcomings, but if others do, I point them out . . . As for me, I have only one dress and two robes, and those are all my shortcomings" (1976:148). Nurmat's response typifies those Luria collected from the traditional and unschooled individuals. The self was discussed in physical and concrete terms. Shortcomings, if they were admitted, were conceived of as material deficiencies.

In contrast, Tekan, age thirty-six and living on a collective farm, was asked, "What good traits and what shortcomings do you know about yourself?" Tekan responded: "I'm neither good nor bad . . . I'm an average person, though I'm weak on literacy and can't write at all, and then I'm very nasty and angry, but still, I don't beat my wife. That's all I can say about myself . . . I forget very fast, I walk out of a room and I forget. I also don't understand very well; yesterday, I was given a long explanation, and I didn't understand anything. If I were educated, I would do everything well. I have to change this shortcoming in education. I don't want to change anything in my character; if I study it'll change by itself" (1976:159). Tekan's response is longer and more complex. The self's cognitive status is rather carefully thought through, and the slightly positive tone of Nurmat's response is in Tekan's case supplanted by a slightly negative and critical tone. Tekan's self is not so good, although Tekan envisions a way in which it will be perfected through education in the future.

In the beginning, the peasants generally failed the task of self-conceptualization assigned to them. Either they refused to make positive or negative characterizations of themselves, or they did so by describing material aspects of their lives. In the next stage, they began to characterize their own qualities on the basis of what other people said. They might say, going by what others said about them, that they were reputed to have such-and-such a fault. A third stage emerged when people measured themselves not against the allegations of others but against the traits or norms characteristic of an "ideal me." In a further stage, the individual "ideal" was frequently replaced by the collective ideal, and now self was taken as membership in a kind. Social norms or demands were seen as imposed on either the individual or the group. A motivology of groups had arisen to stand beside the motivology of individuals. Finally, primarily among younger educated people involved in progressive social life, there occurred a process of singling out and evaluating personal qualities. Something like a psychological frame of reference and simple psychological theories of human nature now existed. Luria assimilated all this to a text by Marx: "At first, man only looked at himself as if in a mirror, except that it is another person. Only by relating to Paul as to one like himself can Peter begin to relate to himself as a person" (1976:145). The pattern of these findings fits the developmental theory that knowledge of self and society are intimately intertwined (Baldwin, 1899; Cooley, 1902; Mead, 1934).

Bernstein distinguished between *elaborated* and *restricted* linguistic codes, which differ in the routinization and predictability of the speech and in "the extent to which each facilitates (elaborated code) or inhibits (restricted code) an orientation to symbolize intent in a verbally explicit form" (1974:25). These codes are functional in different kinds of behavior settings, and they facilitate different kinds of social and self-control. In an elaborated code, individuals wish to transmit a unique individual meaning that they assign to experience. They move to an elaborated code when they want to talk about what they see and know about the world. When they want to make signals about the immediate and obvious world that is right around them and which everybody knows, they use a restricted code. To shift to an elaborated code is to change their social relations with others, to "set themselves off." It means they have a unique understanding and knowledge which they want to tell others about. An elaborated code is ever-so-slightly presumptuous and aloof.

Elaborated codes facilitate the communication of subjective intent. The use of such a code requires that more time be used for speech and more planning be involved in each speech act. But elaborated codes reduce social solidarity. They emphasize the "I" over the "we." Because an elaborated code is verbally complex, hard to create, and hard to listen to, it tends to throw social relationships over into verbal channels.

Bernstein explained what happens when children begin to learn an elaborated code: "From a developmental perspective, an elaborated code user comes to perceive language as a set of theoretical possibilities available for the transmission of unique experience. The concept of self, unlike the concept of self of a speaker limited to a restricted code, will be verbally differentiated, so that it becomes in itself the object of special conceptual activity. In the case of a speaker limited to a restricted code, the concept of self will tend to be refracted through the implications of the status arrangement. Here there is no problem of self *because the problem is not relevant*" (1974:132). When Luria's peasants began living in an environment in which elaborated code was called for and in response began changing cognitively, self similarly became relevant for discussion and problems of self came into view. Something like this happens when children are introduced to elaborate codes, as Bernstein explained:

> As a child learns an elaborated code he learns to scan a particular syntax, to receive and transmit a particular pattern of meaning, to develop a particular verbal planning process, and very early *learns to orient towards the verbal channel.* He learns to manage the role requirements necessary for the effective production of the code. He becomes aware of a certain order of relationships (intellectual, social, and emotional) in his environment, and his experience is transformed by these relations. As the code becomes established through his planning procedures, the developing child voluntarily, through his acts of speech, generates these relations. He comes to perceive language as a set of theoretical possibilities for the presentation of his discrete experience to others. An elaborated code, through its regulation, induces developmentally in its speakers an expectation of separateness and difference from others. It points to the possibilities inherent in a complex conceptual hierarchy for the organization of experience (1974:132–133).

Selection of Social Situations in Childhood

There are two orders of movement in how children "grow up" cognitively. Children explore an ever-widening set of behavior settings and develop action systems that establish them as effective participants in some of these settings and as nonfrequenters of others. At the same time, children extend the world around them into a larger symbolic world stocked with imaginaries. Some of the imaginaries that children deal with are fantasies. Some are what the child's society takes as a broader reality lying over the horizon. The lines between fantasy and reality are not easy to define.

Small children easily and effortlessly make their way out into the complex world of local society, entering and mastering hundreds of behavior settings that have special requirements and special kinds of applicability. This process of entrances and niche-finding is orderly and vital for the future potentiality of the child as a capable adult. Only the shadows of this migration flicker on the walls of the experimental rooms, and to them is attributed cognitive development.

A second migratory process overlaps the first. Not too long after children begin to deal with the three-dimensional reality around them, they begin to contend with the internal relations or microcosms constituted by their make-believe symbolic activity. Children bring the larger world near, as when they put three toy trucks and a tiny gas station on the floor before them and manipulate the world by manipulating the objects. This second process of cognitive development gradually brings children into commerce with large expanses of time, place, and occasion that lie beyond the community. A large part of what is called "verbal ability," "reasoning," "abstraction," and "secondary, process thinking" has to do with the constructive use of imaginaries.

A reasonable examination of children in their milieu calls for some return to a functional view of children's cognitive development. Indeed, a sequence of genetic logics may be entailed in children's attainment of more and more intellectual power as they get older. Present data give little hope that cognitive changes in growing children will be explained by some giant structuralist motor that majestically rolls forth one comprehensive logic after another. But there may be a necessary structural order in which intellectual control is attained in a distinctive context or behavior setting. This would be consistent with the several species of modified genetic logics (Pascual-Leone, 1976; Lawler, 1979, 1981; Fischer, 1980; Siegler, 1981).

Campbell (1974) put forward a possible framework for understanding children's cognitive development. Although evolutionary epistemology encompasses cognitive and social psychology and embodies a functional rather than a structural analysis of the creation of knowingness, it contains some of the elegant philosophical design features characteristic of Piaget's systematics. Perhaps with an explicit consideration of the social contexts of children's development, with a taxonomy or theory of psychological situations, and with a renewed interest in functionalism, it will lead to understanding of the many ways in which children come to know more as they leave the places of children and move toward the places of adults in human society.

Acknowledgments

This book took shape through a study group, organized by Rogoff and Lave, which was sponsored by the Society for Research on Child Development (SRCD) under the auspices of the Foundation for Child Development. The Foundation for Child Development is a private foundation that makes grants to educational and charitable institutions. Its main interests are in research, social and economic indicators of children's lives, advocacy and public information projects, and service experiments that help translate theoretical knowledge about children into policies and practices that affect their daily lives.

The study group was facilitated by Emma Corrigan's organization behind the scenes. The shape of both the book and the study group were influenced in an important manner by Dorothy Holland, Eric Wanner, and the SRCD Committee on Summer Institutes and Study Groups, headed by Thomas Tighe.

The research for Chapter 1 was conducted under a grant from the Ford Foundation. The author's close collaborator in the studies reported was Edward Fahrmeier, who worked with her on all stages of task development and data interpretation. Evelyn Jacob located and developed the field site and conducted an ethnography of literacy in the dairy in the first phase of the research program. Kathryn Rose assisted in interviews and data analysis, and Robert Russell participated in analyzing the pricing and other tasks.

Financial support to conduct the research for Chapter 2 was provided by National Institute of Education Grant #G-78-0177. Assistance in gathering the data was provided by Margaret Crowdes, Alma Hertweck, and Lee Meihls. The Laboratory of Comparative Human Cognition offered a stimulating atmosphere in which to develop ideas. Constructive criticism of this study was made by Aaron V. Cicourel, Michael Cole, James A. Levin, Barbara Rogoff, and Sylvia Scribner.

Research for Chapter 3 was funded by National Institute of Education Grant No. NIE-G-78-0194, and the writing was supported by National Institute of Education Grant No. NIE-G-81-0092. The Center for Human Information Processing at the University of California, San Diego, provided facilities and encouragement to write. Special thanks are due Michael Cole and the Laboratory of Comparative Human Cognition at UCSD for their support. The chapter benefited greatly from skillful data collection by Michael Migalski and from critical readings by Jim Levin, Dorothy Holland, David Lancy, Edwin Hutchins, Aaron Cicourel, Andrea Petitto, and Willett Kempton. Two colleagues influenced its development in ways so crucial that it would have been a different, and lesser, piece of work without their help: Hugh Gladwin and John Comaroff.

Mary Gauvain and Shari Ellis played a helpful role in various phases of the research and writing of Chapter 4. The financial support for this work came from NIH Biomedical Research Support Grant No. RR07092 to the University of Utah.

Chapter 5 was partially supported by a grant from the Spencer Foundation. The figure is reproduced with permission from N. Warren, ed., *Studies in Cross-Cultural Psychology*, vol. 2, © Academic Press, Inc., London.

Chapter 6 is a revised version of the paper "Simplification, Debugging, and Coaching" by Fischer, Burton, and Brown, which appeared in *Proceedings of the Second National Conference of the Canadian Society for Computational Studies of Intelligence*, 1978.

The research reported in Chapter 8 was supported by National Institute of Education Grant No. NIE-G-78-0159. Sheilia Broyles, Karen Johnson, Jean LeBeau, Marilyn Quinsaat, Mitch Rabinowitz, Marti tum Suden, and members of the Laboratory of Comparative Human Cognition made a continuing contribution to this work.

Barbara Allardice did the bulk of the interviewing for Chapter 9, and Herbert Ginsburg did the minor part. Additional interviews were conducted by Kathy Hebbeler and Robert Russell. Some of the interviews are published in Ginsburg, 1982. Further case studies were conducted by Allardice in Rochester and by Ginsburg in Baltimore. Preparation of the chapter was partially supported by National Institute of Education Grant No. NIE-G-78-0163 to Ginsburg. Arthur Baroody, Jane Knitzer, Nancy Kossan, and Robert Russell made helpful comments on an early draft.

Research presented in Chapter 10 was supported by grants from the National Science Foundation (BNS 78-09119) and the National Institute for Mental Health (1 RO1 MH 34723-01).

References

Introduction. *Thinking and Learning in Social Context*

Acredolo, L. P. 1979. Laboratory versus home: the effect of environment on the nine-month-old infant's choice of spatial reference system. *Developmental Psychology* 15:666–667.

Brainerd, C. J. 1978. The stage question in cognitive-development theory. *Behavioral and Brain Sciences* 1:173–181.

Charlesworth, W. R. 1976. Human intelligence as adaptation: an ethological approach. In L. B. Resnick, ed. *The nature of intelligence*. Hillsdale, N.J.: Erlbaum.

Cole, M. 1975. An ethnographic psychology of cognition. In R. W. Brislin, S. Bochner, & W. J. Lonner, eds. *Cross-cultural perspectives on learning*. New York: Wiley.

Cole, M., L. Hood, & R. P. McDermott. 1978a. Concepts of ecological validity: their differing implications for comparative cognitive research. *The Quarterly Newsletter of the Institute for Comparative Human Development* 2:34–37.

Cole, M., L. Hood, & R. P. McDermott. 1978b. Ecological niche picking: ecological invalidity as an axiom of experimental cognitive psychology. University of California, San Diego, and the Rockefeller University.

Cole, M., & S. Scribner. 1975. Theorizing about socialization of cognition. *Ethos* 3:250–268.

DeLoache, J. S. 1980. Naturalistic studies of memory for object location in very young children. *New Directions for Child Development* 10:17–32.

DeLoache, J. S., & A. L. Brown. 1979. Looking for Big Bird: studies of memory in very young children. *The Quarterly Newsletter of the Laboratory of Comparative Human Cognition* 1:53–57.

Feldman, D. H. 1980. *Beyond universals in cognitive development*. Norwood, N.J.: Ablex.

Fischer, K. W. 1980. A theory of cognitive development: the control and construction of hierarchies of skills. *Psychological Review* 87:477–531.

Flavell, J. H. 1977. *Cognitive development*. Englewood Cliffs, N.J.: Prentice-Hall.

282   *References*

Gelman, R. 1978. Cognitive development. *Annual Review of Psychology* 29:297–332.

Gladwin, T. 1970. *East is a big bird*. Cambridge: Harvard University Press.

Gleason, J. B. 1973. Code switching in children's language. In T. E. Moore, ed. *Cognitive development and the acquisition of language*. New York: Academic Press.

Laboratory of Comparative Human Cognition. 1979. Cross-cultural psychology's challenges to our ideas of children and development. *American Psychologist* 34:827–833.

Labov, W. 1970. The logic of non-standard English. In F. Williams, ed. *Language and poverty*. Chicago: Markham.

Lave, J. 1977. Tailor-made experiments and evaluating the intellectual consequences of apprenticeship training. *The Quarterly Newsletter of the Institute for Comparative Human Development* 1:1–3.

McCall, R. B. 1977. Challenges to a science of developmental psychology. *Child Development* 48:333–344.

Parke, R. D. 1979. Interactional designs. In R. B. Cairns, ed. *The analysis of social interactions*. Hillsdale, N.J.: Erlbaum.

Piaget, J. 1970. Piaget's theory. In P. H. Mussen, ed. *Carmichael's manual of child psychology*, vol. 1. New York: Wiley.

Price-Williams, D. R. 1980. Anthropological approaches to cognition and their relevance to psychology. In H. C. Triandis & W. Lonner, eds. *Handbook of cross-cultural psychology*, vol. 3. Boston. Allyn & Bacon.

Reese, H. W. 1977. Discriminative learning and transfer: dialectical perspectives. In N. Datan & H. W. Reese, eds. *Life-span developmental psychology: dialectical perspectives on experimental research*. New York: Academic Press.

Rogoff, B. 1981. Schooling and the development of cognitive skills. In H. C. Triandis & A. Heron, eds. *Handbook of cross-cultural psychology*, vol. 4. Boston: Allyn & Bacon.

———. 1982. Integrating context and cognitive development. In M. E. Lamb & A. L. Brown, eds. *Advances in developmental psychology*, vol. 2. Hillsdale, N.J.: Erlbaum.

Rogoff, B., & M. Gauvain. 1983. The generality of pattern influence skills from experience weaving and in school. University of Utah.

Scribner, S. 1976. Situating the experiment in cross-cultural research. In K. F. Riegel & J. A. Meacham, eds. *The developing individual in a changing world*, vol. 1. Chicago: Aldine.

Scribner, S., & M. Cole. 1981. *The psychology of literacy*. Cambridge: Harvard University Press.

Shatz, M., & R. Gelman. 1977. Beyond syntax: the influence of conversational constraints on speech modifications. In C. E. Snow & C. A. Ferguson, eds. *Talking to children*. Cambridge: Cambridge University Press.

Siegel, A. W. 1977. "Remembering" is alive and well (and even thriving) in empiricism. In N. Datan & H. W. Reese, eds. *Life-span developmental psychology: dialectical perspectives on experimental research.* New York: Academic Press.

Siegler, R. S. 1981. Developmental sequences within and between concepts. *Monographs of the Society for Research in Child Development* 46(2, no. 189).

Todd, C. M., & M. Perlmutter. 1980. Reality recalled by preschool children. *New Directions for Child Development* 10:69–85.

Vygotsky, L. S. 1978. *Mind in society.* Cambridge: Harvard University Press.

Weisz, J. R. 1978. Transcontextual validity in developmental research. *Child Development* 49:1–12.

Wellman, H. M., & S. C. Somerville. 1980. Quasi-naturalistic tasks in the study of cognition: the memory-related skills of toddlers. *New Directions for Child Development* 10:33–48.

Wohlwill, J. F. 1981. Ecological representativeness in developmental research: a critical view. Paper presented at meetings of Society for Research in Child Development, Boston.

1. Studying Working Intelligence

Aristotle. 1963. Book I, Metaphysics. In R. Bambrough, ed. *The philosophy of Aristotle.* New York: Mentor.

Bamberger, J., & D. A. Schon. 1976. The figural formal transaction: a parable of generative metaphor. Mimeo. Cambridge: Division for Study and Research in Education, MIT.

Bartlett, F. 1958. *Thinking.* New York: Basic Books.

Bronfenbrenner, U. 1979. *The ecology of human development.* Cambridge: Harvard University Press.

Brown, A. L. 1977. Development, schooling and the acquisition of knowledge about knowledge. In R. C. Anderson, R. J. Spiro, & W. E. Montague, eds. *Schooling and the acquisition of knowledge.* Hillsdale, N.J.: Erlbaum.

Brown, A. L., & L. A. French. 1979. Commentary. In D. W. Sharp, M. Cole, & C. Lave, eds. Education and cognitive development: the evidence from experimental research. *Monographs of the Society for Research in Child Development* 44(1–2, no. 178):101–108.

Chase, W. G., & H. A. Simon. 1973. Perception in chess. *Cognitive Psychology* 4:55–81.

Childs, C. P., & P. M. Greenfield. 1980. Informal modes of learning and teaching: the case of Zinacanteco weaving. In N. Warren, ed. *Advances in cross-cultural psychology,* vol. 2. London: Academic Press.

Cole, M. 1979. Reply. In D. W. Sharp, M. Cole, & C. Lave, eds. Education and cognitive development: the evidence from experimental research. *Monographs of the Society for Research in Child Development* 44(1–2, no. 178):109–112.

Cole, M., L. Hood, & R. McDermott. 1978. Ecological niche picking:

ecological invalidity as an axiom of experimental cognitive psychology. Univ. of Cal., San Diego, and The Rockefeller University.

Cole, M., & S. Scribner. 1974. *Culture and thought.* New York: Wiley.

Dasen, P. R. 1977. Introduction. In P. R. Dasen, ed. *Piagetian psychology: cross-cultural contributions.* New York: Gardner Press.

deGroot, A. D. 1966. Perception and memory versus thought: some old ideas and recent findings. In B. Kleinmuntz, ed. *Problem-solving: research, method and theory.* New York: Wiley.

Ginsburg, H. P., J. K. Posner, & R. L. Russell. 1981. The development of knowledge concerning written arithmetic: a cross-cultural study. *International Journal of Psychology* 16:13–34.

Goody, J., ed. 1968. *Literacy in traditional societies.* New York: Cambridge University Press.

———. 1977. *The domestication of the savage mind.* New York: Cambridge University Press.

Greenfield, P. M. 1972. Oral and written languages: the consequences for cognitive development in Africa, the United States, and England. *Language and Speech* 15:169–178.

———. 1966. On culture and equivalence. In J. S. Bruner, R. R. Olver, P. M. Greenfield, et al., eds. *Studies in cognitive growth.* New York: Wiley.

Havelock, E. A. 1963. *Preface to Plato.* Cambridge: Harvard University Press.

Hayes, J. R., & H. A. Simon. 1977. Psychological differences among problem isomorphs. In N. J. Castellan, D. B. Pisoni, & G. R. Potts, eds. *Cognitive theory,* vol. 2. Hillsdale, N.J.: Erlbaum.

Hutchins, E. 1979. Conceptual structures in pre-literate Pacific navigation. Paper presented at Social Science Research Council, San Diego, Cal.

Inkeles, A., & D. H. Smith. 1974. *Becoming modern.* Cambridge: Harvard University Press.

James, W. 1950. *The principles of psychology,* vol. 2. New York: Dover. Originally published 1890.

Klahr, D. 1979. Self-modifying production systems as models of cognitive development. Paper presented at Biennial Meeting of Society for Research in Child Development, San Francisco.

Klahr, D., & M. Robinson. 1981. Formal assessment of problem-solving and planning processes in preschool children. *Cognitive Psychology* 13:1–36.

Laboratory of Comparative Human Cognition. 1979. Cross-cultural psychology's challenges to our ideas of children and development. *American Psychologist* 34:827–833.

Laurendeau-Bendavid, M. 1977. Culture, schooling and cognitive development: a comparative study of children in French Canada and Rwanda. In P. Dasen, ed. *Piagetian psychology: cross-cultural contributions.* New York: Gardner Press.

Lave, J. 1977. Cognitive consequences of traditional apprenticeship training in West Africa. *Anthropology and Education Quarterly* 8:177–180.

Mehan, H. 1979. *Learning lessons.* Cambridge: Harvard University Press.

Neisser, U. 1976. General, academic, and artificial intelligence. In L. B. Resnick, ed. *The nature of intelligence.* Hillsdale, N.J.: Erlbaum.

Newell, A., & H. A. Simon. 1972. *Human problem-solving.* Englewood Cliffs, N.J.: Prentice-Hall.

Olson, D. R. 1977. From utterance to text: the bias of language in speech and writing. *Harvard Educational Review* 47:257–281.

Olson, D. R., & E. Bialystok. 1980. Mental representations of space: the representation of objects and the representation of form. In B. de Gelder, ed. *Knowledge and representation.* London: Routledge and Kegan Paul.

Olson, D. R., & N. Nickerson. 1978. Language development through the school years: learning to confine interpretation to the information conventionalized in the text. In K. E. Nelson, ed. *Children's language,* vol. 1. New York: Gardner Press.

Piaget, J. 1950. *The psychology of intelligence.* London: Routledge and Kegan Paul.

Reed, H. J., & J. Lave. 1979. Arithmetic as a tool for investigating relations between culture and cognition. *American Ethnologist* 6:568–582.

Resnick, L. B. 1976. Task analysis in instructional design: some cases from mathematics. In D. Klahr, ed. *Cognition and instruction.* Hillsdale, N.J.: Erlbaum.

Rogoff, B. 1981. Schooling and the development of cognitive skills. In H. C. Triandis & A. Heron, eds. *Handbook of cross-cultural psychology,* vol. 4. Boston: Allyn and Bacon.

Scribner, S. 1974. Developmental aspects of categorized recall in a West African society. *Cognitive Psychology* 6:475–494.

———. 1977. Literacy as a cultural practice. Paper presented at American Anthropological Association Annual Meeting, Houston.

———. 1978. The concept of practice in research on culture and thought. Paper presented at Soviet-American Conference on the Psychological Theory of Activity, Institute of Psychology, Moscow.

Scribner, S., & M. Cole. 1973. Cognitive consequences of formal and informal education. *Science* 182:553–559.

Scribner, S., & M. Cole. 1981. *The psychology of literacy.* Cambridge: Harvard University Press.

Scribner, S., & E. Fahrmeier. 1982. *Practical and theoretical arithmetic.* Working Paper 3, Industrial Literacy Project. New York: The Graduate School and University Center, CUNY.

Sharp, D. W., M. Cole, & C. Lave. 1979. Education and cognitive development: the evidence from experimental research. *Monographs of the Society for Research in Child Development* 44(1–2, no. 178).

Siegler, R. S. 1980. Recent trends in the study of cognitive development: variations on a task-analytic theme. *Human Development* 23:278–285.

Simon, H. A. 1975. The functional equivalence of problem-solving skills. *Cognitive Psychology* 7:268–288.

————. 1976. Identifying basic abilities underlying intelligent performance of complex tasks. In L. Resnick, ed. *The nature of intelligence.*
Hillsdale, N.J.: Erlbaum.

Simon, H. A., & S. K. Reed. 1976. Modelling strategy shifts in a problem-
solving task. *Cognitive Psychology* 8:86–97.

Stevenson, H. W., T. Parker, A. Wilkinson, B. Bonnevaux, & M. Gonzalez.
1978. Schooling, environment, and cognitive development: a cross-
cultural study. *Monographs of the Society for Research in Child Development* 43(3, no. 175).

Vygotsky, L. S. 1962. *Thought and language.* Cambridge: M.I.T. Press.

————. 1978. *Mind in society.* Cambridge: Harvard University Press.

Wagner, D. A. 1978. Memories of Morocco: the influence of age, schooling
and environment on memory. *Cognitive Psychology* 10:1–28.

Wertheimer, M. 1959. *Productive thinking.* Ed. Michael Wertheimer.
New York: Harper.

2. Institutional Decision-Making

Allison, G. 1971. *Essence of decision.* Boston: Little, Brown.

Bartlett, F. D. 1958. *Thinking.* New York: Basic Books.

Becker, H. 1963. *Outsiders.* New York: Free Press.

Benson, J. K. 1977. Innovation and crisis in organizational analysis. *Sociological Quarterly* 18:3–16.

Cicourel, A. V. 1980. Three models of discourse. *Discourse Processes*
3:100–132.

Cole, M., & K. Traupmann, 1981. Comparative cognitive research: learning from a learning disabled child. In *Minnesota Symposia on Child
Psychology.* vol. 14. Hillsdale, N.J.: Erlbaum.

D'Andrade, R. G. In press. Cultural meaning systems. In Richard
Schweder, ed. *Essays on the social origins of mind, self and emotion.*
Chicago: University of Chicago Press.

Elstein, A. S., L. S. Shulman, & S. V. Sprafke. 1978. *Medical problem
solving.* Cambridge: Harvard University Press.

Garfinkel, H. 1967. *Studies in ethnomethodology.* New York: Prentice-
Hall.

Goffman, E. 1961. *Asylums: essays on the social situation of mental
patients and other inmates.* Garden City, N.Y.: Anchor Books.

Heap, J. 1980. Description in ethnomethodology. *Human Studies* 3(1):87–
106.

Inhelder, B., & J. Piaget. 1958. *The growth of logical thinking from childhood to adolescence.* New York: Basic Books.

Janis, I., & L. Mann. 1978. *Decision making.* New York: Free Press.

Katz, D., & R. L. Kahn. 1978. *The social psychology of organizations.* New
York: Wiley.

Laboratory of Comparative Human Cognition. 1981. Culture and intelligence. In R. Sternberg, ed. *Handbook of intelligence.* New York:
Cambridge University Press.

Lakoff, G., & M. Johnson. 1980. *Metaphors we live by.* Chicago: University of Chicago Press.

Lave, J. 1979. A model of mundane arithmetic problem solving. Paper presented at SSRC Conference on Cultural Representations of Knowledge, La Jolla, Cal.

Levin, J. A. 1981. Everyday problem solving. Paper presented at Third Annual Cognitive Science Meetings, Berkeley, Cal.

Levin, J., & Y. Kareev. 1980. Problem solving in everyday situations. *Quarterly Newsletter of the Laboratory of Comparative Human Cognition* 2(3):47–52.

March, J. A., & J. P. Olsen. 1976. *Ambiguity and choice in organizations.* Bergen: Universitetsforlaget.

Mehan, H. 1979. *Learning lessons.* Cambridge: Harvard University Press.

———. 1983. The role of language and the language of role in practical decision making. *Language in Society* 12(3):1–39.

Mehan, H., et al. 1981. Identifying handicapped students. In S. B. Bacharach, ed. *Organizational behavior in schools and school districts.* New York: Praeger.

Mehan, H., A. Hertweck, S. E. Combs, & P. J. Flynn. 1982. Teachers' interpretations of students' behavior. In L. C. Wilkinson, ed. *Communicating in the classroom.* New York: Academic Press.

Meihls, J. L. 1981. Handicapping students. Paper presented at Second Annual Ethnography in Education Forum, Philadelphia, Pa.

Norman, D. A., & D. G. Bobrow. 1975. On data-limited and resource-limited processes. *Cognitive Psychology* 7:44–64.

Parsons, T. 1932. *The structure of social action.* Glencoe, Ill.: Free Press.

Pepper, S. 1944. *World hypotheses.* Berkeley: University of California Press.

Quinn, N. 1976. A natural system used in Mfantse litigation settlement. *American Ethnologist* 3:331–351.

Rosenhan, D. L. 1973. On being sane in insane places. *Science* 179:250–258.

Scheff, T. J. 1966. *Being mentally ill: a sociological theory.* Chicago: Aldine.

Schelling, T. 1950. *Strategies of conflict.* New York: Oxford University Press.

Schutz, A. 1943. The problem of rationality in the social world. *Economica* 10:142–143.

———. 1962. *Collected papers I: the problem of social reality.* The Hague: Martinus Nijoff.

———. 1964. *Collected papers II: studies in social theory.* The Hague: Mouton.

Scribner, S. 1977. Modes of thinking and ways of speaking: culture and logic reconsidered. In P. N. Johnson-Laird & P. C. Wason, eds. *Thinking: readings in cognitive science.* Cambridge: Cambridge University Press.

Shweder, P. A. 1977. Likeness and likelihood in everyday thought: magical thinking in judgments about personality. *Current Anthropology* 18:637–648.

Simon, H. A. 1976. *Discussion: cognitive and social behavior.* Hillsdale, N. J.: Erlbaum.

Simon, N. 1949. *Administrative behavior.* New York: Free Press.

Tversky, A. 1972. Elimination by aspects. *Psychological Review* 79:281–299.

Tversky, A., & D. Kahneman. 1974. Judgement under uncertainty: heuristics and biases. *Science* 185 (September):1124–1131.

Wason, P. 1977. The theory of formal operations: a critique. In B. A. Gerber, ed. *Piaget and knowing.* London: Routledge and Kegan Paul.

Watkins, J. 1970. Imperfect rationality. In R. Borger & F. Cioffi, eds. *Explanation in the behavioral sciences.* Cambridge: Cambridge University Press.

Weber, M. 1947. *The theory of social and economic organization.* Trans. A. M. Henderson & T. Parsons. New York: Free Press.

Weick, K. 1976. Educational organizations as loosely coupled systems. *Administrative Science Quarterly* 21:1–19.

Witkin, H. A., & J. W. Berry 1975. Psychological differentiation in cross-cultural perspective. *Journal of Cross-Cultural Psychology* 6:4–87.

3. *The Dialectic of Arithmetic in Grocery Shopping*

Barker, R. G. 1963. On the nature of the environment. Kurt Lewin memorial award address, 1963. *Journal of Social Issues* 19:17–38.

———. 1968. *Ecological psychology: concepts and methods for studying the environment of human behavior.* Stanford: Stanford University Press.

Barker, R. G., & H. F. Wright. 1954. *Midwest and its children: the psychological ecology of an American town.* Evanston, Ill.: Row, Peterson.

Bartlett, F. C. 1958. *Thinking: an experimental and social study.* New York: Basic Books.

Bronfenbrenner, U. 1979. *The ecology of human development: experiments by nature and design.* Cambridge: Harvard University Press.

Bronfenbrenner, U., & M. A. Mahoney, eds. 1975. *Influences on human development.* 2nd ed. Hinsdale, Ill.: Dryden Press.

Cole, M., L. Hood, & R. McDermott. 1978. Ecological niche picking: ecological invalidity as an axiom of experimental cognitive psychology. University of California, San Diego, and the Rockefeller University.

de la Rocha, O. In preparation. The use of arithmetic in the context of dieting: a study of practical problem solving. Ph.D. diss. University of California, Irvine.

Laboratory of Comparative Human Cognition. 1981. Culture and cognitive development. In J. V. Wertsch, ed. *Culture, cognition and communication.* Cambridge: Cambridge University Press.

Lave, J. In preparation. Culture and cognitive theory.

Murtaugh, M. 1984. A hierarchical decision model of American grocery shopping. Ph.D. diss. University of California, Irvine.

Neisser, U. 1976. *Cognition and reality: principles and implications of cognitive psychology.* San Francisco: Freeman.

Schank, R., & R. Abelson. 1977. *Scripts, plans, goals and understanding: an inquiry into human knowledge structures.* Hillsdale, N.J.: Erlbaum.

Wertsch, J. V. 1979. The regulation of human action and the origins of inner speech. In G. Zivin, ed. *The development of self-regulation through speech.* New York: Wiley.

———. 1981. Trends in Soviet cognitive psychology. *Storia e critica della psicologia* 2(2).

4. Adult Guidance of Cognitive Development

Bartlett, F. C. 1958. *Thinking: an experimental and social study.* New York: Basic Books.

Bernstein, L. E. 1981. Language as a product of dialogue. *Discourse Processes* 4:117–147.

Brainerd, C. J. 1978. The stage question in cognitive-development theory. *Behavioral and Brain Sciences* 1:173–181.

Brown, A. 1979. Theories of memory and the problems of development: activity, growth, and knowledge. In L. S. Cermak & F. I. M. Craik, eds. *Levels of processing and human memory.* Hillsdale, N.J.: Erlbaum.

Bruner, J. S. 1981. Intention in the structure of action and interaction. In L. P. Lipsitt, ed. *Advances in infancy research,* vol. 1. Norwood, N.J.: Ablex.

Burstein, M. H. 1981. Concept formation through the interaction of multiple models. *Proceedings of the third annual conference of the Cognitive Science Society.* Berkeley, Cal.

Burton, R. R., & J. S. Brown. 1979. An investigation of computer coaching for informal learning activities. *International Journal of Man-Machine Studies* 11:5–24.

Butterworth, G., & E. Cochran. 1980. Towards a mechanism of joint visual attention in human infancy. *International Journal of Behavioral Development* 3:253–272.

Cazden, C. 1979. Peekaboo as an instructional model: discourse development at home and at school. In *Papers and reports on child language development,* no. 17. Stanford University, Department of Linguistics.

Cole, M., & P. Griffin. 1980. Cultural amplifiers reconsidered. In D. R. Olson, ed. *The social foundations of language and thought.* New York: Norton.

D'Andrade, R. G. 1981. The cultural part of cognition. *Cognitive Science* 5:179–195.

DeLoache, J., & A. Brown. 1979. Looking for Big Bird: studies of memory in very young children. *The Quarterly Newsletter of the Laboratory of Comparative Human Cognition* 1:53–57.

Dunkin, M., & B. Biddle. 1974. *The study of teaching.* New York: Holt, Rinehart & Winston.

Feldman, D. H. 1980. *Beyond universals in cognitive development.* Norwood, N.J.: Ablex.

Gick, M. L., & K. J. Holyoak. 1980. Analogical problem solving. *Cognitive Psychology* 12:306–355.

Glick, J. 1978. Cognition and social cognition: an introduction. In J. Glick & K. A. Clarke-Stewart, eds. *The development of social understanding.* New York: Gardner Press.

Greenfield, P. M. 1980. Toward an operational and logical analysis of intentionality: the use of discourse in early child language. In D. R. Olson, ed. *The social foundations of language and thought.* New York: Norton.

Greenfield, P. M. & J. Lave. 1982. Cognitive aspects of informal education. In D. Wagner & H. Stevenson, eds. *Cultural perspectives on child development.* San Francisco: Freeman.

Hay, D. F. 1980. Multiple functions of proximity seeking in infancy. *Child Development* 51:636–645.

Hogbin, H. I. 1970. A New Guinea childhood: from weaning until the eighth year in Wogeo. In J. Middleton, ed. *From child to adult.* New York: Natural History Press.

Kaye, K. 1979. The development of skills. In G. Whitehurst & B. Zimmerman, eds. *The functions of language and cognition.* New York: Academic Press.

Kuipers, B. 1979. On representing common-sense knowledge. In N. V. Findler, ed. *Associative networks.* New York: Academic Press.

Laboratory of Comparative Human Cognition. 1980. Culture and cognitive development. University of California, San Diego.

Lave, J. In preparation. Tailored learning: education and cognitive skills among tribal craftsmen in West Africa.

Lempers, J. D. 1979. Young children's production and comprehension of nonverbal deictic behaviors. *Journal of Genetic Psychology* 135:93–102.

McNamee, G. D. 1980. The social origins of narrative skills. PhD. dissertation, Northwestern University.

Mehan, H. 1976. Assessing children's school performance. In J. Beck, C. Jenks, N. Keddie, & M. F. D. Young, eds. *Worlds apart.* London: Collier Macmillan.

Mehan, H., & M. M. Riel. In press. Teachers' and students' instructional strategies. In L. L. Adler, ed. *Issues in cross-cultural research.* New York: Academic Press.

Messer, D. J. 1980. The episodic structure of maternal speech to young children. *Journal of Child Language* 7:29–40.

Ochs, E. 1979. Introduction: what child language can contribute to pragmatics. In E. Ochs & B. Schieffelin, eds. *Developmental pragmatics.* New York: Academic Press.

Petrie, H. G. 1979. Metaphor and learning. In A. Ortony, ed. *Metaphor and thought.* Cambridge: Cambridge University Press.

Rogoff, B. 1982a. Integrating context and cognitive development. In M. E. Lamb & A. L. Brown, eds. *Advances in developmental psychology,* vol. 2. Hillsdale, N.J.: Erlbaum.

————. 1982b. Mode of instruction and memory test performance. *International Journal of Behavioral Development* 5:33–48.

Rogoff, B., S. Ellis, & W. Gardner. In press. The adjustment of maternal-child instruction according to child's age and task. *Developmental Psychology.*

Ruddle, K., & R. Chesterfield. 1978. Traditional skill training and labor in rural societies. *The Journal of Developing Areas* 12:389–398.

Scribner, S., & M. Cole. 1973. Cognitive consequences of formal and informal education. *Science* 182:553–559.

Siegler, R. S. 1981. Developmental sequences within and between concepts. *Monographs of the Society for Research in Child Development* 46:(2, no. 189).

Snow, C. 1977. Mother's speech research: from input to interaction. In C. E. Snow & C. A. Ferguson, eds. *Talking to children.* Cambridge: Cambridge University Press.

Sorce, J. F., R. N. Emde, & M. Klinnert. 1981. Maternal emotional signaling: its effect on the visual cliff behavior of one-year-olds.

Turvey, M. 1974. Constructive theory, perceptual systems, and tacit knowledge. In W. B. Weimer & D. S. Palermo, eds. *Cognition and the symbolic processes.* Hillsdale, N.J.: Erlbaum.

Vygotsky, L. S. 1962. *Thought and language.* Cambridge: M.I.T. Press.

————. 1978. *Mind in society.* Cambridge: Harvard University Press.

Wertsch, J. 1979. From social interaction to higher psychological processes. *Human Development* 22:1–22.

Wertsch, J. V., & C. A. Stone. 1979. A social interactional analysis of learning disabilities remediation. Paper presented at International Conference of Association for Children with Learning Disabilities, San Francisco.

Wood, D. J. 1980. Teaching the young child: some relationships between social interaction, language, and thought. In D. R. Olson, ed. *The social foundations of language and thought.* New York: Norton.

Wood, D., J. S. Bruner, & G. Ross. 1976. The role of tutoring in problem solving. *Journal of Child Psychology and Psychiatry* 17:89–100.

Wood, D., H. Wood, & D. Middleton. 1978. An experimental evaluation of four face-to-face teaching strategies. *International Journal of Behavioral Development* 2:131–147.

Zukow, P. G., J. Reilly, & P. M. Greenfield. 1982. Making the absent present: facilitating the transition from sensorimotor to linguistic communication. In K. Nelson, ed. *Children's language,* vol. 3. New York: Gardner Press.

5. *A Theory of the Teacher in the Learning Activities of Everyday Life*

Brown, A. L. 1975. The development of memory: knowing, knowing about knowing, and knowing how to know. In H. W. Reese, ed. *Advances in child development and behavior*, vol. 10. New York: Academic Press.

———. 1979. Theories of memory and the problems of development: activity, growth, and knowledge. In L. S. Cermak & F. I. M. Craik, eds. *Levels of processing in human memory*. Hillsdale, N.J.: Erlbaum.

Childs, C. P., & P. M. Greenfield. 1980. Informal modes of learning and teaching: the case of Zinacanteco weaving. In N. Warren, ed. *Studies in cross-cultural psychology*, vol. 2. London: Academic Press.

Chomsky, N. 1965. *Aspects of a theory of syntax*. Cambridge: M.I.T. Press.

Greenfield, P. M., & J. Lave. 1982. Cognitive aspects of informal education. In D. Wagner & H. Stevenson, eds. *Cultural perspectives on child development*. San Francisco: Freeman.

Greenfield, P. M., & J. H. Smith. 1976. *The structure of communication in early language development*. New York: Academic Press.

Hatch, E., S. Peck, & J. Wagner-Gough. 1979. A look at process in child second language acquisition. In E. Ochs & B. B. Schieffelin, eds. *Developmental pragmatics*. New York: Academic Press.

Hickman, M., & J. V. Wertsch. 1978. Adult-child discourse in problem solving situations. *Papers from the fourteenth regional meeting, Chicago Linguistic Society*. Chicago: Chicago Linguistic Society.

Hunt, J. McV. 1961. *Intelligence and experience*. New York: Ronald Press.

Kunihara, S., & J. J. Asher. 1965. The strategy of the total physical response: an application to learning Japanese. *International Review of Applied Linguistics* 3:278–289.

Mehan, H. 1979. *Learning lessons: social organization in the classroom*. Cambridge: Harvard University Press.

Ochs, E., B. B. Schieffelin, & M. L. Platt. 1979. Propositions across utterances and speakers. In E. Ochs & B. B. Schieffelin, eds. *Developmental pragmatics*. New York: Academic Press.

Piaget, J. 1951. *Play, dreams, and imitation in childhood*. New York: Norton.

———. 1952. *The origins of intelligence in children*. New York: International University Press.

———. 1954. *The construction of reality in the child*. New York: Basic Books.

Reilly, J., P. G. Zukow, & P. M. Greenfield. 1978. Facilitating the transition from sensorimotor to linguistic communication. Paper presented at International Congress of Child Language, Tokyo.

Skinner, B. F. 1938. *The behavior of organisms: an experimental analysis*. New York: Appleton-Century-Crofts.

Vygotsky, L. S. 1962. *Thought and language*. Cambridge: M.I.T. Press.

———. 1966. Development of the higher mental functions. In *Psychological research in the U.S.S.R.* Moscow: Progress Publishers.

———. 1978. *Mind in society: the development of higher psychological processes.* Cambridge: Harvard University Press.

Wertsch, J. V. 1979a. Adult-child interaction as a source of self-regulation in children. Paper presented at Conference on Growth of Insight During Childhood, University of Wisconsin, Madison.

———. 1979b. The social interactional origins of metacognition. Paper presented at Biennial Meeting of Society for Research in Child Development, San Francisco.

Wood, D., H. Wood, & D. Middleton. 1978. An experimental evaluation of four face-to-face teaching strategies. *International Journal of Behavioral Development* 2:131–147.

Wood, D. J., J. S. Bruner, & G. Ross. 1976. The role of tutoring in problem solving. *Journal of Child Psychology and Psychiatry* 17:89–100.

Zukow, P. G., J. Reilly, & P. M. Greenfield, 1982. Making the absent present: facilitating the transition from sensorimotor to linguistic communication. In K. Nelson, ed. *Children's language*, vol. 3. New York: Gardner Press.

6. Skiing as a Model of Instruction

Abelson, H., & A. A. di Sessa. 1981. *Turtle geometry: the computer as a medium for exploring mathematics.* Cambridge: M.I.T. Press.

Austin, Howard. 1974. A computational view of the skill of juggling. Massachusetts Institute of Technology, AI Memo no. 330.

Carlo. 1974. *The juggling book.* New York: Random House.

Brown, J. S. 1982. Learning-by-doing revisited for electronic learning environments. In M. A. White, ed. *The future of electronic learning.* Hillsdale, N.J.: Erlbaum.

Brown, J. S., & R. R. Burton. 1978. Diagnostic models for procedural bugs in basic mathematical skills. *Cognitive Science* 2:155–191.

DVSL (Deutscher Verband fuer das Skilehowesen). 1977. Skilehoplan, vols. 1–7. Munich: BLV Verlagsgesellschaft.

Fischer, G. 1977. Das Loesen Komplexer Problemanf-gaben furh naive Beuutzer mit Hilfe des interaktiven Programmierens. Darmstadt: FG CUU.

Lave, J. 1977. Cognitive consequences of traditional apprenticeship training in West Africa. *Anthropology and Education Quarterly* 8(3):177–180.

Papert, S. 1976. Some poetic and social criteria for education design. Massachusetts Institute of Technology, AI Memo no. 373.

———. 1978. Computer-based micro-worlds as incubators for powerful ideas. Massachusetts Institute of Technology, AI Laboratory.

———. 1980. *Mindstorms: children, computers, and powerful ideas.* New York: Basic Books.

Simon, Herbert. 1969. *The sciences of the artificial.* Cambridge: M.I.T. Press.

VanLehn, K., & J. S. Brown. 1980. Planning nets: a representation for formalizing analogies and semantic models for procedural skills. In R. E. Snow, P. A. Frederico, & W. E. Montague, eds. *Aptitude learning and instruction, vol. 2: Cognitive process analyses of learning and problem-solving.* Hillsdale, N.J.: Erlbaum.

7. *The Creation of Context in Joint Problem-Solving*

Arns, Flavio Jose. 1980. Joint problem solving activity in adult-child dyads: a cross-cultural study. Dissertation, Northwestern University.

Chomsky, N. 1968. *Language and mind.* New York: Harcourt, Brace & World.

Cole, M., & S. Scribner. 1974. *Culture and thought.* New York: Wiley.

Davydov, V. V., & L. A. Radzikhovskii. In press. L. S. Vygotsky's theory and the activity-oriented approach in psychology. In J. V. Wertsch, ed. *Culture, communication, and cognition: Vygotskian perspectives.* New York: Cambridge University Press.

Fortes, M. 1938. Education in Taleland. *Africa* 11(Supplement):4.

Goffman, E. 1974. *Frame analysis: an essay on the organization of experience.* Cambridge: Harvard University Press.

Laosa, L. M. 1978. Maternal teaching strategies in Chicano families of varied educational and socio-economic levels. *Child Development* 49:1129–1135.

———. 1979. Maternal teaching strategies in Chicano and Anglo-American families: the influence of culture and education on maternal behavior. Educational Testing Service.

Lave, J. 1980. A comparative approach to educational forms and learning processes. Paper presented at Annual Meeting of American Anthropological Association.

———. In preparation. Tailored learning: education and cognitive skills among tribal craftsmen in West Africa.

Leontiev, A. N. 1972. *Problemy razvitiya psyikhiki* (Problems in the development of mind). Moscow: Izdatel'stvo Moskovskogo Universiteta. Trans. *Problems of the development of the mind.* Moscow: Progress, 1981.

———. 1975. *Deyatel'nost'. Soznanie. Lichnost'* (Activity. Consciousness. Personality). Moscow: Izdatel'stvo Politicheskoi Literatury. Trans. *Activity, consciousness, and personality.* Englewood Cliffs, N.J.: Prentice-Hall, 1978.

———. 1981. The problem of activity in psychology. In J. V. Wertsch, ed. *The concept of activity in Soviet psychology.* Armonk, N.Y.: Sharpe.

Luria, A. R. 1982. *Language and cognition.* New York: Wiley Interscience.

Marx, Karl. 1977. *Capital: a critique of political economy*, vol. 1. New York: Vintage Books.

Mead, G. H. 1934. *Mind, self and society.* Chicago: University of Chicago Press.

Smirnov, A. A. 1975. *Razvitie i sovremennoe sostoyanie psikhologicheskoi nauki v SSSR* (The development and current state of psychology in the USSR). Moscow: Pedagogika.

Vygotsky, L. S. 1956. *Izbrannye psikhologicheskie issledovaniya* (Selected psychological research). Moscow: Izdatel'stvo Akademii Pedagogicheskikh Nauk RSFSR.

———. 1978. *Mind in society: the development of higher psychological processes.* Cambridge: Harvard University Press.

———. 1981. The genesis of the higher mental functions. In J. V. Wertsch, ed. *The concept of activity in Soviet psychology.* Armonk, N.Y.: Sharpe.

Wertsch, J. V. 1981. The concept of activity in Soviet psychology: an introduction. In J. V. Wertsch, ed. *The concept of activity in Soviet psychology.* Armonk, N.Y.: Sharpe.

———. In press. A state of the art review of Soviet research in cognitive psychology. *Storia e Critica della Psicologia.*

Wertsch, J. V. & P. Schneider. 1980. Variations of adults' directives to children in a problem solving situation. Northwestern University.

8. *Social Constraints in Laboratory and Classroom Tasks*

Abelson, R. P. 1981. Psychological status of the script concept. *American Psychologist* 36(7):715–730.

Bartlett, F. C. 1958. *Thinking.* New York: Basic Books.

Brown, A. L., & R. A. Ferrara. In press. Diagnosing zones of proximal development. In J. Wertsch , ed. *Culture, communication, and cognition: Vygotskian perspectives.* New York: Academic Press.

Brown, A. L., & L. A. French. 1979. The zone of potential development: implications for intelligence testing in the year 2000. *Intelligence* 3:255–277.

Cole, M., L. Hood, & R. P. McDermott. 1978. Ecological niche picking: ecological invalidity as an axiom of experimental cognitive psychology. University of California, San Diego, and The Rockefeller University.

Cole, M., & K. Traupmann. 1981. Comparative cognitive research: learning from a learning disabled child. In *Minnesota Symposia on Child Psychology,* vol. 14. Hillsdale, N.J.: Erlbaum.

Gearhart, M., & D. Newman. 1980. Learning to draw a picture: the social context of an individual activity. *Discourse Processes* 3:169–184.

Gick, M. L., & K. J. Holyoak. 1980. Analogical problem solving. *Cognitive Psychology* 12:306–355.

Griffin, P., D. Newman, & M. Cole. 1981. *Activities, actions and formal operations: a Vygotskian analysis of a Piagetian task.* Paper presented at meetings of International Society for the Study of Behavioral Development, Toronto.

Inhelder, B., & J. Piaget. 1958. *The growth of logical thinking from childhood to adolescence.* New York: Basic Books.

Laboratory of Comparative Human Cognition. 1978. Cognition as a residual category in anthropology. *Annual Review of Anthropology* 7:51–69.

————. 1979. What's cultural about cross-cultural cognitive psychology? *Annual Review of Psychology* 30:145–172.

Lave, J. 1980. What's special about experiments as contexts for thinking. *The Quarterly Newsletter of the Laboratory of Comparative Human Cognition* 2(4):86–91.

Newman, D., P. Griffin, & M. Cole. In preparation. Learning in interaction: contributions to a cognitive science of education.

Newman, D., M. Riel, & L. Martin. 1983. Cultural practices and Piaget's theory: the impact of a cross-cultural research program. In D. Kuhn & J. A. Meacham, eds. *On the development of developmental psychology.* Basel: Karger.

Piaget, J., & B. Inhelder. 1975. *The origin of the idea of chance in children.* New York: Norton.

Reed, S. K., G. W. Ernst, & R. Banerji. 1974. The role of analogy in transfer between similar problem states. *Cognitive Psychology* 6:436–450.

Rumelhart, D. E. 1980. Schemata: the building blocks of cognition. In R. Spiro, B. Bruce, & W. Brewer, eds. *Theoretical issues in reading comprehension.* Hillsdale N.J.: Erlbaum.

Vygotsky, L. S. 1978. *Mind in society: the development of higher psychological processes.* Cambridge: Harvard University Press.

9. Children's Difficulties with School Mathematics

Binet, A. 1969. The perception of lengths and numbers. In R. H. Pollack & M. W. Brenner, eds. *The experimental psychology of Alfred Binet.* New York: Springer.

Brown, A. 1978. Knowing when, where, and how to remember: a problem of metacognition. In R. Glaser, ed. *Advances in instructional psychology.* New York: Halsted Press.

Brown, A. L., & L. A. French. 1979. The zone of potential development: implications for intelligence testing in the year 2000. In R. J. Sternberg & D. K. Detterman, eds. *Human intelligence: perspectives on theory and measurement.* Norwood, N.J: Ablex.

Brown, J. S., & R. R. Burton. 1978. Diagnostic models for procedural bugs in basic mathematical skills. *Cognitive Science* 2:155–192.

Cole, M., & J. S. Bruner. 1971. Cultural differences and inferences about psychological processes. *American Psychologist* 26:866–876.

Feuerstein, R. 1980. *Instrumental enrichment.* Baltimore: University Park Press.

Fuson, K. C., & J. W. Hall. 1983. The acquisition of early number word meanings. In H. P. Ginsburg, ed. *The development of mathematical thinking.* New York: Academic Press.

Gelman, R., & C. R. Gallistel. 1978. *The child's understanding of number.* Cambridge: Harvard University Press.

Ginsburg, H. P. 1972. *The myth of the deprived child: poor children's intellect and education.* Englewood Cliffs, N.J.: Prentice-Hall.

——. 1981. The clinical interview in psychological research on mathematical thinking: aims, rationales, techniques. *For the Learning of Mathematics* 1:4–11.

——. 1982. *Children's arithmetic.* Austin, Tex.: Pro-Ed.

Ginsburg, H. P., J. K. Posner, & R. L. Russell. 1981a. The development of mental addition as a function of schooling and culture. *Journal of Cross-cultural Psychology* 12:163–178.

Ginsburg, H. P., J. K. Posner, & R. L. Russell. 1981b. Mathematics learning difficulties in African children: a clinical interview study. *The Quarterly Newsletter of the Laboratory of Comparative Human Cognition* 3:8–11.

Ginsburg, H. P., & R. L. Russell. 1981. Social class and racial influences on early mathematical thinking. *Monographs of the Society for Research in Child Development* 46(6, serial no. 193).

Hebbeler, K. 1977. Young children's addition. *Journal of Children's Mathematical Behavior* 1:108–121.

Hunt, J. McV. 1964. The psychological basis for using pre-school enrichment as an antidote for cultural deprivation. *Merrill-Palmer Quarterly* 10:209–248.

Jensen, A. R. 1969. How much can we boost I.Q. and scholastic achievement? *Harvard Educational Review* 39:1–123.

Kirk, G. E., J. McV. Hunt, & F. Volkmar. 1975. Social class and preschool language skill, vol. V: Cognitive and semantic mastery of number. *Genetic Psychology Monographs* 92:131–153.

Labov, W. 1972. *Language in the inner city.* Philadelphia: University of Pennsylvania Press.

Ogbu, J. U. 1978. *Minority education and caste.* New York: Academic Press.

Papert, S. 1980. *Mindstorms: children, computers, and powerful ideas.* New York: Basic Books.

Petitto, A. L., & H. P. Ginsburg. 1982. Mental arithmetic in Africa and America: strategies, principles, and explanations. *International Journal of Psychology* 17:81–102.

Piaget, J. 1970. *Science of education and the psychology of the child.* New York: Oreon Press.

Posner, J. K. 1982. The development of mathematical knowledge in two West African societies. *Child Development* 53:200–208.

Russell, R. L., & H. P. Ginsburg. In press. A cognitive analysis of children's mathematics difficulties. *Cognition and Instruction.*

Starkey, P., & R. G. Cooper. 1980. Perception of numbers by human infants. *Science* 210:1033–1035.

Vygotsky, L. S. 1978. *Mind in society: the development of higher psychological processes.* Cambridge: Harvard University Press.

Weinstein, M. L. 1978. Dyscalculia: a psychological and neurological approach to learning disabilities in mathematics in school children. Ph.D. dissertation, University of Pennsylvania.

Wertheimer, M. 1954. *Productive thinking.* New York: Harper.

10. *Children's Reasoning and Peer Relations*

Altmann, G. 1974. Observational study of behavior: sampling methods. *Behavior* 49:227–267.

Bornstein, M. R., A. S. Bellack, & M. Hersen. 1977. Social skills training for unassertive children: a multiple-baseline analysis. *Journal of Applied Behavioral Analysis* 10:183–195.

Bruner, J. 1974. The organization of early skilled action. In M. P. M. Richards, ed. *The integration of the child into a social world.* London: Cambridge University Press.

Clark, R. A., & J. G. Delia. 1976. The development of functional persuasive skills in childhood and early adolescence. *Child Development* 47:1008–1014.

Cooke, T. P., & T. Apolloni. 1976. Developing positive social-emotional behavior: a study of training and generalization effects. *Journal of Applied Behavior Analysis* 9:64–78.

Corsaro, W. 1979. "We're friends, right?": children's use of access rituals in a nursery school. *Language in Society* 8(3):315–336.

Damon, W. 1977. *The social world of the child.* San Francisco: Jossey-Bass.

Delia, J. G., S. L. Kline, & B. R. Burleson. 1979. The development of persuasive communication strategies in kindergartners through twelfth-graders. *Communication Monographs* 46:241–256.

Eckman, P., & W. V. Friesen. 1969. Nonverbal leakage and clues to deception. *Psychiatry* 32:88–106.

Forbes, D. L. 1978. Recent research on children's social cognition: a brief review. *New Directions for Child Development* 1:123–139.

Forbes, D. L., & D. Danaher. 1982. Sex differences in children's conflict behavior: conflict resolution vs. conflict mitigation. Harvard University.

Forbes, D. L., & M. Greenberg, eds. 1982. *New directions in child development: children's planning strategies.* San Francisco: Jossey-Bass.

Forbes, D. L., & M. Katz. In preparation. Getting acquainted: responses to unfamiliar peers at ages five and seven.

Forbes, D. L., M. Katz, & B. Paul. 1982. Children's plans for joining play: an analysis of structure and function. In D. Forbes & M. Greenberg, eds. *New directions in child development: children's planning strategies.* San Francisco: Jossey-Bass.

Forbes, D., M. Katz, & B. Paul. In press. Frame talk: a dramatistic analysis of children's fantasy play. In E. Mueller & C. Cooper, eds. Developmental Psychology Series. New York: Academic Press.

Forbes, D. L., & D. A. Lubin. 1981a. The development of applied strategies in children's social behavior. Paper presented at Biennial Meetings of Society for Research in Child Development, Boston.

Forbes, D. L., & D. A. Lubin. 1981b. The impact of interpretive procedures on peer interaction. Paper presented at Fourth International Conference on Culture and Communication, Philadelphia.

Forbes, D. L., & D. A. Lubin. In press. Verbal social reasoning and observed persuasion strategies in children's social behavior. In H. Sypher & J. Applegate, eds. *Understanding interpersonal communication: social cognitive and strategic processes in children and adults.*

Forbes, D. L., D. A. Lubin, & D. Anderegg. 1980. Third party entry behavior. Harvard University.

Hartup, W. W. 1978. Children and their friends. In H. McGurk, ed. *Issues in childhood social development.* London: Methuen.

Haslett, B. 1980. "I'll give you a knuckle sandwich:" preschoolers' resolution of conflict. Paper presented at Annual Meeting of Speech Communication Association.

Hoffman, M. L. 1977. Personality and social development. *Annual Review of Psychology* 28:295–321.

Lubin, D. A. 1977. The development of children's techniques of persuasion: an analysis of behavior sequences. Doctoral thesis, Harvard University.

Miller, G. A., E. Galanter, & K. H. Pribram. 1960. *Plans and the structure of behavior.* New York: Holt, Rinehart & Winston.

Oden, S., & S. R. Asher. 1977. Coaching children in skills for friendship making. *Child Development* 48:495–506.

Piaget, J. 1950. *The psychology of intelligence.* New York: Harcourt, Brace.

Putallaz, M., & J. Gottman. 1981. An interactional model of children's entry into peer groups. *Child Development* 52:986–994.

Rosenthal, R., ed. 1979. *Skill in nonverbal communication: individual differences.* Cambridge: Oelgeschlager, Gunn & Hain.

Schank, R., & R. Abelson. 1977. *Scripts, plans, goals and understanding.* Hillsdale, N.J.: Erlbaum.

Shantz, C. U. 1975. The development of social cognition. In E. M. Hetherington. ed. *Review of child development research.* vol. 5. Chicago: University of Chicago Press.

Shatz, M., & R. Gelman. 1973. Adaptation of speech as a function of age of listener: egocentrism revisited. *Monographs of the Society for Research in Child Development* 38(5):1–38.

Sullivan, H. S. 1953. *The interpersonal theory of psychiatry.* New York: Norton.

Werner, H. 1948. *Comparative psychology of mental development.* New York: Science Editions.

11. *Cognitive Development in Time and Space*

Acredolo, L. P. 1977. Developmental changes in the ability to coordinate perspectives of a large-scale space. *Developmental Psychology* 13:1–8.

Allen, G. L., K. C. Kirasic, A. W. Siegel, & J. F. Herman. 1979. Developmental issues in cognitive mapping: the selection and utilization of environmental landmarks. *Child Development* 50:1062–1070.

Arbib, M. 1972. *The metaphorical brain: an introduction to cybernetics as artificial intelligence and brain theory.* New York: Wiley-Interscience.

Bakan, D. 1971. Adolescence in America: from idea to social fact. In J. Kagan and R. Coles, eds. *Twelve to sixteen: early adolescence.* New York: Norton.

Baldwin, J. M. 1906 (1895). *Mental development in the child and the race,* 3rd ed. New York: Macmillan.

———. 1899. *Social and ethical interpretations in mental development: a study in social psychology,* 2nd ed. New York: Macmillan.

———. 1930. In C. Murchison, ed. *A history of psychology in autobiography,* vol. 1. Worcester, Mass.: Clark University Press.

Barker, R. G., & L. S. Barker, 1963. Social actions in the behavior streams of American and English children. In R. G. Barker, ed. *The stream of behavior.* New York: Appleton-Century-Crofts.

Barker, R. G., & H. F. Wright. 1954. *Midwest and its children: the psychological ecology of an American town.* Evanston, Ill.: Row, Peterson.

Basseches, M. 1978. Beyond closed-system problem-solving: a study of meta-systematic aspects of mature thought. Ph.D. dissertation, Department of Psychology and Social Relations, Harvard University.

Beane, W. C., & W. G. Doty, eds. 1975. *Myths, rites, symbols: a Mircea Eliade reader.* New York: Harper Colophon.

Bearison, D. J. 1969. Role of measurement operations in the acquisition of conservation. *Developmental Psychology* 1:653–660.

Berger, P. L., & T. Luckmann, 1967. *The social construction of reality.* New York: Anchor.

Bernstein, B. 1974. *Class, codes, and control.* New York: Schocken Books.

Berry, J. W. 1966. Temne and Eskimo perceptual skills. *International Journal of Psychology* 1:207–229.

Bloom, L., P. Lightbown, & L. Hood. 1975. Structure and variation in child language. *Monographs of the Society for Research in Child Development* 40(no. 160).

Bossard, J. H. S. 1948. *The sociology of child development.* New York: Harper.

Bronfenbrenner, U. 1974. The origins of alienation. *Scientific American* 231:53–61.

———. 1977. Toward an experimental psychology of human development. *American Psychologist* 32:513–531.

———. 1979. *The ecology of human development: experiments by nature and design.* Cambridge: Harvard University Press.

Bronfenbrenner, U., & A. C. Crouter. 1983. The evolution of research models in field studies of human development. In *Carmichael's Manual of Child Psychology,* 4th ed. New York: Wiley.

Burke, K. 1973. (1941). *The philosophy of literary form.* 3rd ed. Berkeley: University of California Press.

Calhoun, D. H. 1973. *Intelligence of a people.* Princeton: Princeton University Press.

Campbell, D. T. 1974. Evolutionary epistemology. In P. A. Schilpp, ed. *The library of living philosophers,* vol. 14: *The philosophy of Karl Popper.* LaSalle, Ill.: Open Court.

Cassirer, E. 1944. The concept of group and the theory of perception. *Philosophy and Phenomenological Research* 5:1–35.

Clanchy, M. T. 1979. *From memory to written record: England 1066–1307.* Cambridge: Harvard University Press.

Clark, H. 1973. Space, time, semantics, and the child. In T. E. Moore, ed. *Cognitive development and the acquisition of language.* New York: Academic Press.

Cole, M., J. Gay, J. A. Glick, & D. W. Sharp. 1971. *The cultural context of learning and thinking.* New York: Basic Books.

Cole, M., L. Hood, & R. McDermott. 1978. Ecological niche picking: ecological invalidity as an axiom of experimental cognitive psychology. University of California, San Diego, and The Rockefeller University.

Cole, M., & B. Means. 1981. *Comparative studies of how people think: an introduction.* Cambridge: Harvard University Press.

Cole, M., & K. Traupmann. 1981. Comparative cognitive research: learning from a learning disabled child. In *Minnesota Symposia on Child Psychology,* vol. 14. Hillsdale, N.J.: Erlbaum.

Coleman, J. S. 1961. *The adolescent society.* New York: Free Press.

Cooley, C. H. 1902. *Human nature and the social order.* New York: Charles Scribner's Sons.

Douglas, M., ed. 1973. *Rules and meanings: the anthropology of everyday knowledge.* New York: Penguin.

Downs, R. M., & D. Stea. 1977. *Maps in mind.* New York: Harper & Row.

Eisenstein, E. L. 1980. *The printing press as an agent of change.* Cambridge: Cambridge University Press.

Eliade, M. 1959. *The sacred and the profane: the nature of religion.* Trans. W. R. Trask. New York: Harcourt Brace Jovanovich.

Ellenberger, H. 1970. *The discovery of the unconscious.* New York: Basic Books.

Erikson, E. H. 1968. *Identity, youth, and crisis.* New York: Norton.

Fischer, K. W. 1980. A theory of cognitive development: the control and construction of hierarchies of skills. *Psychological Review* 87:477–531.

Fishbein, H. D. 1976. *Evolution, development, and children's learning.* Pacific Palisades, Cal.: Goodyear.

Flavell, J. H. 1977. *Cognitive development.* Englewood Cliffs, N.J.: Prentice-Hall.

Gleason, J. B. 1973. Code switching in children's language. In T. E. Moore, ed. *Cognitive development and the acquisition of language.* New York: Academic Press.

Goodman, N. 1976. *Languages of art.* Indianapolis: Hackett.

Goody, J., ed. 1968. *Literacy in traditional societies.* Cambridge: Cambridge University Press.

———. 1977. *The domestication of the savage mind.* New York: Cambridge University Press.

Goody, J., & I. Watt. 1968. The consequences of literacy. In J. Goody, ed. *Literacy in traditional societies.* Cambridge: Cambridge University Press.

Gould, P., & R. White. 1974. *Mental maps.* London: Penguin.

Gould, S. 1980. *The panda's thumb.* New York: Norton.

Hardwick, D. A., C. W. McIntyre, & H. L. Pick, Jr. 1976. The content and manipulation of cognitive maps in children and adults. *Monographs of the Society for Research in Child Development* 41(no. 166).

Hart, R. A. 1979. *Children's experience of place.* New York: Irvington.

Herman, J. F. 1980. Children's cognitive maps of large-scale spaces: effects of exploration, direction, and repeated experience. *Journal of Experimental Child Psychology* 29:126–143.

Hood, L., & L. Bloom. 1979. What, when, and how about why: a longitudinal study of early expressions of causality. *Monographs of the Society for Research in Child Development* 44(no. 181).

Innis, H. A. 1951. *The bias of communication.* Toronto: University of Toronto Press.

James, W. 1950 (1890). *The principles of psychology,* vol. 1. New York: Dover Publications.

———. 1958 (1901–1902). *The varieties of religious experience.* New York: Mentor.

Kirasic, K. C., A. W. Siegel, & G. L. Allen. 1980. Developmental changes in recognition-in-context memory. *Child Development* 51:302–305.

Labov, W. 1970. The study of language in its societal context. *Studium Generale* 23:30–87.

Ladd, F. C. 1970. Black youths view their environment: neighborhood maps. *Environment and Behavior* 2:64–79.

Lane, H. 1976. *The wild boy of Aveyron.* Cambridge: Harvard University Press.

Lawler, R. 1979. One child's learning. Ph.D. dissertation, Artificial Intelligence Laboratory, M.I.T.

———. 1981. The progressive construction of mind. *Cognitive Science* 5:1–30.

Ley, D. 1972. The black inner city as a frontier outpost: images and behavior of a North Philadelphia neighborhood. Ph.D. dissertation, Pennsylvania State University.

Livingston, R. B. 1967. Reinforcement. In G. C. Quarton, T. Melnechuk, & F. O. Schmitt, eds. *The neurosciences: a study program.* New York: Rockefeller University Press.

Lorenz, K. 1966. *On aggression.* New York: Harcourt Brace Jovanovich.

Luria, A. R. 1961. *The role of speech in the regulation of normal and abnormal behavior.* New York: Liveright.

————. 1976. *Cognitive development: its cultural and social foundations.* Cambridge: Harvard University Press.

Mead, G. H. 1934. *Mind, self, and society.* Chicago: University of Chicago Press.

Munn, N. D. 1973. *Walbiri iconography: graphic representation and cultural symbolism in a Central Australian society.* Ithaca: Cornell University Press.

Munroe, R. L., & R. H. Munroe. 1971. Effect of environmental experience on spatial ability in an East African society. *Journal of Social Psychology* 83:15–22.

Nerlove, S. B., R. H. Munroe, & R. L. Munroe. 1971. Effect of environmental experience on spatial ability: a replication. *Journal of Social Psychology* 84:3–10.

Olson, D. 1970. Language and thought: aspects of a cognitive theory of semantics. *Psychological Review* 77:257–273.

Olson, D. R., & J. S. Bruner. 1974. Learning through experience and learning through media. In D. R. Olson, ed. *Media and symbols: the forms of expressions, communication, and education.* 73rd Handbook of the National Society for the Study of Education. Chicago: University of Chicago Press.

Pascual-Leone, J. 1976. Metasubjective problems of constructive cognition: forms of knowing and their psychological mechanism. *Canadian Psychological Review* 17:110–125.

Peirce, C. S. 1978 (1931). In C. Hartshorne & P. Weiss, eds. *Collected papers,* vol II: *Elements of logic.* Cambridge: Harvard University Press.

Piaget, J. 1926. *The language and thought of the child.* New York: Harcourt, Brace.

————. 1942. *Classes, relations et nombres.* Paris: Vrin.

————. 1949. *Traite de logique.* Paris: Colin.

————. 1952. *Essai sur les transformations des operations logiques.* Paris: Presses Univer. France.

————. 1952. *Play, dreams, and imitation in childhood.* New York: Norton.

————. 1953a (1941). *The child's conception of number.* New York: Humanities Press.

————. 1953b. *Logic and psychology.* Manchester: Manchester University Press.

————. 1954. *The child's construction of reality.* New York: Basic Books.

————. 1970a (1946). *The child's conception of movement and speed.* New York: Basic Books.

————. 1970b. *The child's conception of time.* New York: Basic Books.

Piaget, J., & B. Inhelder. 1956 (1948). *The child's conception of space.* New York: Humanities Press.

Piaget, J., & B. Inhelder. 1958. *The growth of logical thinking from childhood to adolescence.* New York: Basic Books.

Piaget, J., & B. Inhelder. 1964. *The early growth of logic in the child.* New York: Harper and Row.

Piaget, J., & B. Inhelder. 1976 (1951). *The origin of the idea of chance in children.* New York: Norton.

Piaget, J., B. Inhelder, & A. Szeminska. 1960. *The child's conception of geometry.* New York: Basic Books.

Plumb, J. H. 1971. The great change in children. *Horizon* 13:4–13.

Prince, M. 1900. The problem of multiple personalities. *Proceedings of the Society for Psychical Research* 15:466–483.

———. 1906. *The dissociation of a personality: a biographical study in abnormal psychology.* New York: Longman.

———. 1925. The problem of personality: how many selves have we? *Pedagogical Seminary* 32:266–292.

Rheingold, H. L., & C. O. Eckerman. 1970. The infant separates himself from his mother. *Science* 168:78–90.

Riegel, K. F. 1973. Dialectic operations: the final period of cognitive development. *Human Development* 16:346–360.

Rogoff, B., N. Newcombe, N. Fox, & S. Ellis. 1980. Transitions in children's roles and capabilities. *International Journal of Psychology* 15:181–200.

Rogoff, B., M. J. Sellers, S. Pirrotta, N. Fox, & S. H. White. 1975. Age of assignment of roles and responsibilities to children: a cross-cultural survey. *Human Development* 18:353–369.

Romanes, G. J. 1889. *Mental evolution in man: origin of human faculty.* New York: Appleton.

Royce, J. 1894. *The world and the individual.* New York, Macmillan.

Schallenberger, M. E. 1894. A study of children's rights as seen by themselves. *Pedagogical Seminary* 3:87–96.

Schoggen, M., L. S. Barker, & R. G. Barker, 1963. Structure of the behavior of American and English children. In R. G. Barker, ed. *The stream of behavior.* New York: Appleton-Century-Crofts.

Scribner, S., & M. Cole. 1973. Cognitive consequences of formal and informal education. *Science* 182:553–559.

Scribner, S., & M. Cole. 1981. *The psychology of literacy.* Cambridge: Harvard University Press.

Sechenov, I. M. 1973 (1878). Elements of thought. In A. A. Subkov, ed. *I. M. Sechenov: biographical sketch and essays.* New York: Arno Press.

Shatz, M., & R. Gelman. 1973. The development of communicative skills. *Monographs of the Society for Research in Child Development* 38(no. 5).

Shatz, M., & R. Gelman. 1977. Beyond syntax: the influence of conversational constraints on speech modification. In C. E. Snow & C. A. Ferguson, eds. *Talking to children.* Cambridge: Cambridge University Press.

Siegel, A. W. 1981. The externalization of cognitive maps by children and adults: in search of ways to ask better questions. In L. S. Liben, A.

Patterson, & N. Newcombe, eds. *Spatial representation and behavior across the life span: theory and application.* New York: Academic Press.

Siegel, A. W., G. L. Allen, & K. C. Kirasic. 1979. Children's ability to make bi-directional distance comparisons: the advantage of thinking ahead. *Developmental Psychology* 15:656–657.

Siegel, A. W., & S. H. White. 1975. The development of spatial representation of large-scale environments. In H. W. Reese, ed. *Advances in child development and behavior,* vol. 10. New York: Academic Press.

Siegel, A. W., & S. H. White. 1982. The child study movement: early growth and development of the symbolized child. In H. Reese, ed. *Advances in child development and behavior,* vol. 17. New York: Academic Press.

Siegler, R. S. 1981. Developmental sequences within and between concepts. *Monographs of the Society for Research in Child Development* 46(no. 189).

Sigel, I. E., & R. R. Cocking. 1977. *Cognitive development from childhood to adolescence: a constructivist perspective.* New York: Holt, Rinehart, and Winston.

Snow, C. E., & C. A. Ferguson, eds. 1977. *Talking to children.* Cambridge: Cambridge University Press.

Thigpen, C. H., & H. Cleckley. 1954. A case of multiple personality. *Journal of Abnormal Psychology* 49:135–151.

Tyack, D. B. 1974. *The one best system: a history of American urban education.* Cambridge: Harvard University Press.

Vygotsky, L. S. 1962 (1934). *Thought and language.* Cambridge: M.I.T. Press.

———. 1978. *Mind in society.* Cambridge: Harvard University Press.

Wapner, S. 1980a. Toward an analysis of transactions of persons-in-a-high-speed-society. Paper presented at Symposium on Man and a High-Speed Society, International Association of Traffic and Safety Science, Tokyo, Japan.

———. 1980b. Transactions of persons-in-environments: some critical transitions. Clark University.

Wapner, S., B. Kaplan, & R. Ciottone. 1981. Self-world relationships in critical environment transitions: childhood and beyond. In L. S. Liben, A. Patterson, & N. Newcombe, eds. *Spatial representation and behavior across the life span: theory and application.* New York: Academic Press.

Werner, H. 1957 (1948). *Comparative psychology of mental development.* New York: International Universities Press.

Werner, H., & B. Kaplan. 1963. *Symbol formation.* New York: Wiley.

White, R. 1959. Motivation reconsidered: the concept of competence. *Psychological Review* 66:297–333.

White, S. H. 1978. Psychology in all sorts of places. In R. A. Kasschau & F. S. Kessel, eds. *Houston symposium,* vol. I: *Psychology and society: in search of symbiosis.* New York: Holt, Rinehart & Winston.

———. 1980. Cognitive competence and performance in everyday environments. *Bulletin of the Orton Society* 30:29–45.

White, S. H., & D. Pillemer. 1979. Childhood amnesia and the development of a socially accessible memory system. In J. F. Kihlstrom & F. J. Evans, eds. *Functional disorders of memory.* Hillsdale, N.J.: Erlbaum.

Whiting, B. B. 1980. Culture and social behavior: a model for the development of social behavior. *Ethos* 8:95–116.

Yamamoto, T., S. Wapner, & D. A. Stevens. 1980. Exploration and learning of topographical relationships by the rat. *Bulletin of the Psychonomic Society* 15:99–102.

Index